I0901134

IMAGES
of America

MANASQUAN

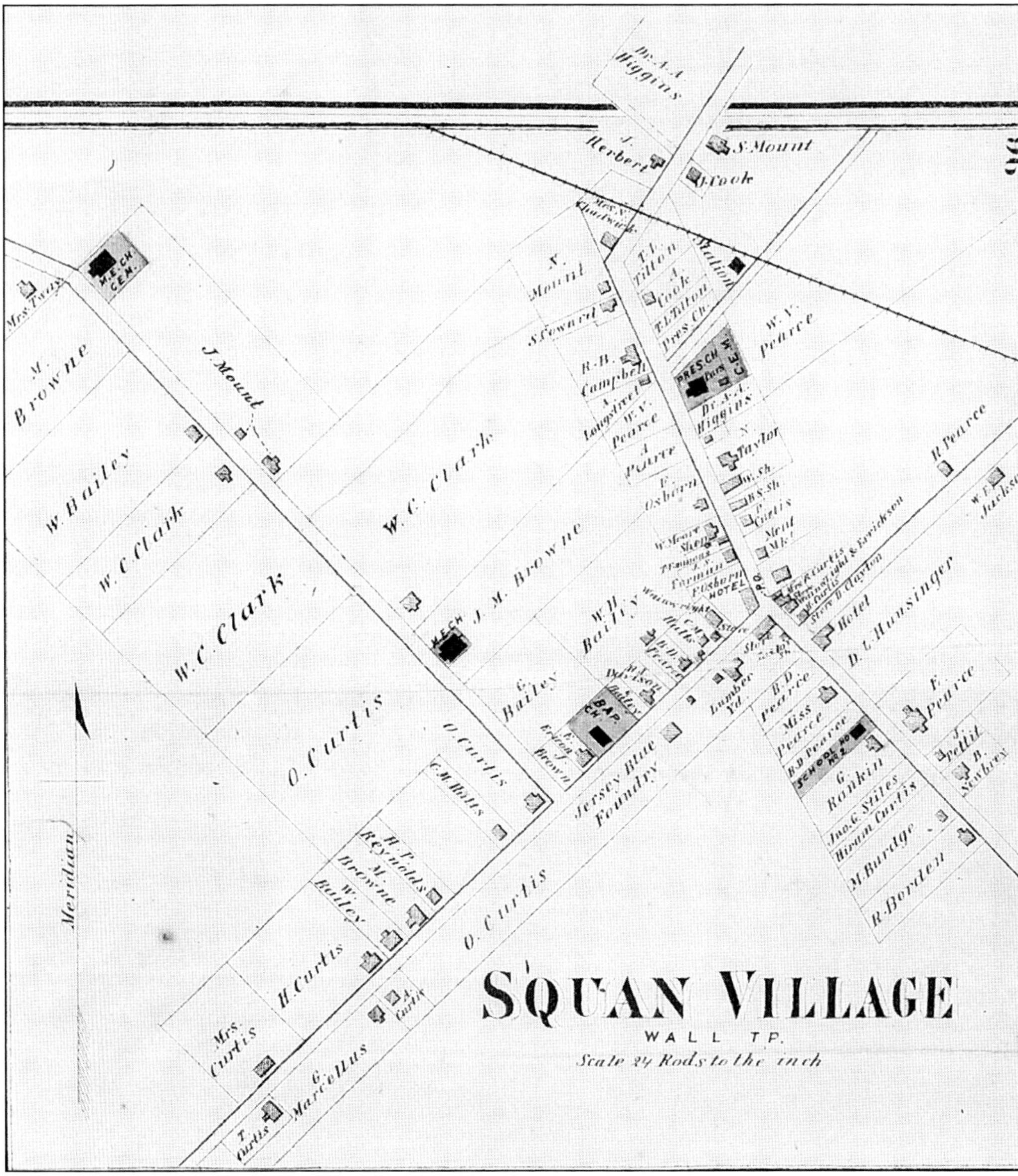

This map, reproduced from the *Atlas of Monmouth County, New Jersey* (published in 1873 by Beers, Comstock, and Cline, New York City), illustrates the development of the community before its incorporation as a borough in 1887.

IMAGES
of America

MANASQUAN

Mary A. Birckhead Ware

ARCADIA
PUBLISHING

ISBN 978-0-7385-9019-6

Published by Arcadia Publishing
Charleston, South Carolina

Printed in the United States of America

For all general information contact Arcadia Publishing at:
Telephone 843-853-2070
Fax 843-853-0044
E-mail sales@arcadiapublishing.com
For customer service and orders:
Toll-Free 1-888-313-2665

Visit us on the Internet at www.arcadiapublishing.com

For my parents

Contents

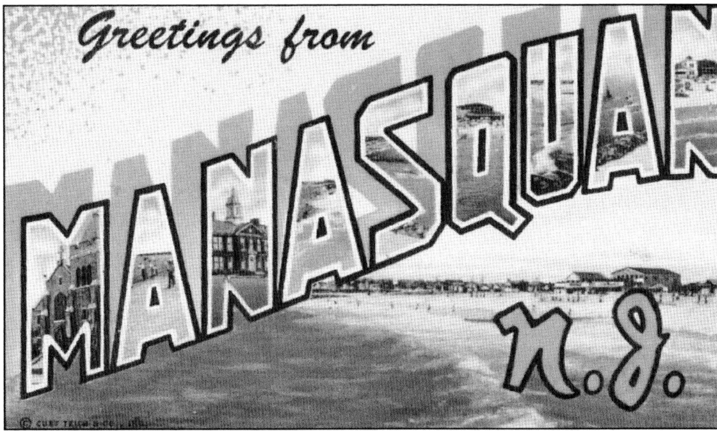

Acknowledgments

As a lifelong Manasquan resident, I cherish the many summer days spent at the beach, parades through town, the sound of the foghorn at night, riding bicycles along the Glimmer Glass, and ice skating at Mac's Pond as wonderful experiences. At the age of seven, after my grandmother Esther M. Barss began sending postcards to me, I started a postcard collection—and a special interest in those of the Manasquan area. I've also been an active member of the Squan Village Historical Society since its establishment. When I first saw the Images of America series, I knew this was a perfect opportunity to share "my Manasquan," the hometown we all know and love.

The book would never have progressed to completion without the encouragement and assistance of friends, local writers, and historians. Wesley V. Banse Sr. and his wife, Grace, welcomed my frequent calls and visits to their home and shared hours with me discussing the borough's history. Wes, Holly Peterson, and Iva Messick all offered their writing and editing expertise. Also, fellow historical society members offered help—in particular, Alice Skokos, James N. Height, Raymond Pettit, George Williams, Thomas Keiderling, Frank and Jean Applegate, and J. Marshall Brown.

Other area residents generously shared stories, photographs, and postcards for the book, including Grace B. Dickson, my aunt; Esther Riddle Mills and her family; L. Warren Randolph; Boyd and Nelda Davis; Shirley Carroll; Herbert Muller; William Zavalas; Melinda and Stanley Saminski; Bankston and Hilda Brooman; Harriet G. Brown; John Geiser; Steven E. Phillips; Linda J. Fitzgerald; Eugene and Florence Croddick; Dale Wooley; Arthur Birdsall; Jerry Woolley; Kathy Ferris Heim; and George Scheller.

Recognition is extended to all of the area writers, photographers, and historians who took the time to document the events, activities, and changes in landscape that make Manasquan such a wonderful place. This book could not have been written without the contributions of those who compiled the *Golden Jubilee* and *Diamond Jubilee* books, and *Manasquan 1887–1987*—all excellent sources of Manasquan history. Many editions of the *Coast Star*, which has chronicled Manasquan for more than 100 years, also served as a valuable resource.

Lastly, and most importantly, many thanks to my father and mother, Thomas and Virginia Birckhead, who have instilled in me a wonderful sense of community pride and a great interest in reading, learning, and sharing knowledge, both local and global; and to my husband, Charles Ware, who has patiently lived with old photographs, negatives, newspapers, and postcards spread around the house for months!

Foreword

The zealously devoted and energetic compiler of these photographs and their captions has captured for following generations a dessert-slice serving of what was once the entire pie—an unusually scenic, tranquil spot in the best of locations, peopled by compatible, hard-working villagers on one square mile of earth called Manasquan, New Jersey.

It was, and currently remains, an American early-nineteenth-century seaside village adapting selectively to the hucksters of twentieth-century lifestyles while simultaneously retaining pride in its heritage.

Those preceding generations who have lived as part of, or have learned, the past history of Manasquan will leaf though this book with growing recognition and nostalgia for what was once the "Camelot" atmosphere of a fondly remembered family home, neighborhood, or a kindly pastor, doctor, shopkeeper, or even, perhaps, a long-kept local tradition.

That the town's inhabitants have always exhibited pride in their community is best illustrated, perchance, by a tale recorded by the late Karl Eggiman, former editor of the now defunct *Manasquan Herald.*

In 1888, it seems, there was a snowbound group in deep discussion of the merits of 'Squan while gathered 'round the cherry-red, pot-bellied stove in the former Curtis and Davison general store. One sage was reported as saying, "I hear they are building up quite a town over yon." Another asked, "Over where?" The first replied, "Over in Pennsylvaniyah." "What's it called?" persisted the second. "Phillydelphy," was the response. "Wal," the other retorted, "t'wont amount to nothin. It's too dang far from Squan." Today, that man would be unanimously selected as head of the chamber of commerce.

Most Manasquanians observed by this writer still match the spirit and fervor of that former secular elder. By their pride in the town and exhibited desire to keep—as long as possible—the merited tranquility and homespun quality of family life, they have built upon a solid foundation laid by far-seeing past residents.

The neatly kept business section, the well-maintained century-old homes, the beachfront accommodations for visitors, the clipped greenery of well-used parks, the spires of seven churches and the activity surrounding their doors, educational facilities that are spacious with supportive, interested staffs, all are incalculable assets immediately recognizable by a visitor to the area. The numerous service organizations handling extracurricular activity such as provisions for a library, first aid, firefighting, safety and security, the memorials to those who have devotedly served their nation, state, and community, also are tremendous benefits to the community. And all such assets are a tribute to those who, in the past, set the desired standards.

What lies ahead? Change is inevitable.

Like a movie thriller, Megalopolis, that huge, all-encroaching dragon whose ponderous feet inexorably crush into bits and pieces unsuspecting hamlets, villages, and towns, sits a-waiting, held at bay by would-be St. Georges who are spurred to action by reminders of a highly desirable way of life—reminders such as found in this book.

In New Jersey, especially, we have the example of what happens to communities who forgot their heritage—heritage hard-won by stalwart and active pillars of community and church. That crowded area northwest of the Raritan River testifies to the disappearance of vestiges of individual communities with unique beginnings of settlements by Dutch, German, Norwegian, Italian, Irish, and Welsh immigrant families.

We cannot turn the clock back at any time, but we can slow its hands by remembrance and appreciation of previous years, months, days, and hours. And then, passing on, to the next generation, why those times counted in our lives. Mary Birckhead Ware has done just that in this work.

As lyricist Alan Jay Lerner delightfully put it to music for our adaptation—"Each evening from December to December, before you drift asleep upon your cot, think back to all the tales that you remember—of Camelot. Ask every person if he's heard the story, and tell it strong and clear if he has not, that once there was a fleeting wisp of glory—called Camelot."

Don't let it be forgot, that once there was a spot—called Manasquan.

Wesley V. Banse Sr.
Historian, Borough of Manasquan
December 1997

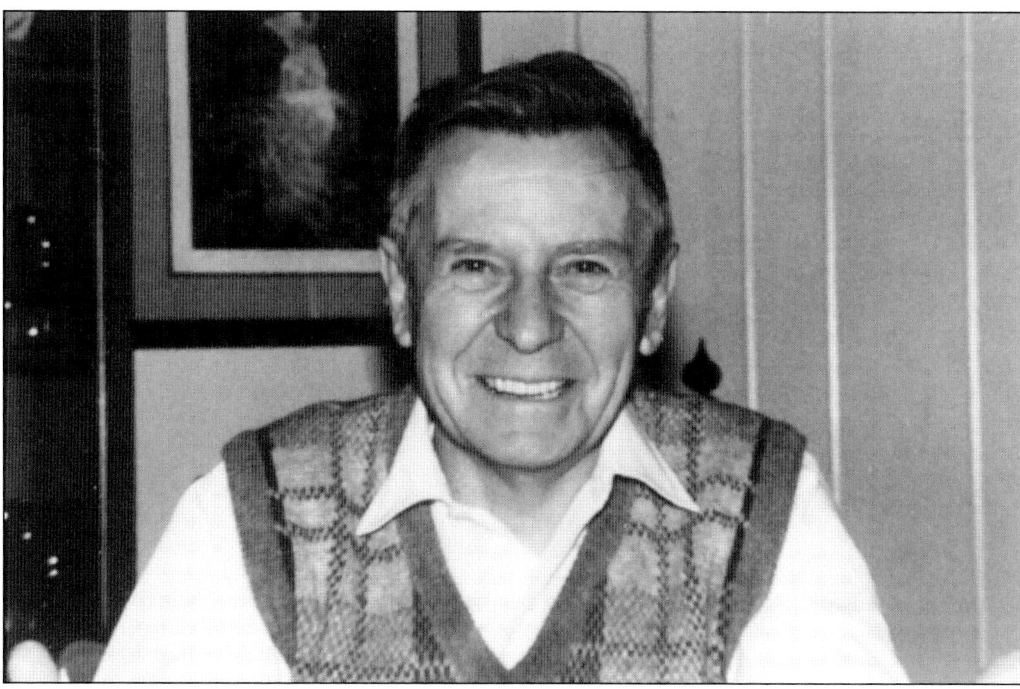

One

Celebrations and Observances

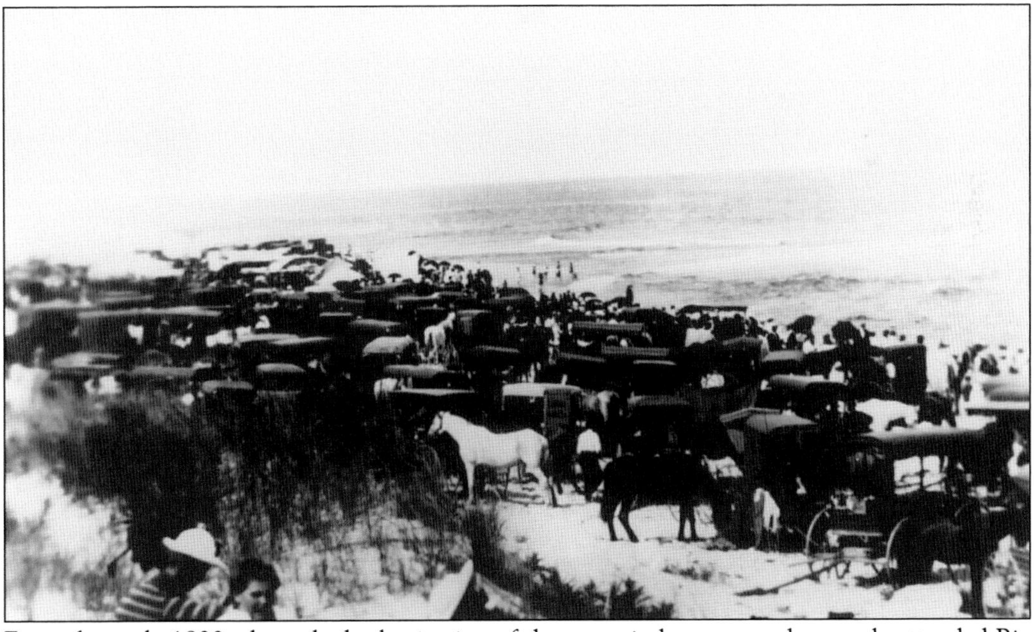

From the early 1800s through the beginning of the twentieth century, thousands attended Big Sea Day festivities—also known as Salt Water Day. The custom, however, ceased about 1915 because townspeople complained of rowdiness and overcrowding caused by the summer visitors. Since the Centennial celebration in 1987, Big Sea Day has been once again declared a part of the community calendar.

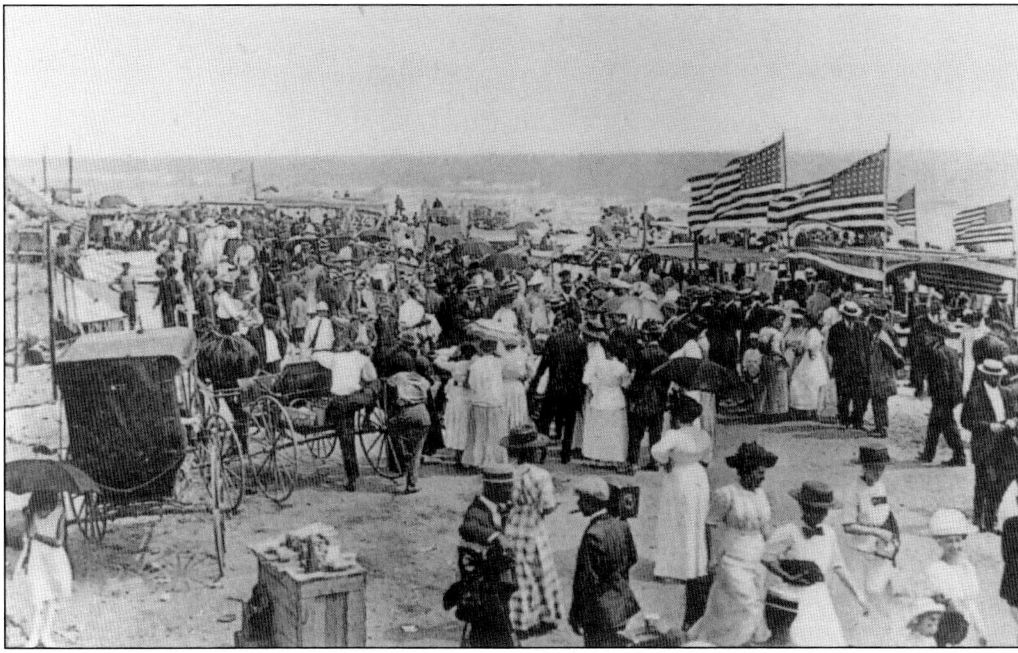

Big Sea Day was observed annually on the second Saturday in August. Farmers and their families traveled from miles to enjoy the festivities on the beaches at Manasquan. They would camp, picnic, drink, and dance, as well as swim in the ocean. The custom followed the Lenni Lenape Indians, who held an annual clambake at the seaside.

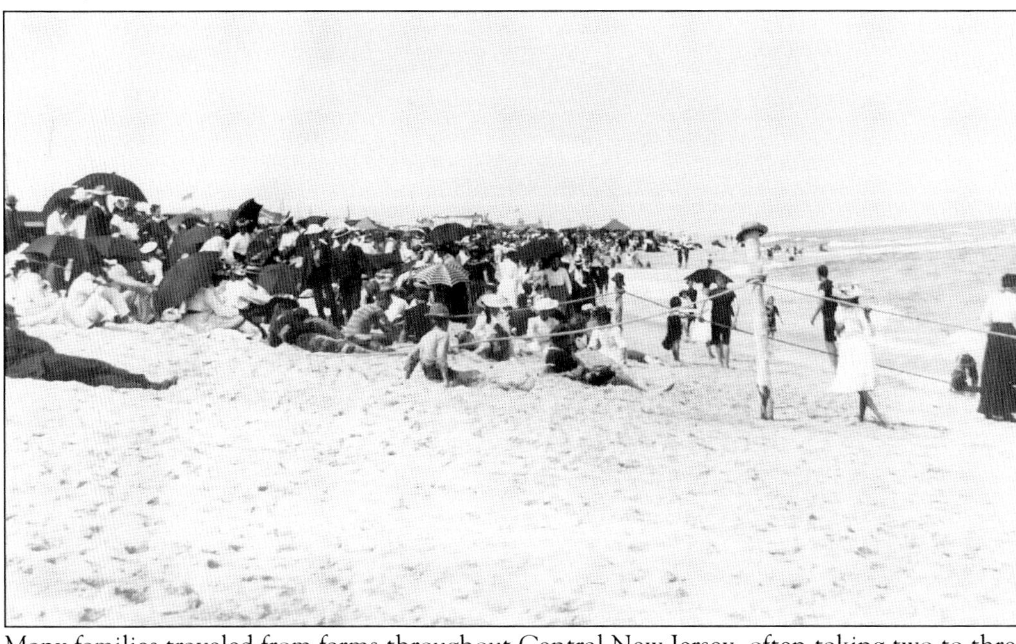

Many families traveled from farms throughout Central New Jersey, often taking two to three days to arrive at the festivities. They slept with their horses and wagons and many wore their homespun, heavy, daily work clothes the entire time—including in and out of the sea. Little Sea Day was held the following Saturday for persons who had stayed on the farm to tend to the animals.

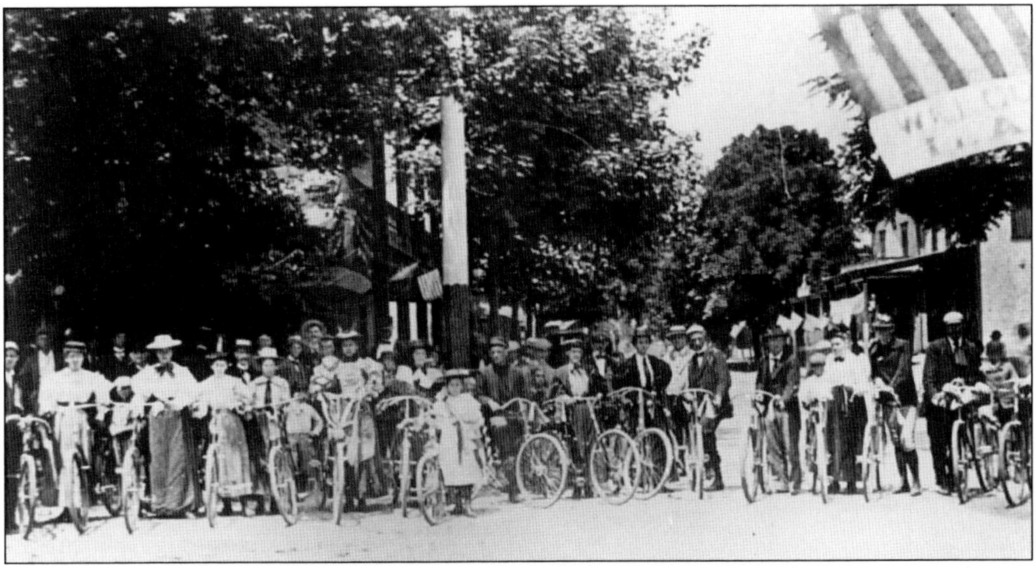

Arthur A. Zimmerman Jr., a borough resident who had been a world champion cyclist in the United States, Canada, Europe, Mexico, and Australia, helped make bicycle racing a highlight of Manasquan holiday activities. In 1869, Mr. Zimmerman was born in Camden, New Jersey, and moved to Manasquan before his feet could reach the pedals of a bicycle. By 1891, he had earned 52 first place awards, 10 for second, and 3 third place honors in national and international competition.

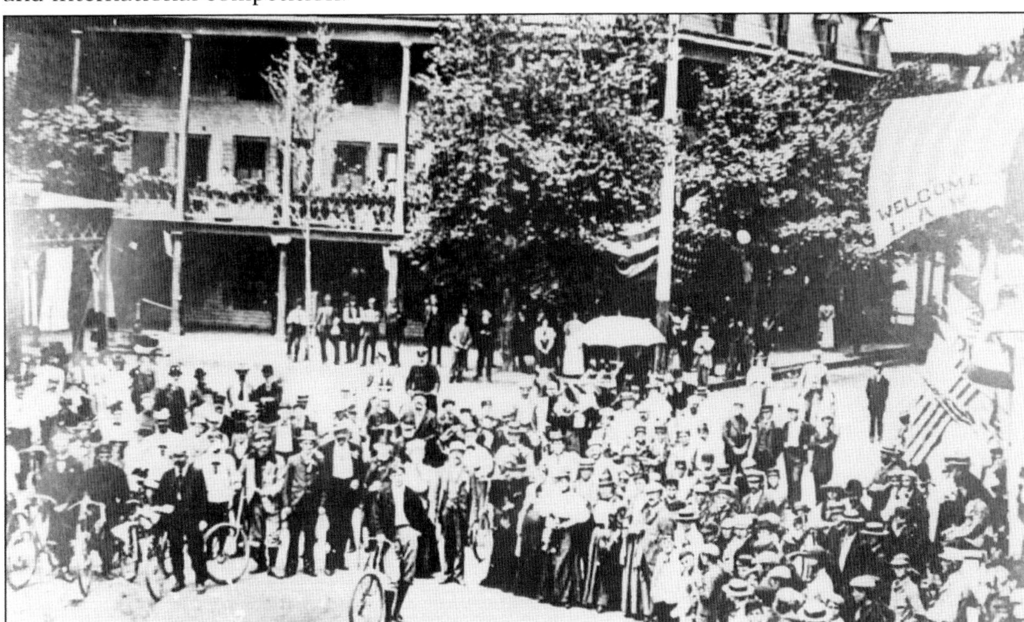

Members of the League of American Wheelman are welcomed in Manasquan by Arthur A. Zimmerman Jr. (center), a one-time world champion bicycle rider, and other members of the community. In the 1880s, Mr. Zimmerman created and manufactured the "Zimmy," a bicycle made for speed in its design. Coupled with the name of the world champion, the bicycle was a bestseller for years. Mr. Zimmerman died in 1936.

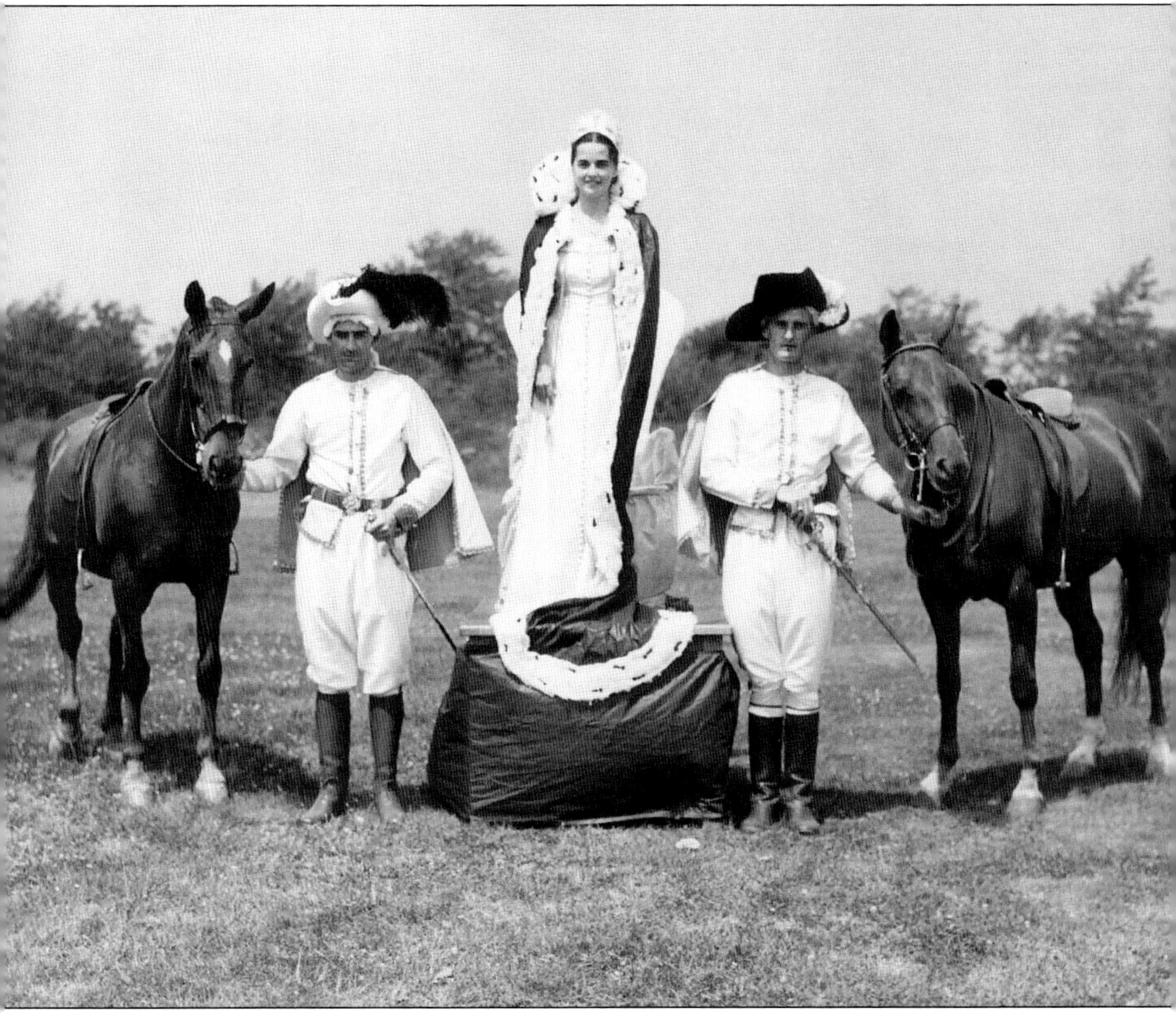

During the Golden Jubilee held in 1937, Marvin Paxson (left), Miss Esther Riddle, and Chase P. Withrow participate in a historical pageant. Mr. Paxson, who represented the State of New Jersey, traced his ancestry back 200 years to the Quaker settlers of Manasquan's shores; and Mr. Withrow, who represented Monmouth County, was a great-grandson of Joel Parker, New Jersey governor during the early part of the Civil War. Miss Riddle, who later became Mrs. Mills, represented Manasquan, thus earning the title Miss Manasquan. The pageant, featuring vignettes from the town's incorporation and history, was directed by Mrs. Frieda Schadt and produced as part of the anniversary festivities.

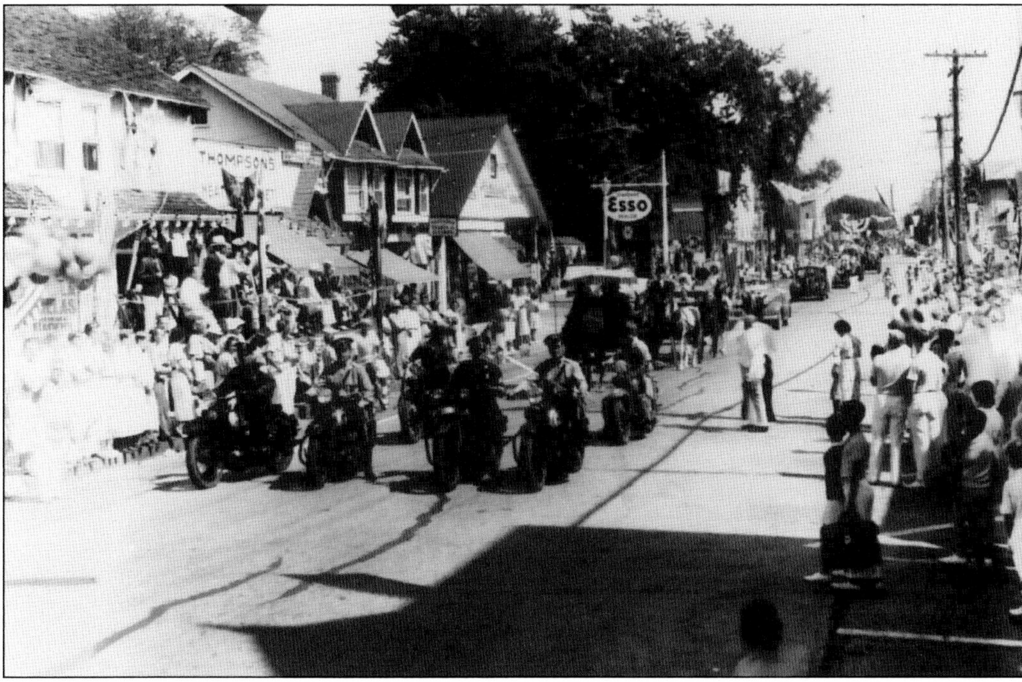

A representative group from the New Jersey State Police opened the 50th anniversary parade leading the way for the mayor, floats, bands, and other attractions. Mayor Lloyd C. Riddle served as general chairman of the jubilee. Wilbur D. Crosley, supervising principal of the borough schools, was the parade chairman. The festivities were held August 11–15, 1937.

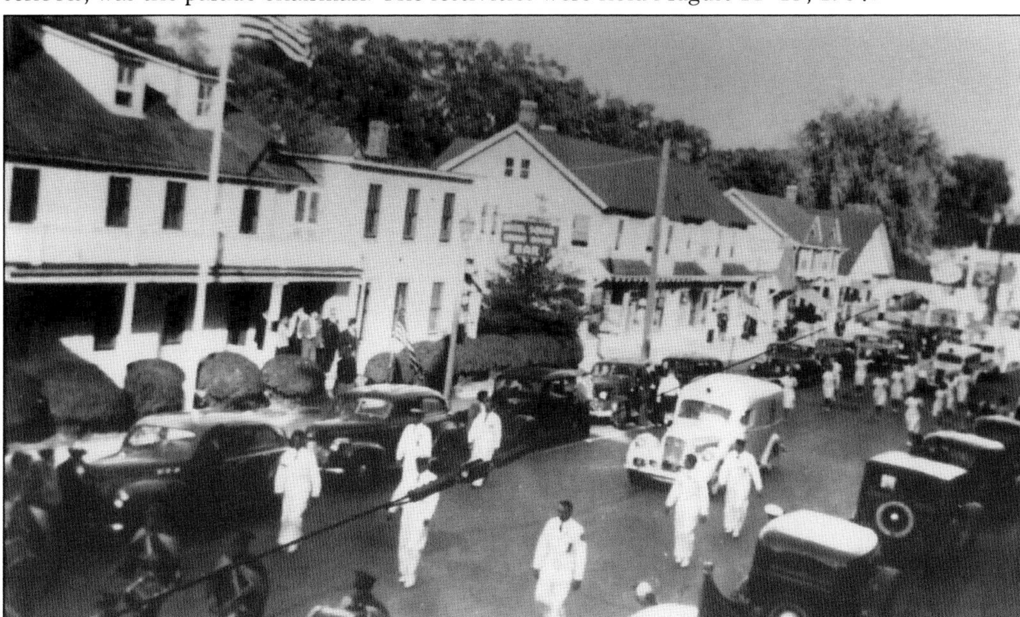

Members of the Manasquan First Aid Squad march past the Squan House during the 1937 celebration. The first aid squad was established by 14 firemen on July 22, 1929, when there were only two other volunteer squads in the United States. Andrew S. Jackson served as the first president of the squad. The squad's first ambulance was a 1929 panel truck converted for use.

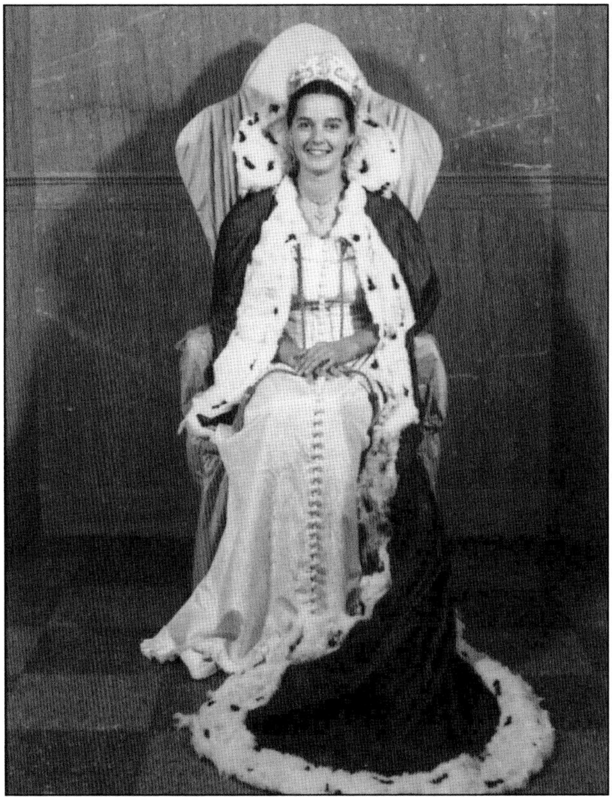

In ermine robe and crown, Miss Esther Riddle serves as queen of Manasquan during Golden Jubilee festivities. A native of Manasquan, she was graduated from the borough's schools. Miss Riddle, whose father served as mayor, was employed in 1937 as an English teacher at Southern Maryland High School in Baltimore, and she returned to her hometown to serve in a lead position in the historical pageant.

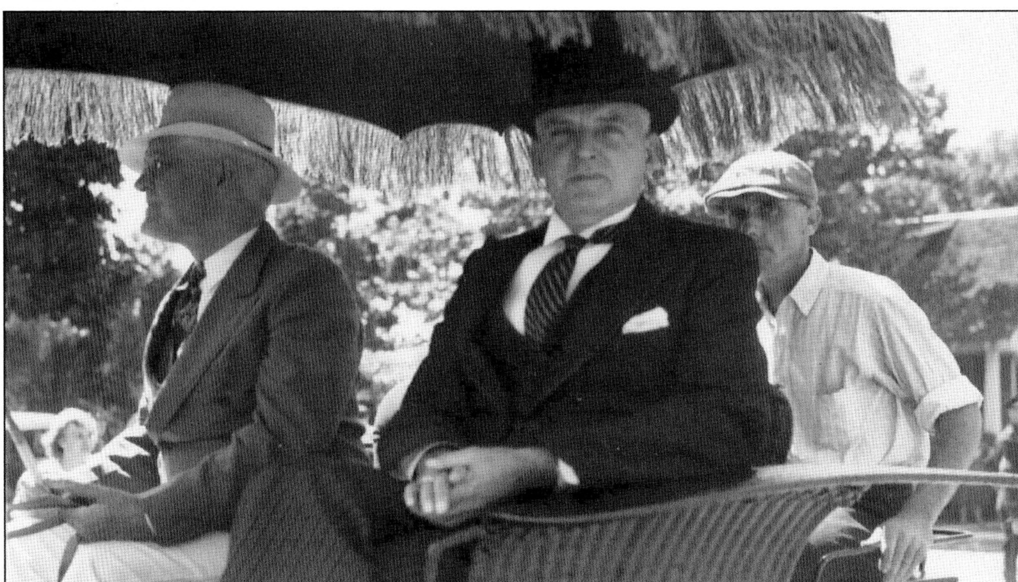

Mayor Lloyd C. Riddle (right), chairman of the celebration committee for the borough's 50th anniversary of incorporation, is escorted by Howard Height, who drives his surrey during the parade. Mr. Riddle served as mayor from 1922 until 1938. Mr. Height owned and operated the first Ford dealership in Monmouth County with offices at Main Street and Taylor Avenue (Route 71).

A souvenir book was published for the 1937 Golden Jubilee containing a program of events for the August 11–15 celebration. Articles in the program included a history of the borough, as well as other stories of local interest and advertisements. Some activities planned for the gala were a pageant, water events, a parade, band concert, and fishermen's casting contest.

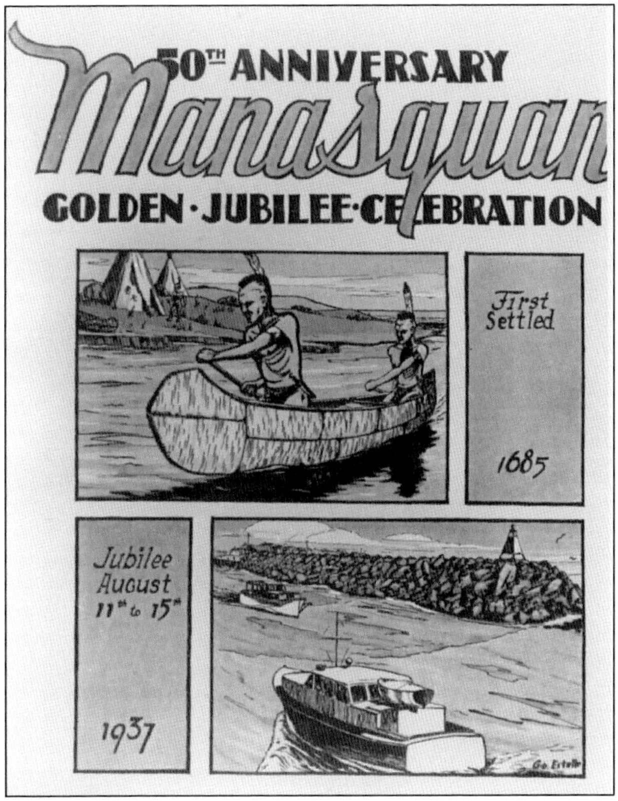

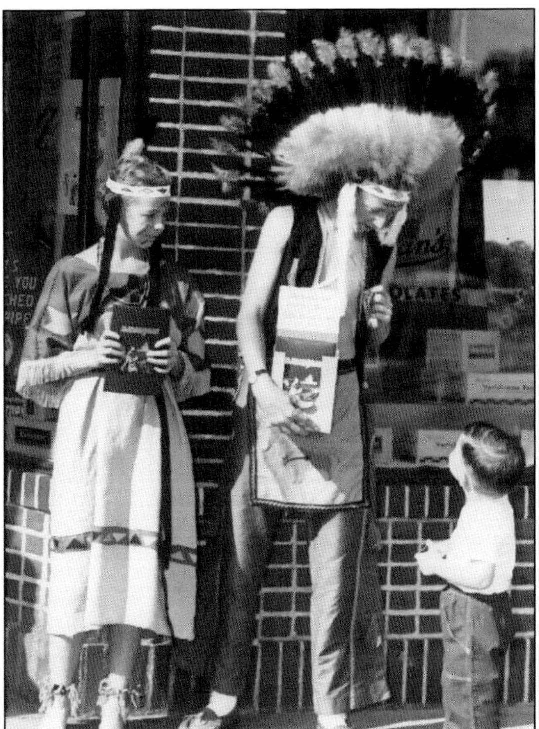

Representing summer settlement of the Lenni Lenape Indians on the shores of Manasquan, this couple in Native American dress talk with youngsters about the history of the borough. As part of the community's anniversary celebration in 1962, a 200-page souvenir volume on the history of Manasquan was published. Proceeds from the sale of the book helped offset costs of celebration events.

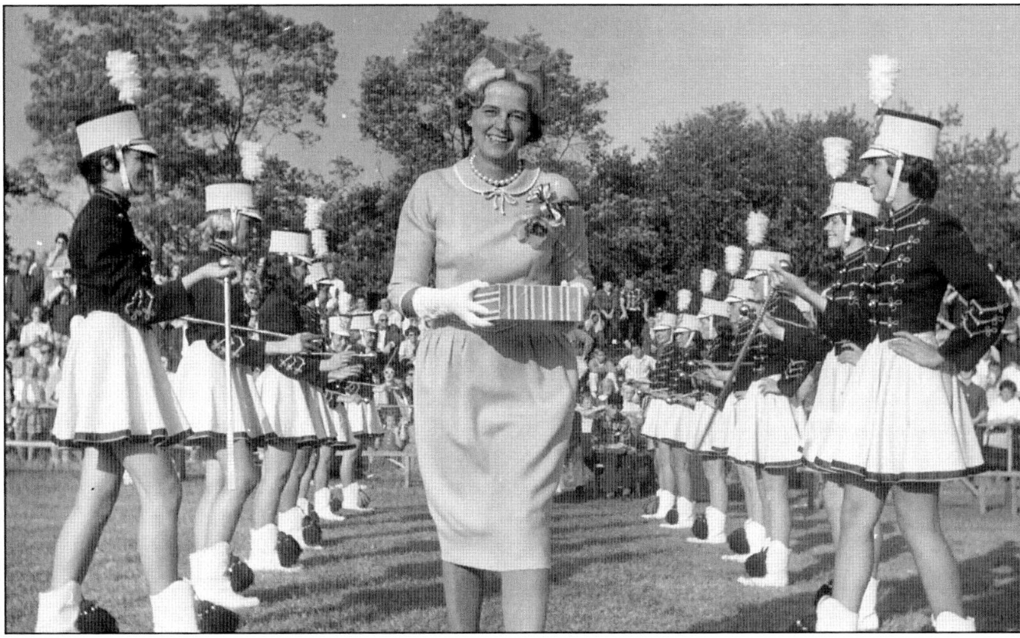

Mrs. Esther Riddle Mills, daughter of a former Manasquan mayor, passes through the ceremonial Manasquan High School guard of honor on the high school football field during the 75th anniversary of the Borough of Manasquan in 1962. Mrs. Mills returned to her hometown from Toronto, Canada, to take part in the gala.

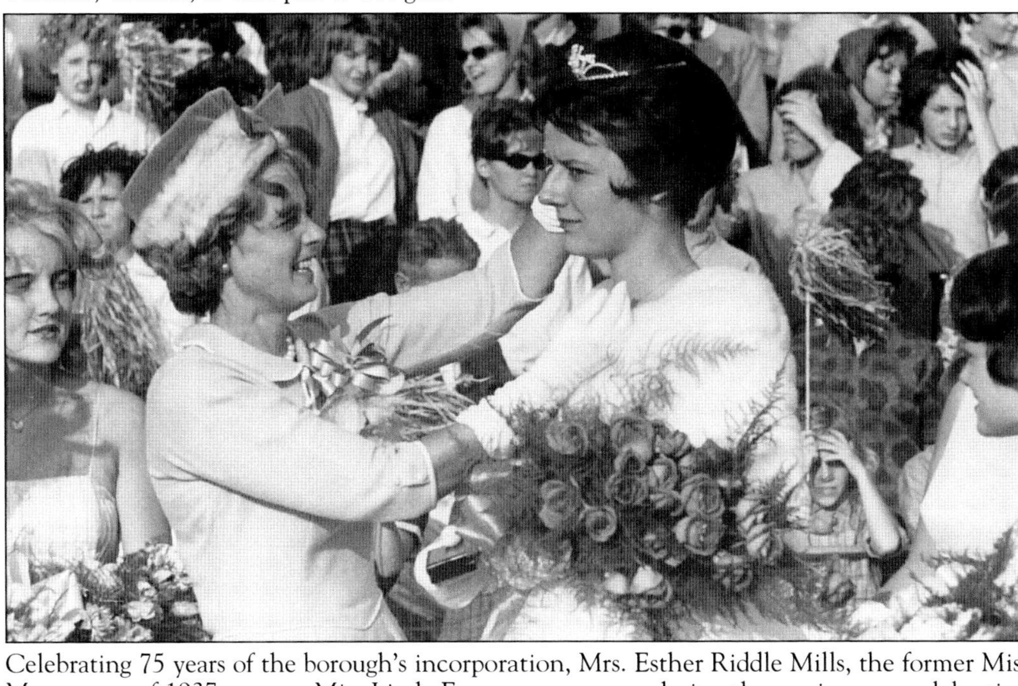

Celebrating 75 years of the borough's incorporation, Mrs. Esther Riddle Mills, the former Miss Manasquan of 1937, crowns Miss Linda Evans, new queen, during the anniversary celebration held on the Manasquan High School football field during half-time festivities. Members of Miss Evans's court included Miss Dodi Buhler, Miss Kathy Morris, Miss Mary Beth Dillon, and Miss Nancy Roberts.

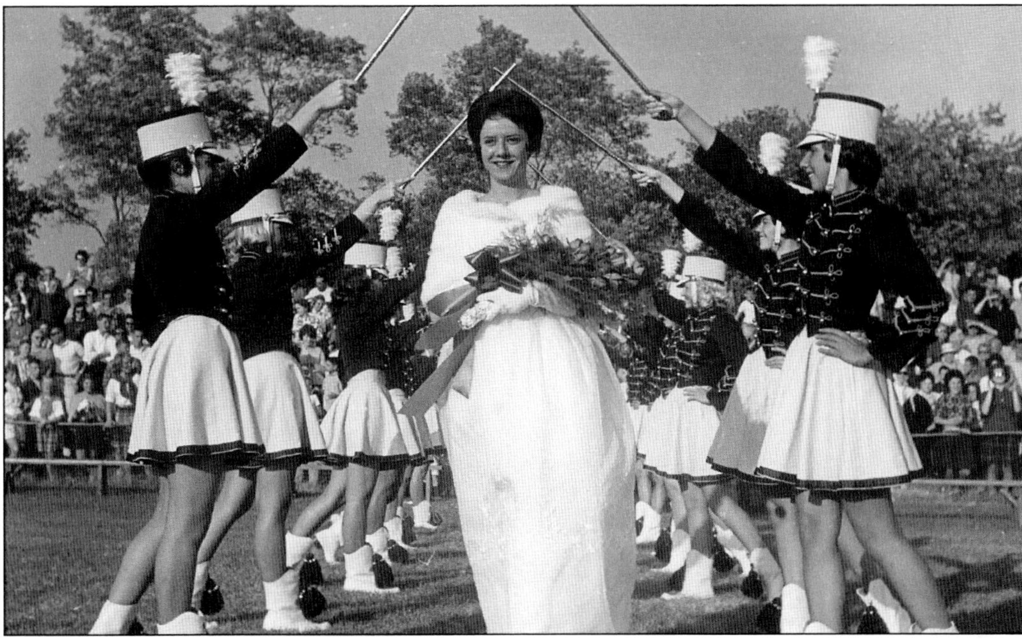

Miss Linda Evans, queen of the Diamond Jubilee held in 1962, smiles as she emerges from archway formed for her by Manasquan High School twirlers during half-time ceremonies at Manasquan–Toms River football game on the field at the borough high school. The Big Blue Warriors downed the Toms River Indians 27 to 14.

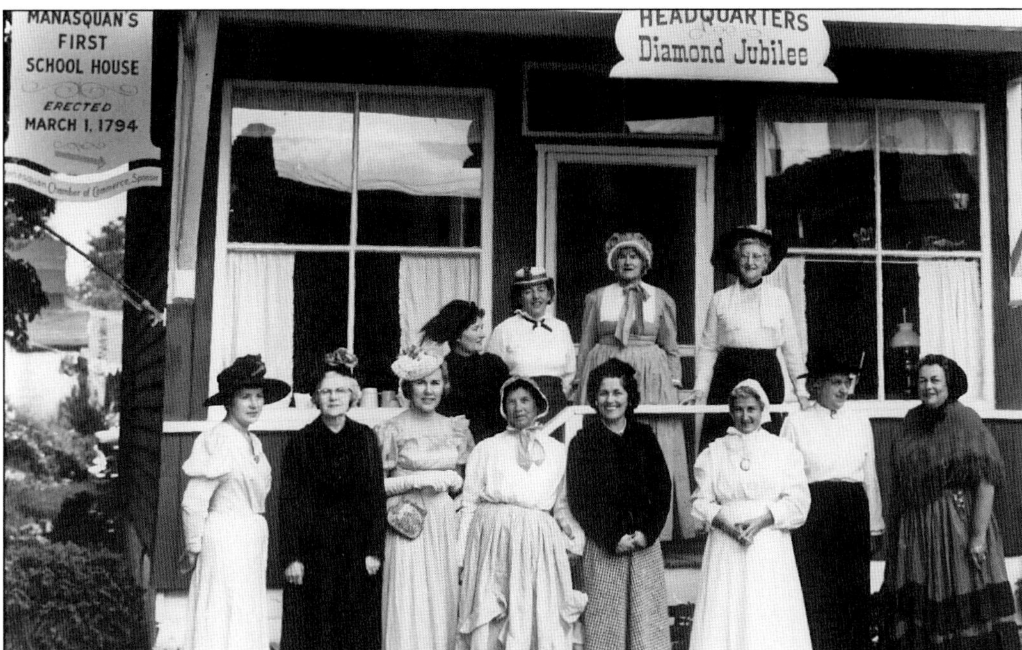

Members of the hospitality committee for the borough celebration, dressed in period costume, gather outside the Diamond Jubilee headquarters. Events during the gala included a parade, fishing contest, Historymobile at the Manasquan Public Library, flower show, Big Sea Day festivities, and a family barbecue for the entire town.

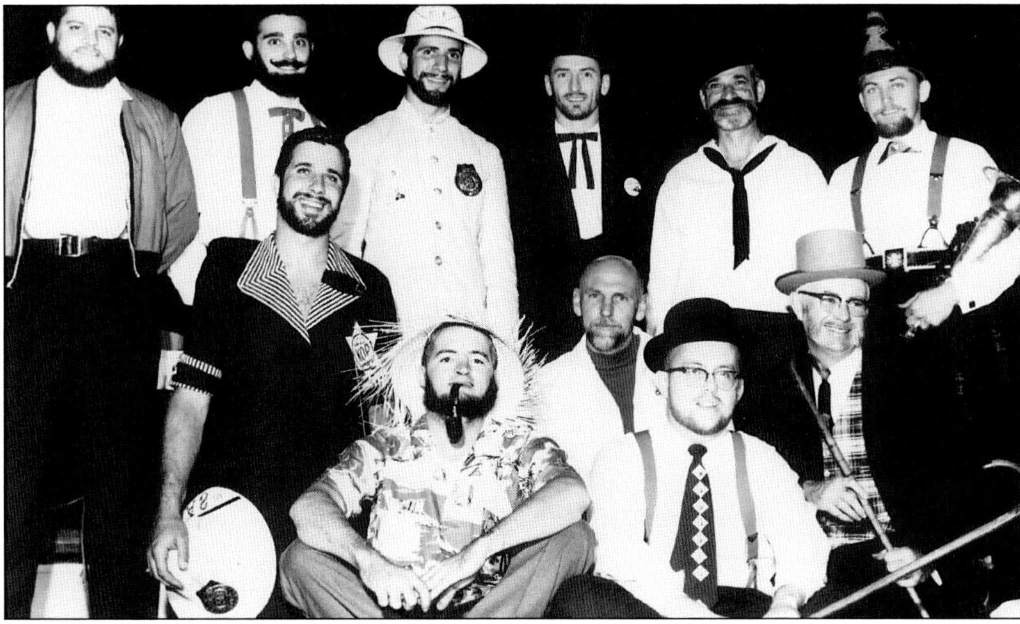

"Brothers of the Brush" exhibit beards grown for the Diamond Jubilee in 1962. According to Sal Maraziti (standing, second from right), chairman of the beard growers' events, prizes were given in a variety of categories. Left to right are (front row) Sal Maraziti Jr., Clifford Ferguson, Roy Hains, Ed Oliver, and Bob Fitzgerald; (standing) Jerry Caggiano, George R. Dempsey Jr., Peter Maraziti, John C. Ebner Jr., Mr. Maraziti, and Eugene Bialas.

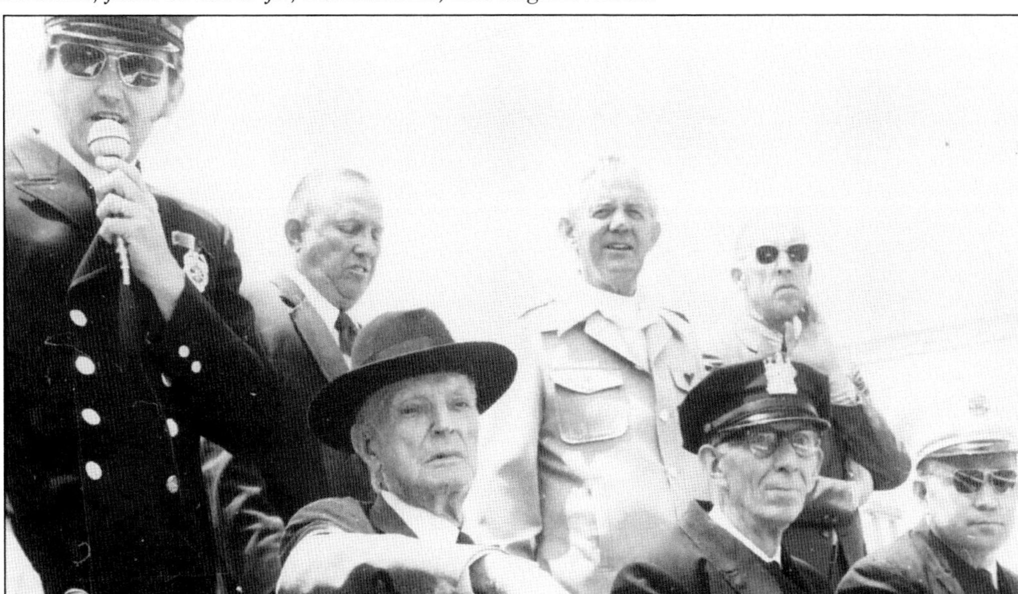

Enjoying the parade marking the 75th anniversary of the Borough of Manasquan, Eugene Bialas, a fireman, announces floats and parade attractions as (from left to right) Mayor Stuart Hancock; former Mayor Lloyd C. Riddle; George J. Dvorak; George LaFetra, a fireman; Councilman Breckenridge Jones; and Robert Gardner, secretary and treasurer of Manasquan Hook & Ladder Co. No. 1, look on.

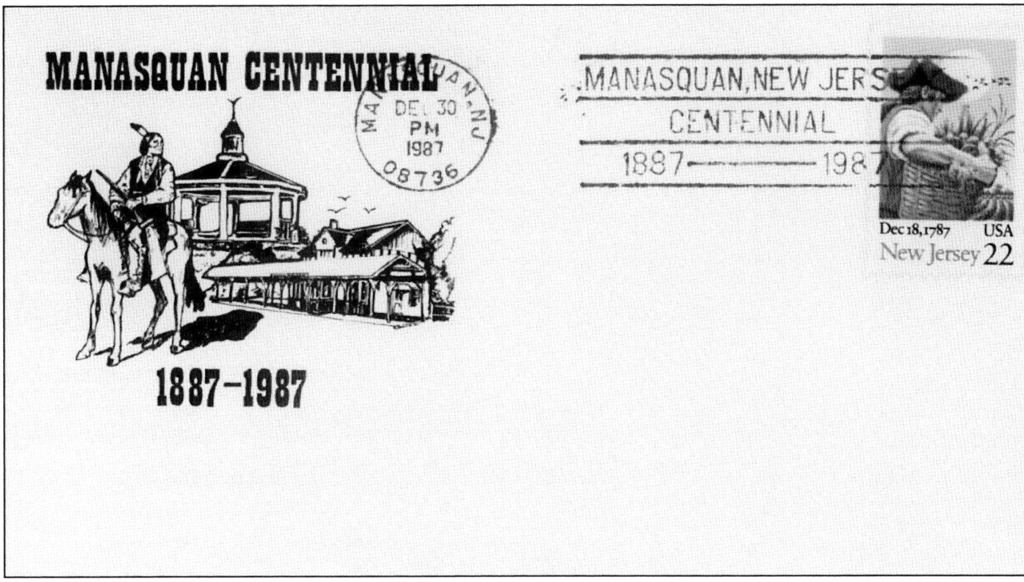

Members of the Manasquan Centennial Committee arranged a first-day cover and stamp cancellation for the Borough of Manasquan on December 30, 1987, the 100th anniversary of the incorporation of the town. Historical records indicate that Manasquan, which has been interpreted from Native American tongue to mean "isle of the squaws," was settled in 1685. The illustration was the creation of Melinda Saminski, a member of the Manasquan Centennial Committee and borough resident.

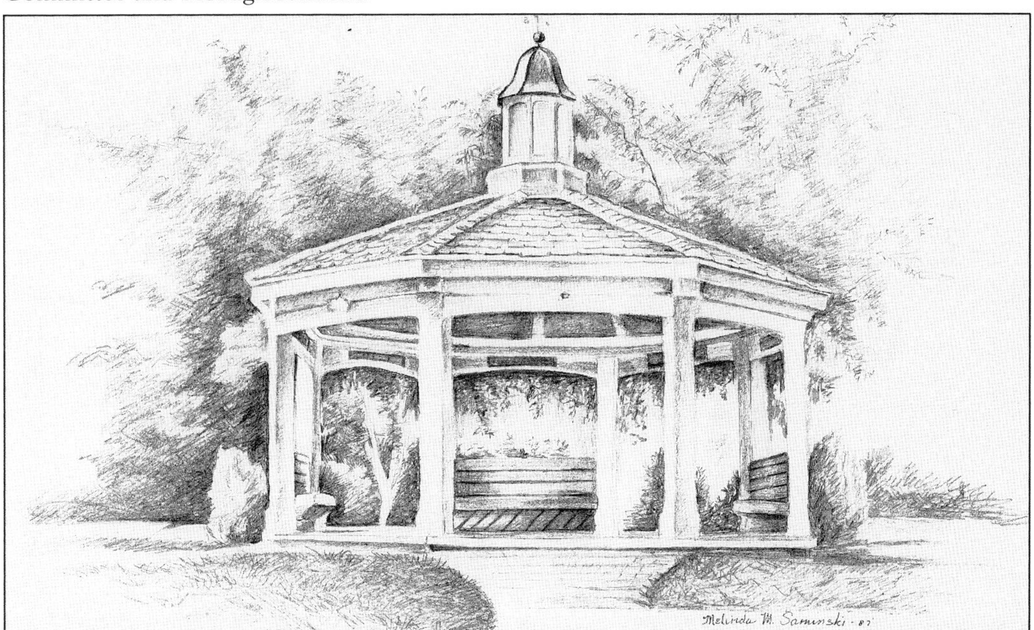

This rendering of the Manasquan Centennial Memorial Gazebo was also illustrated by artist Melinda Saminski. The gazebo was constructed for the 100th anniversary of the borough in 1987. Joel Parker and William W. Donovan (a former borough mayor), co-chairmen of the Centennial Permanent Memorial Committee, said the committee chose a gazebo as a memorial because in the mid- to late 1800s important events took place in a community's gazebo.

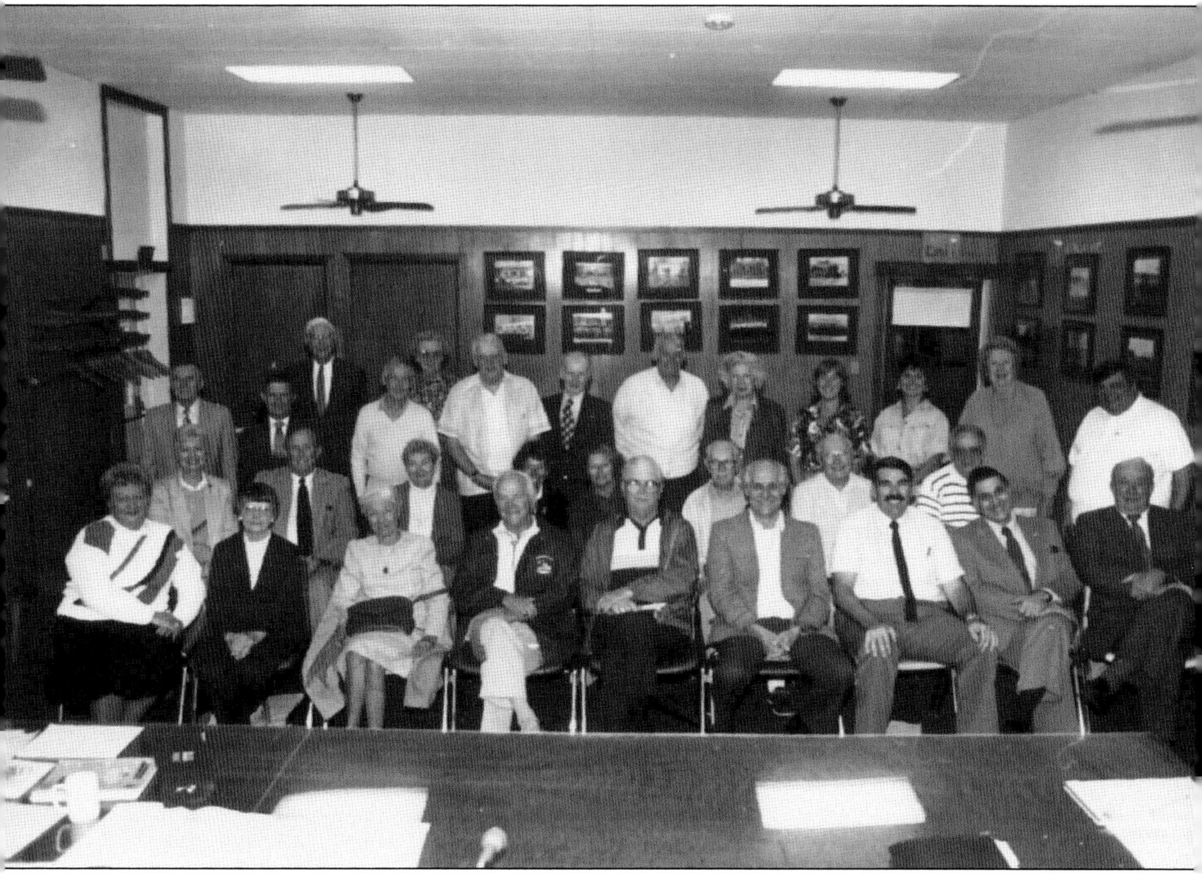

Some members of the Manasquan Centennial Committee meet in Borough Hall during 1987. More than 300 area residents from at least 22 organizations participated in planning and executing the festivities. Members of the Centennial Steering Committee were Iva Messick, chairwoman of the committee and the first president of the Squan Village Historical Society; John Evans, vice chairman; Raymond Pettit, treasurer; and Alyce May and Wesley V. Banse Sr. (borough historian), recording secretaries. Other steering committee members were George Skokos, Elizabeth Coder, George L. Tootell, George Williams, Kenneth Miller, Terance Kelleher, and Dorothy Decker. Events were planned throughout the year with most activities held October 3–10. Many members of the Centennial Committee were also charter members of the Squan Village Historical Society founded the prior year.

Mrs. Esther Riddle Mills, the former Miss Manasquan of 1937, is joined by Thomas S. Birckhead Jr., editor and publisher of the *Coast Star*, and his daughter, Mary, during the borough's Centennial celebration in 1987. Mrs. Mills, a Manasquan native whose father served as mayor of the community, returned once again to Manasquan for the gala from her home in Toronto, Canada.

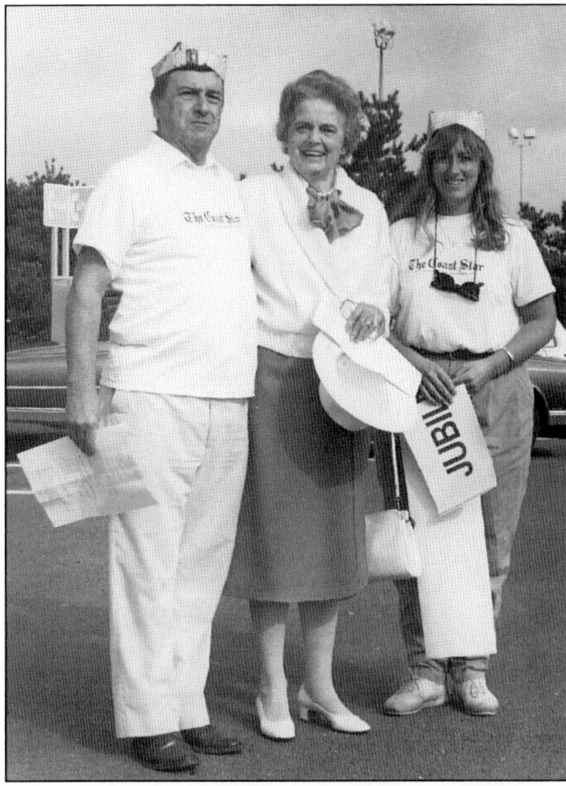

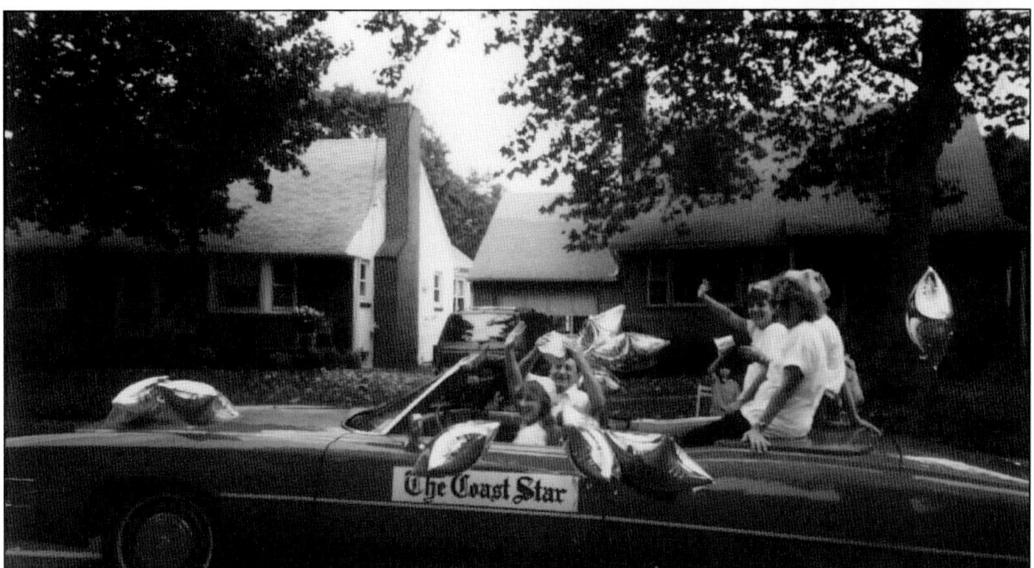

Members of the staff of the *Coast Star*, one of New Jersey's oldest continually published newspapers since 1877 with offices at 13 Broad Street, travel the parade route in a Cadillac lent by Mr. and Mrs. Boyd C. Davis of Manasquan and Pennsylvania. Mary A. Birckhead drives the car, while her father, Thomas S. Birckhead Jr., editor and publisher of the newspaper and a native of Manasquan, rides beside her. Other passengers (from left to right) are Dawn M. Vrabel, Joseph Lee, and Susan Ruane.

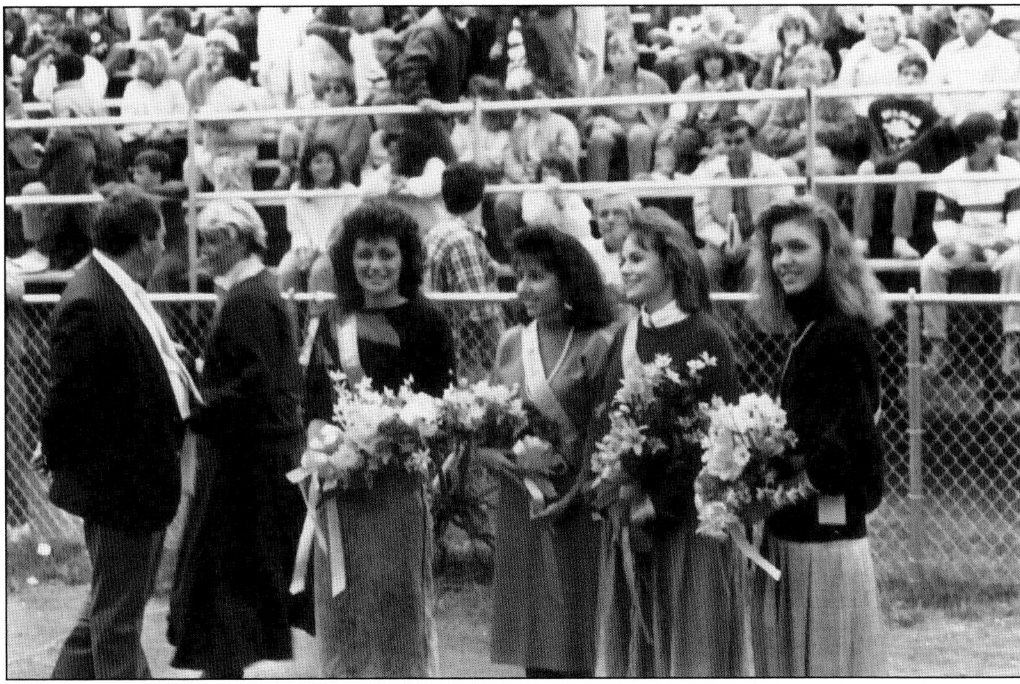

Miss Joan Raffetto (fourth from left), daughter of Mr. and Mrs. Theodore Raffetto, takes part in the Centennial events. Miss Raffetto was selected for the title of Miss Centennial as part of the festivities. She is joined by (from left to right) Mayor John L. Winterstella; his wife, Judy; and Miss Jill Blakeney, a member of the court; Miss Raffetto; and Miss Jessica Danish and Miss Jill Dalton, also members of the court.

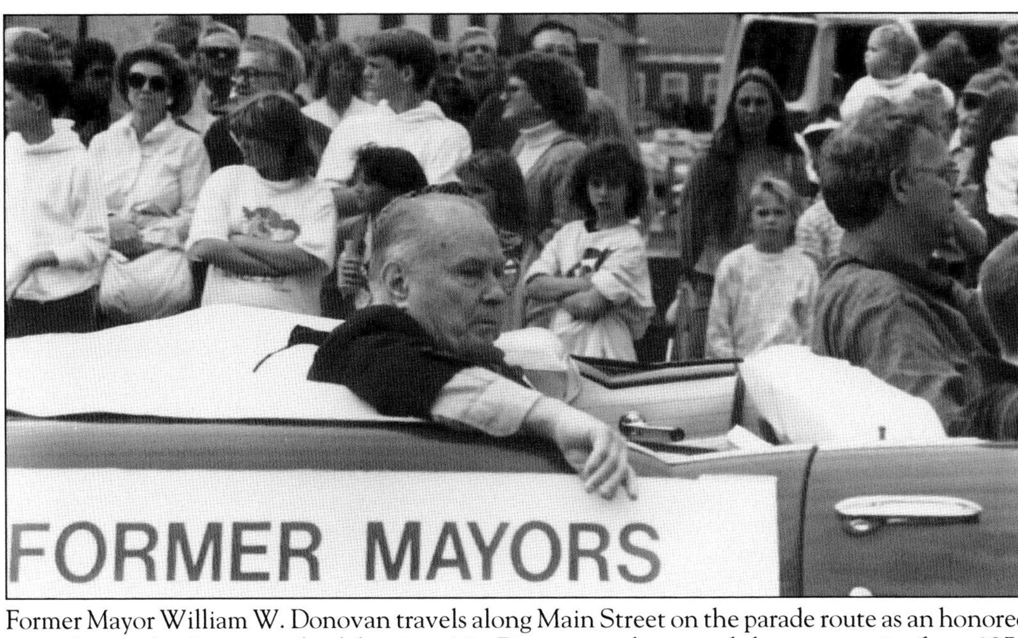

Former Mayor William W. Donovan travels along Main Street on the parade route as an honored guest during the Centennial celebration. Mr. Donovan, who served the community from 1976 until 1983, was one of many special guests who participated in the Centennial festivities.

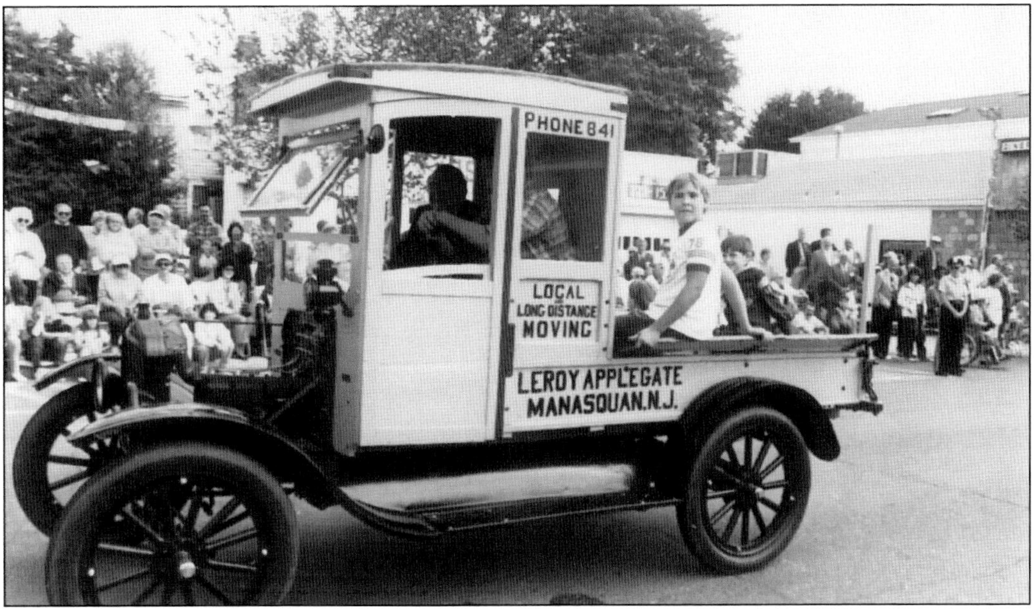

A bright yellow 1921 Model T Ford truck once owned by Leroy Applegate glides through the borough during the 1987 Centennial celebration. Applegate Moving & Storage Co. was established in 1906. During the summer months, Frank Applegate, Leroy's son, remembers his father transporting trunks and baggage from the Sea Girt and Spring Lake rail depots to the hotels in those communities.

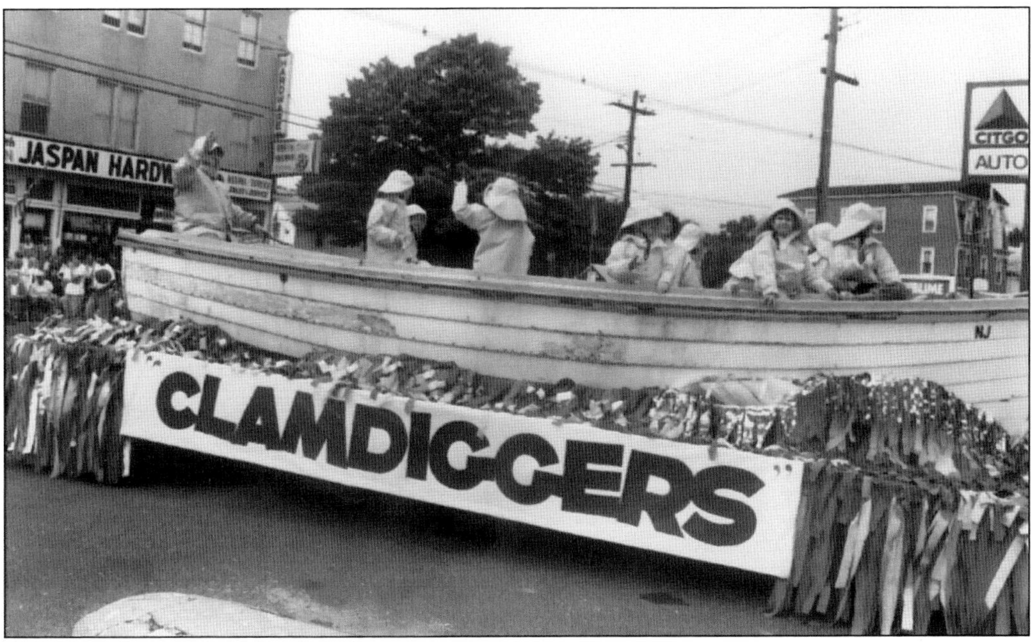

Clamdiggers—a local term used to describe natives of the Shore area—circumnavigate the corner of Main and Broad Streets during Centennial parade. As Manasquan was once a shipbuilding and fishing community, a representative sea captain is perched at the stern as young clamdiggers greet area residents. The float was entered by the Ward Wight Agency, a Manasquan real estate firm owned by the Ward Wight family.

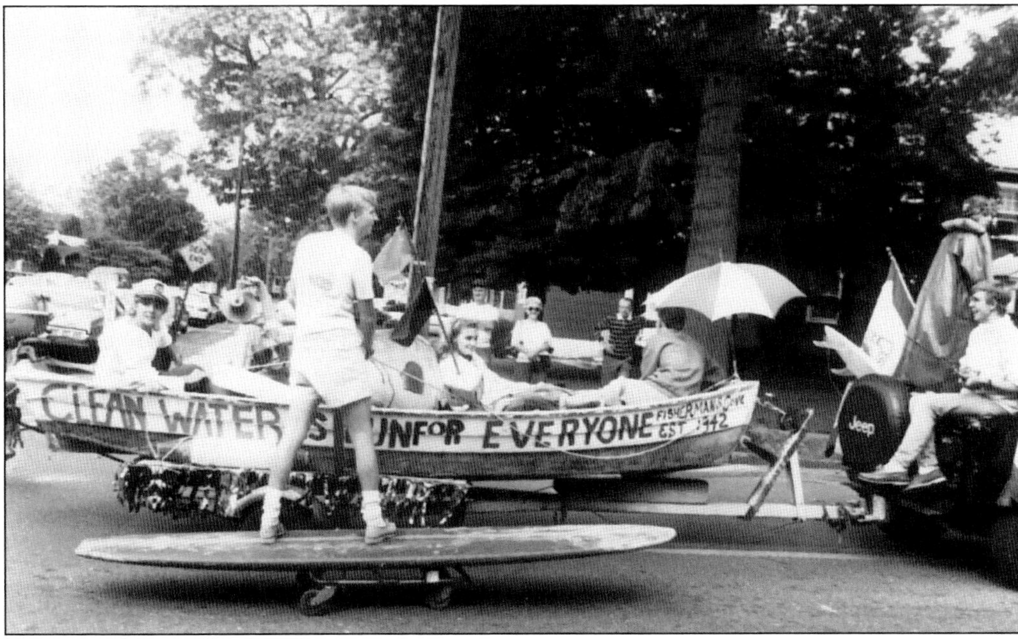

It's smooth sailing—and surfing— for members of the Danish family and friends on this Centennial float. The Danish family operated a bait shop at Fisherman's Cove on land leased from the American Timber Company of Sea Girt from 1942 until 1996, when the site—at the corner of Riverside Drive and Third Avenue—was acquired by Monmouth County.

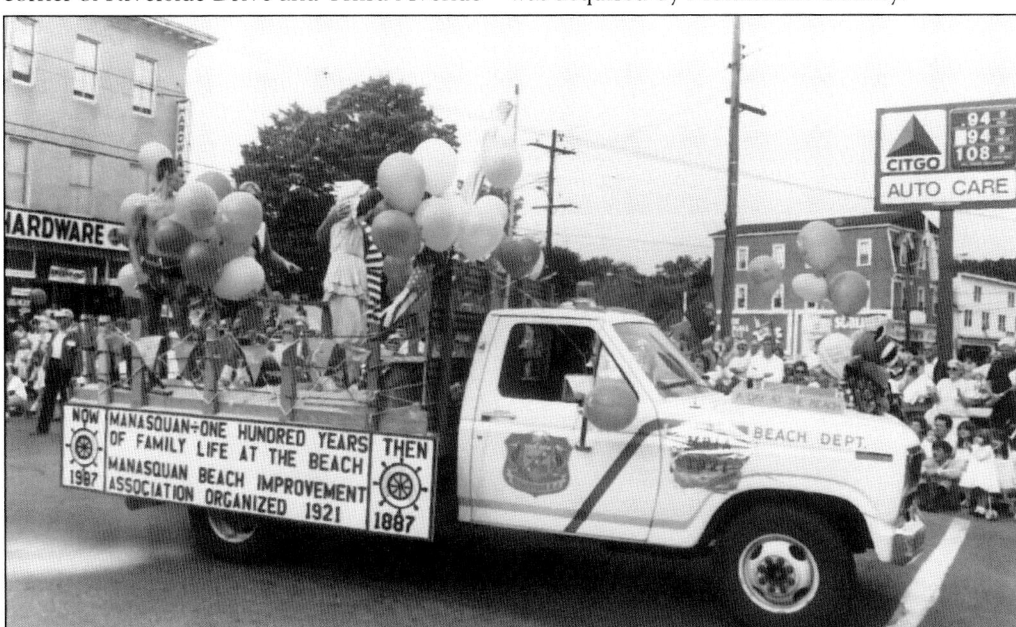

"Manasquan—One Hundred Years of Family Life at the Beach" is the theme of this float entered in the Centennial parade by the Manasquan Beach Improvement Association. Members of the organization, dressed in turn-of-the-century bathing attire, created the float on the back of a borough truck. The association was established in 1921 to protect and preserve the beachfront area of the community for residents and visitors.

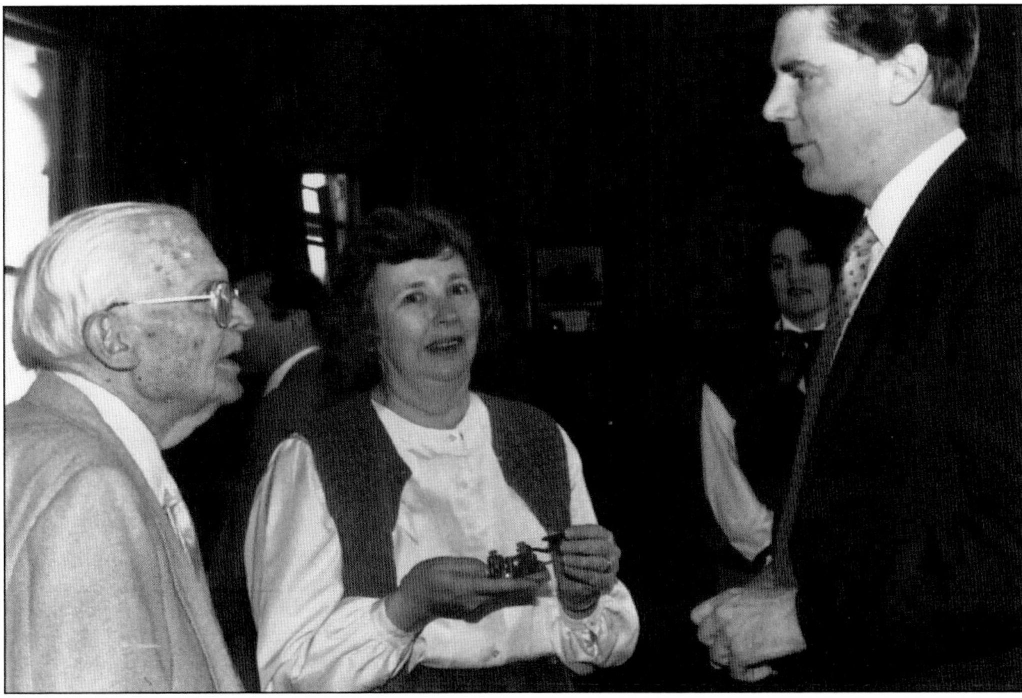

Senator Frank Pallone (right) meets with Mrs. Jean Lee (center), chairwoman of Save Our Station (SOS), a group established in 1984 to restore the Manasquan Railroad Station, and Dr. Donald V. Patterson, whose father served as stationmaster when the station was in the former Sea Plain, North Spring Lake. Dedication services were held in October 1987, upon completion of the restoration project and as part of the borough's Centennial celebration. Senator Pallone worked with the volunteer group to gain government funds for the project.

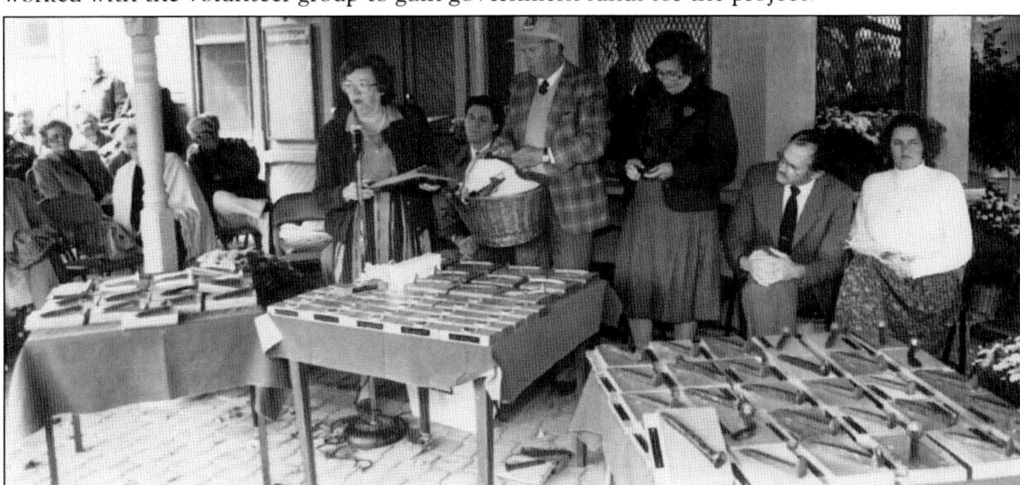

Mrs. Jean Lee, chairwoman of Save Our Station (SOS), and Joel Parker, a member of the group, award gold, silver, and iron spike plaques and coin plaques during Donor Appreciation Day on October 4, 1987, at the rail depot. Assisting the presenters is Mrs. Virginia B. Birckhead. Senator Frank Pallone is seated between Mrs. Lee and Mr. Parker. Richard Thomas and his wife, Deborah (ways and means chairwoman), also participated in the awards ceremony. Plaques were given to those who donated supplies, services, and money.

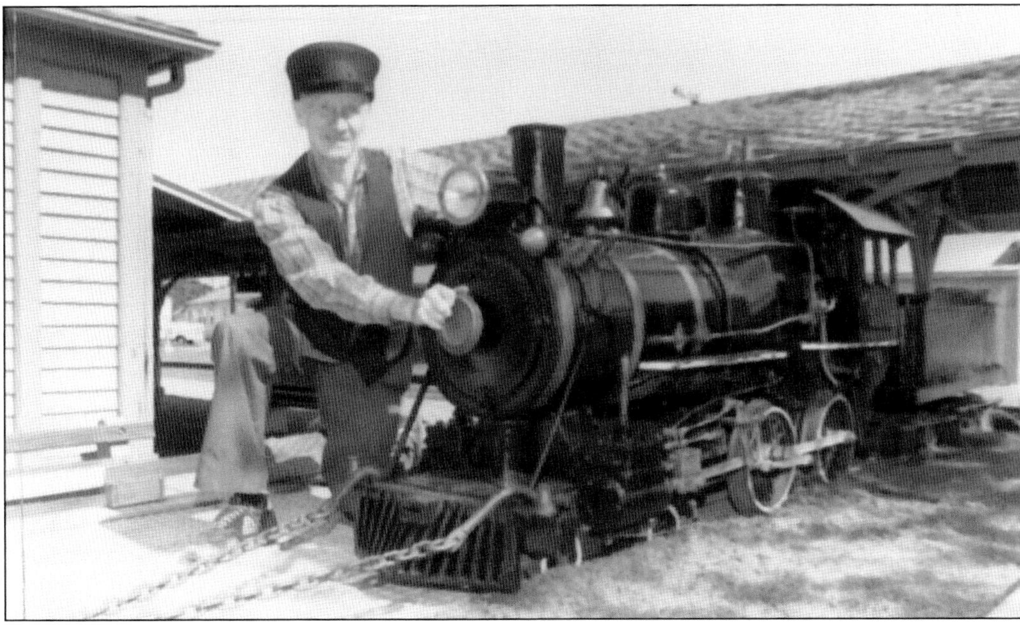

George Williams, a member of Save Our Station (SOS), a group organized in 1984 to restore the deteriorating Manasquan Railroad Station, serves as the engineer on this Centennial parade float. The steam engine—built by Carrey Locomotive Works in Jersey City—was lent to the SOS by the Pine Creek Railroad, Allaire. The float took second place in the parade.

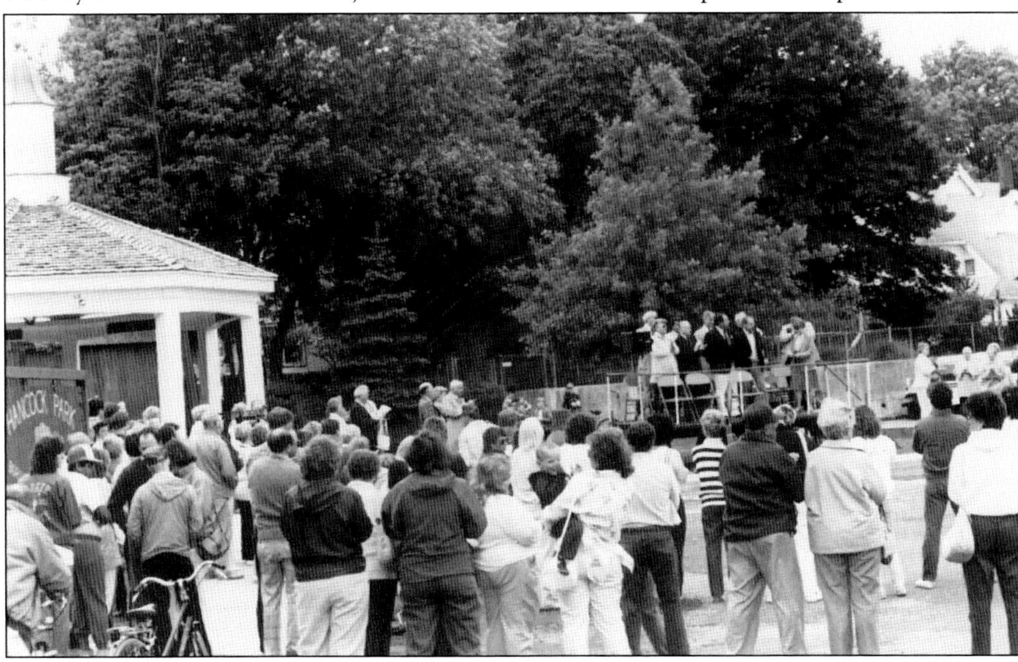

The Centennial Memorial Gazebo in Hancock Park, Old Squan Plaza, was dedicated on May 25, 1987, during Memorial Day ceremonies. The committee, organized to raise funds and oversee construction of the gazebo, dedicated it as a "memorial to former residents who ordered their lives to create the pleasant community we live in, and for those who gave their lives to protect it."

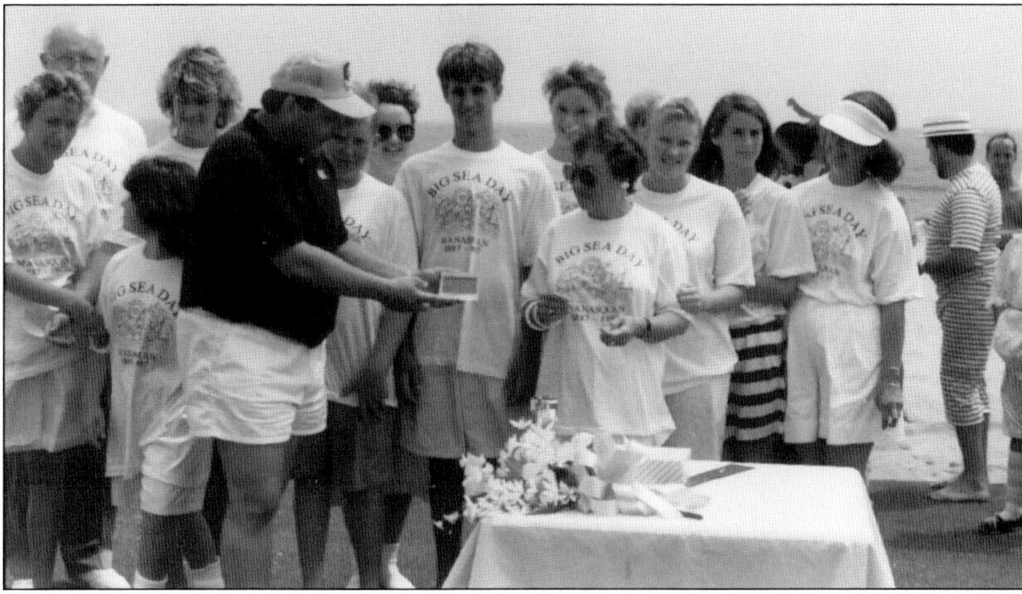

Members of the Croddick family sport Big Sea Day T-shirts during the 1987 Centennial celebration. During Big Sea Day that year, Eugene and Florence Croddick purchased special commemorative T-shirts for their five children, grandchildren, and great-grandchildren, as well as created a display of beach landscape photographs for the Beach Walk, a Centennial event. The Croddicks had been summer residents of Manasquan for 26 years until their home was destroyed by a fire on October 5, 1996.

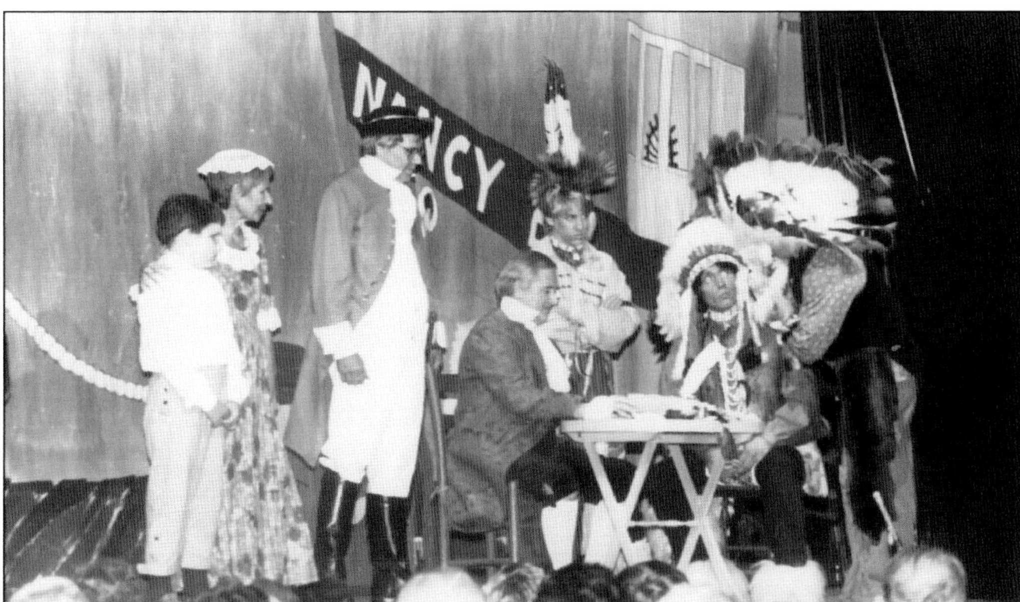

Local residents recreate the April 8, 1665 signing of Monmouth Patent during "Manasquan—A Borough," as part of the historical pageant held during the Centennial festivities. Historical records indicate that the first Europeans in the area made their settlements in the spring or summer of 1664. The pageant highlighted events back to the 1600s in the borough's history.

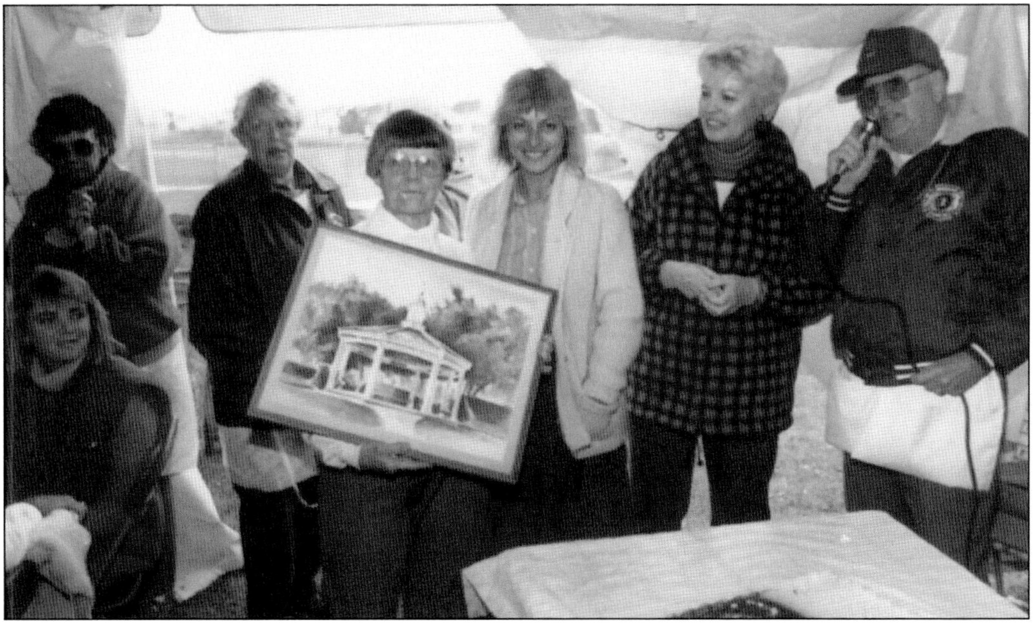

Kenneth Miller (at right), bakemaster, announces special award given to Mrs. Iva Messick (third from left), chairwoman of the Manasquan Centennial celebration and first president of the Squan Village Historical Society. Melinda Saminski presented Mrs. Messick with a watercolor rendering of the newly-constructed Centennial gazebo as a gift on behalf of the Manasquan Centennial Committee. Also participating in the presentation are Constance Watkins, Doris Brittle (at left), and Alyce May (right).

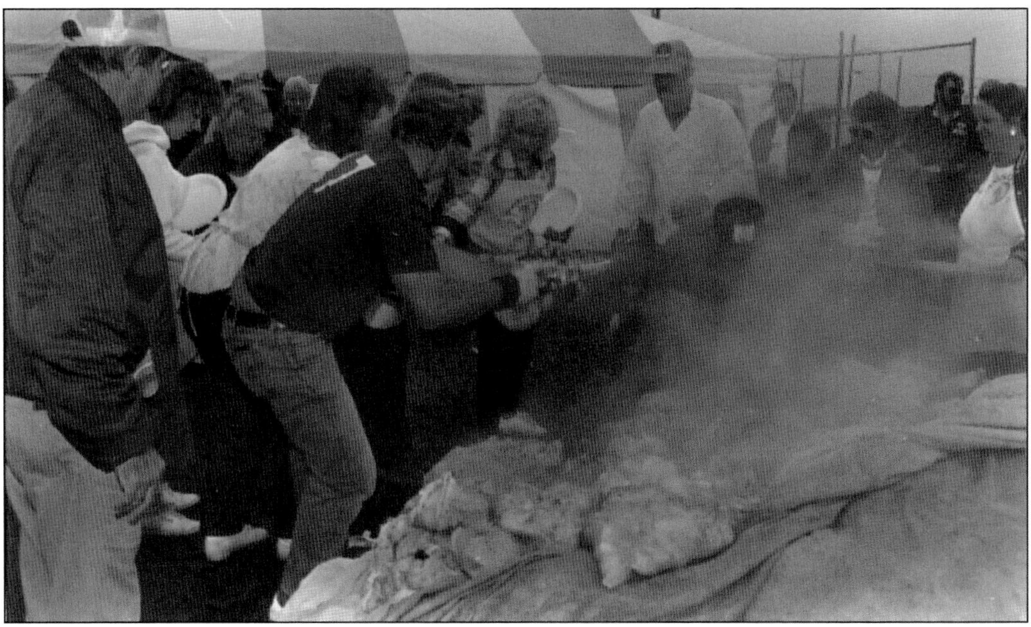

The cooking team performs under direction of Kenneth Miller, bakemaster and borough resident. The old-fashioned clambake at Stockton Park was part of the Centennial festivities. The meal included shellfish and other seafood, chicken, potatoes, corn-on-the-cob, and beverages. Slices from a special birthday cake for Manasquan topped off the meal.

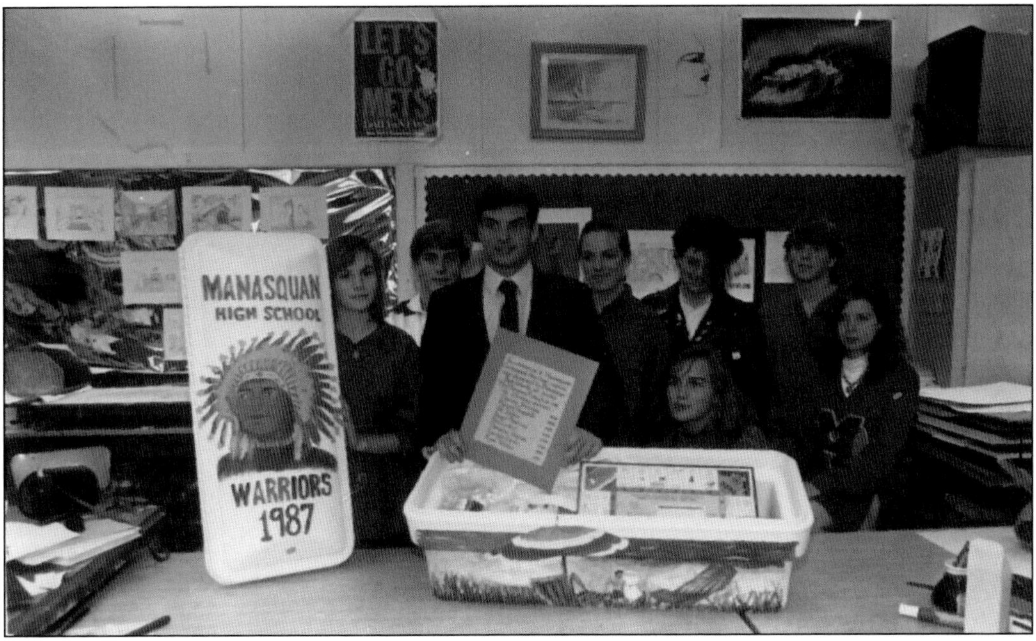

Students from Manasquan High School and their teacher display a time capsule. From left to right are Jill Dalton, Don Lichter, John Yachnik, Mrs. Maryann S. Monaghan (art teacher), Christina Vilacoba, Bridget Patterson (seated), Brian Sassone, and Christine Brennan. The capsule was prepared for the 100th anniversary of the borough and was buried adjacent to the Centennial gazebo. It will be opened in 2037.

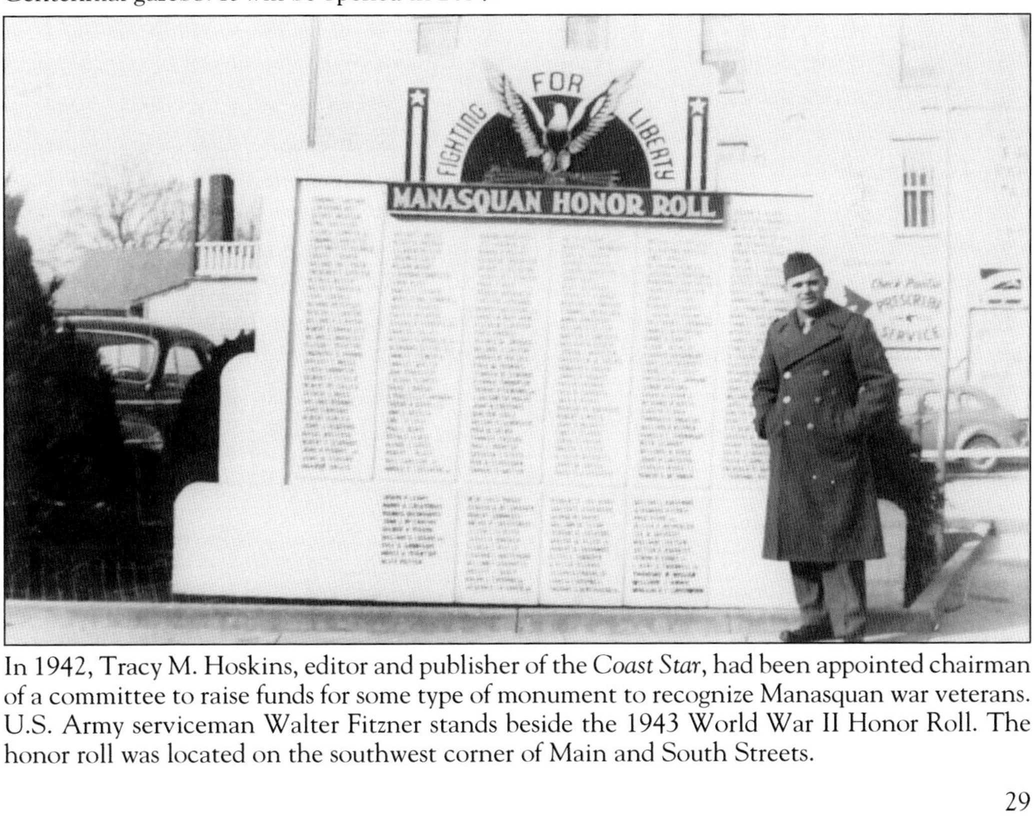

In 1942, Tracy M. Hoskins, editor and publisher of the *Coast Star*, had been appointed chairman of a committee to raise funds for some type of monument to recognize Manasquan war veterans. U.S. Army serviceman Walter Fitzner stands beside the 1943 World War II Honor Roll. The honor roll was located on the southwest corner of Main and South Streets.

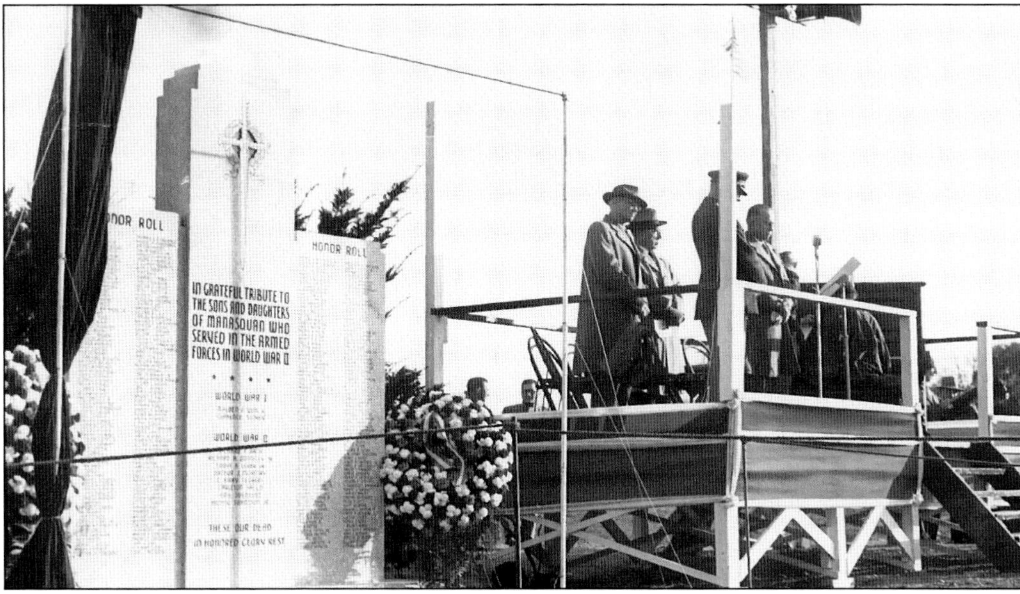

The granite Manasquan War Memorial replacing its wooden predecessor was unveiled on November 12, 1950, during services held at Memorial Park, on the east side of Broad Street across from the high school. Tracy M. Hoskins served as the chairman of the War Memorial Committee and was assisted by Erwood D. McCormack and Robert J. Riddle.

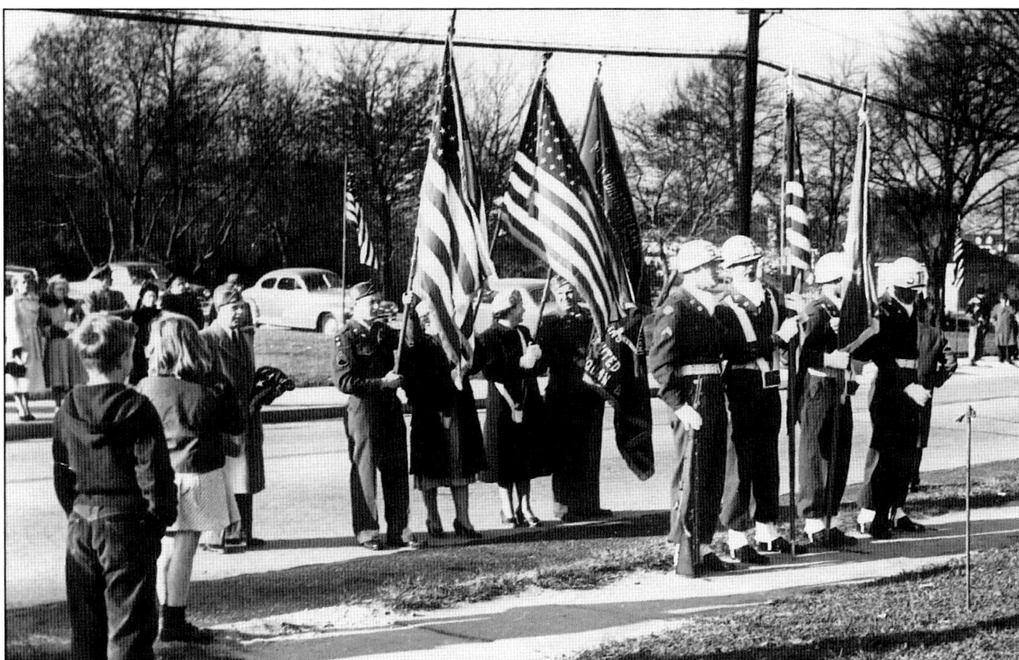

Area residents gather to participate in the dedication of the World War I and II monument. Mayor Raymond R. Baker unveiled the monument while the Manasquan Veterans of Foreign War Post No. 1838 placed a wreath on it. The Manasquan Men's Chorus and the Fort Monmouth Band also participated in the service. The monument was moved on December 7, 1968, to its present location in Old Squan Plaza to allow for the expansion of the schools.

Two

Houses of Worship

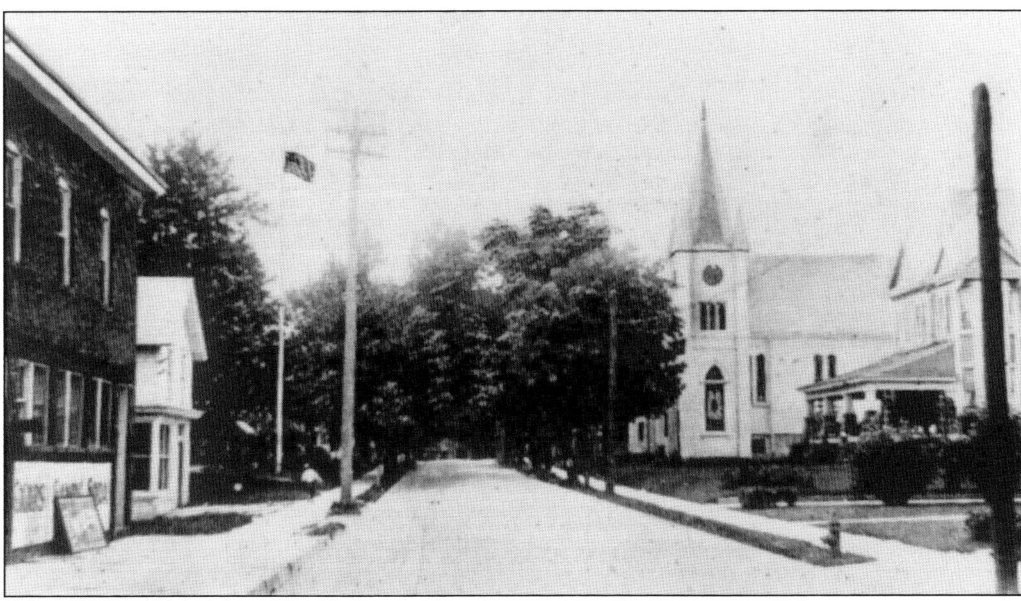

The First Baptist Church of Manasquan—seen about 1930—depicts a sparsely developed South Street. The stained-glass windows on the north and south sides of the sanctuary were contributed as memorials at a cost of $25 each. The large baptismal window facing South Street was donated at a cost of $275.

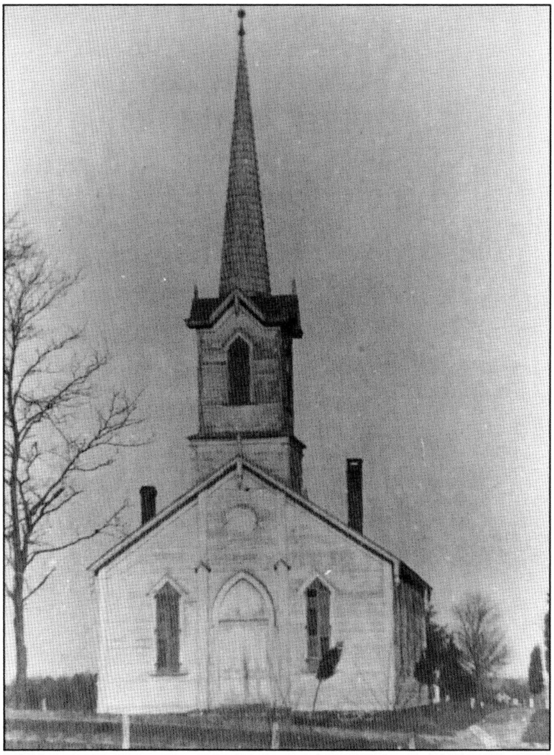

The Ocean Church on the Hill—or the Free Church, as it was also known—that stood adjacent to Atlantic View Cemetery at the top of Church Street was established in 1842–43 as the Union Church for Methodist Episcopalians, Methodist Protestants, Baptists, and Presbyterians who shared the church for several years. By 1898, no longer used for Sunday congregations, it was used solely as a cemetery chapel. In 1922, the church was razed.

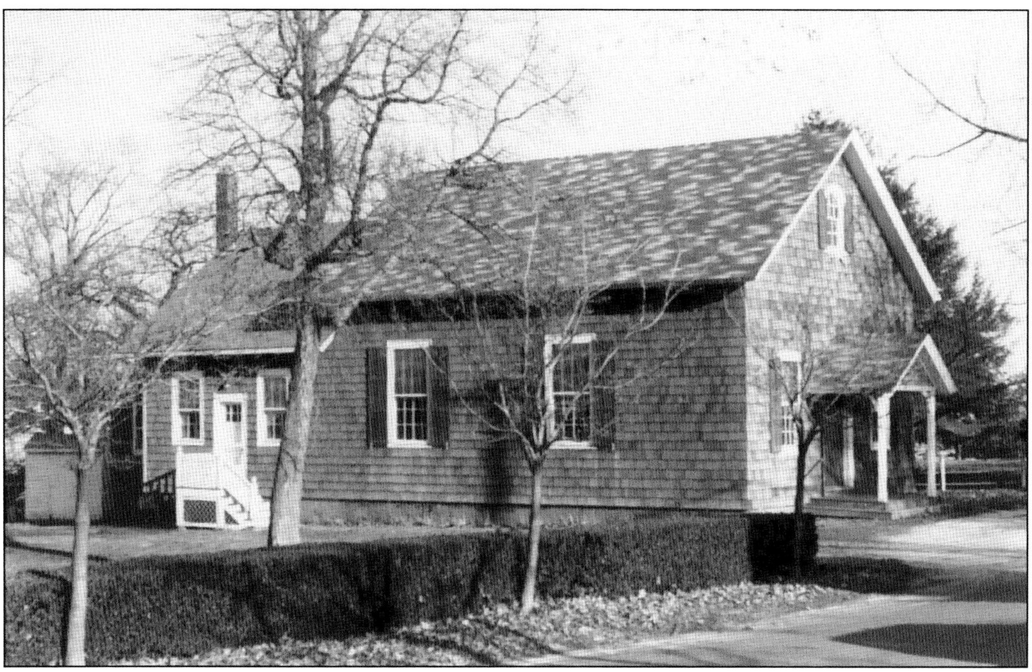

This is a view of the Friends' Meeting House as it is seen today. In 1882, a group met to discuss plans to replace the church and in 1884 the task was accomplished. The burial ground, one of the oldest in Monmouth County, contains many old stones; one of which is still decipherable—that of Joshua Gifford, who died on November 30, 1800.

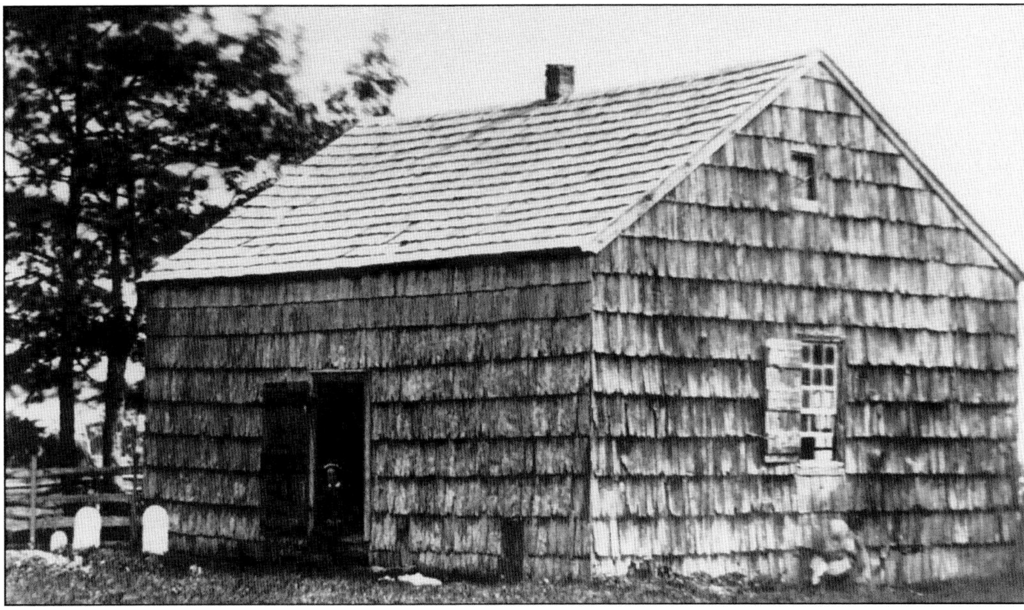

The Friends' Meeting was located in Wall Township but had a great influence on Manasquan and its history. In 1685, Quakers purchased land in the Manasquan area. The first meetinghouse—completed in 1701—was a two-story, 20-by-30-foot building situated just north of the present structure. The second floor of the church was a gallery for children.

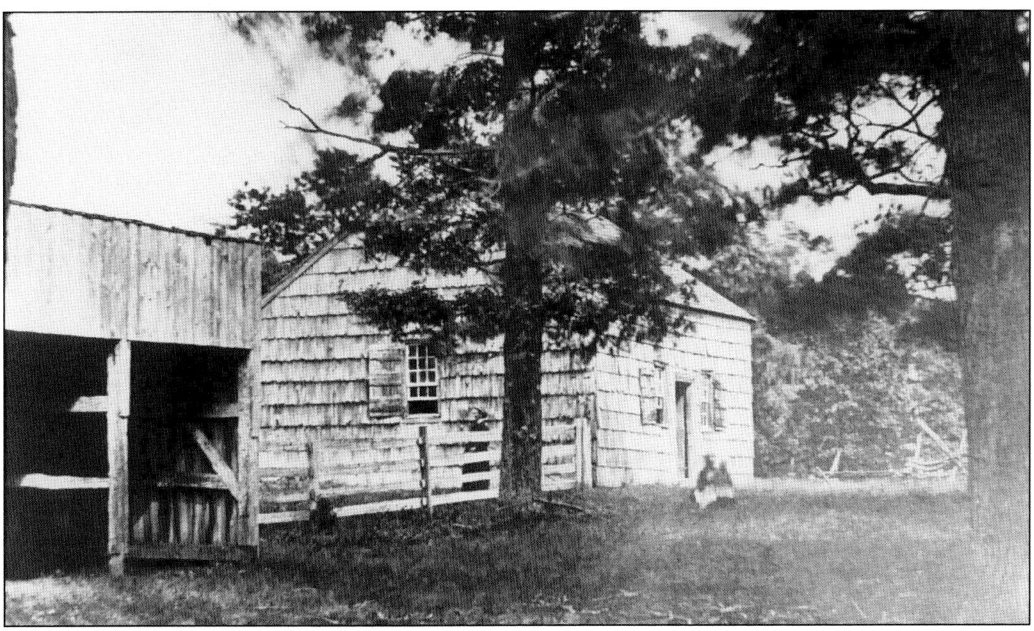

This view of the 1701 Friends' Meeting House shows the carriage house and fenced area for horses. The meetinghouse was modeled after the Shrewsbury (New Jersey) Meeting House. Damage from a storm in August 1808 made the house of worship unsafe, and in 1812, the building was remodeled into a one-story structure.

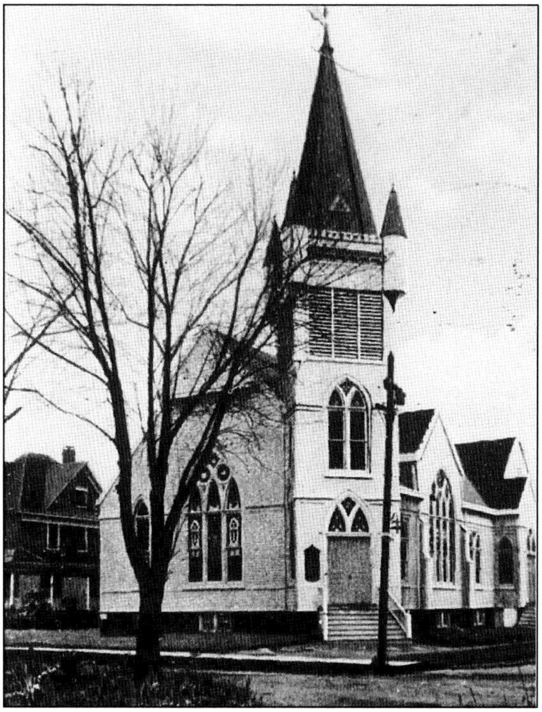

In 1890, the church at the corner of South Street and Marcellus Avenue—a portion of the former G.V. Marcellus farm—was constructed. The original tower on the First Manasquan Bible Church (originally the Methodist Protestant Church) had been copied from architecture from the University of Glasgow, Scotland, with one large spire surrounded by four smaller towers. (But for the sake of safety, the towers were removed following the 1938 hurricane.)

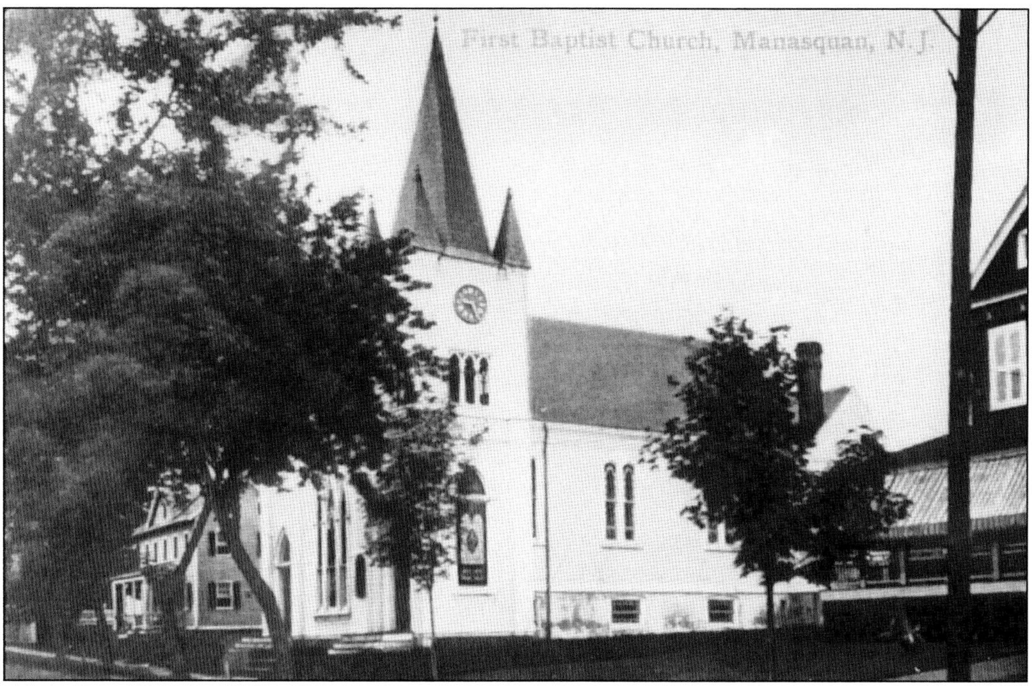

Thirty-seven persons gathered at the farm of John and Elizabeth Havens in Howell Township on October 20, 1804, to sign a covenant to form the Baptist Church of Squan. In 1869, members of the congregation acquired land on South Street and built the Squan Village Baptist Church. On January 16, 1875, the congregation incorporated as the First Baptist Church of Manasquan, and in 1898, the stained-glass windows were added to the structure.

In this 1954 image, the spire from the third Methodist church is removed. The wooden sanctuary (as seen below) had been built on land once owned by Osborn Curtis. The following year the current red brick church with its white pillars was built in its place.

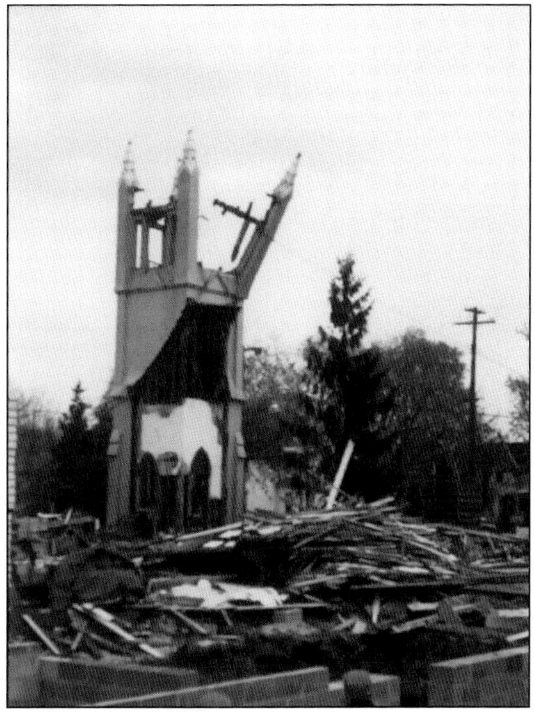

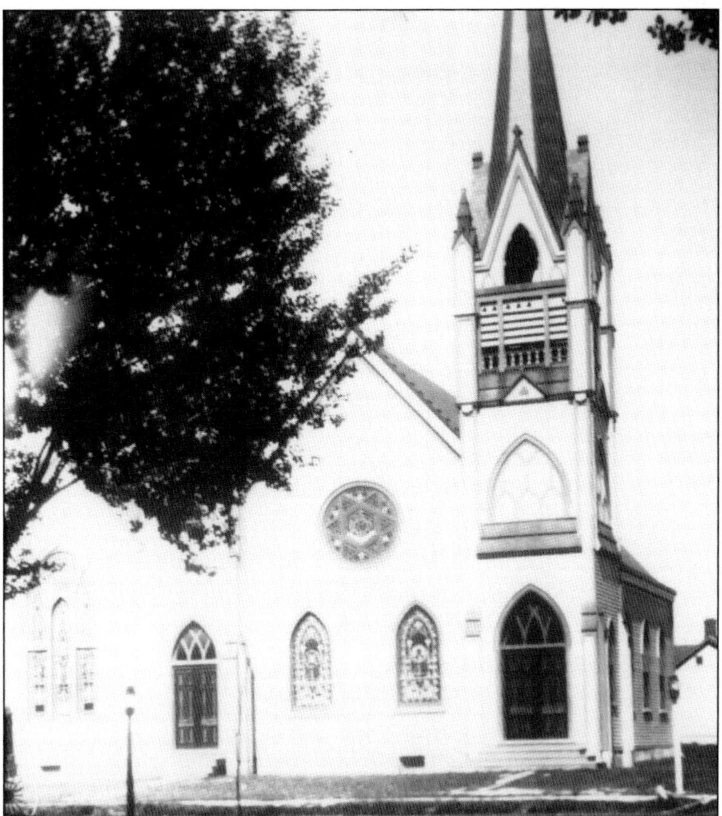

On August 29, 1890, the cornerstone was laid for the Manasquan United Methodist Church at its present site —the southwest corner of South and Church Streets. Prior to this location, two Methodist churches had been built at 36 Church Street, but both were destroyed by fire: one in 1869 and the other in 1890, in which the organ, some song books, and a marble-top stand were salvaged. The church, and its parsonage, were built for $18,000.

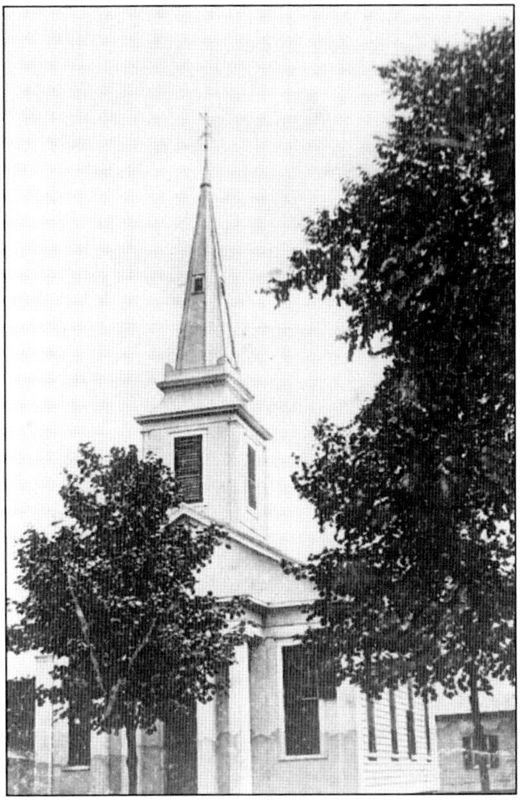

On May 28, 1922, with 27 charter members, the Evangelical Holy Trinity Lutheran Church was organized under direction of the Reverend Walter A. Grunow of Atonement Lutheran Church in Asbury Park. The parishioners applied for a charter of incorporation in 1924, and the charter was recorded in 1926. Church parishioners began holding services in the former Presbyterian church located at the corner of Main Street and Osborn Avenue during September 1922.

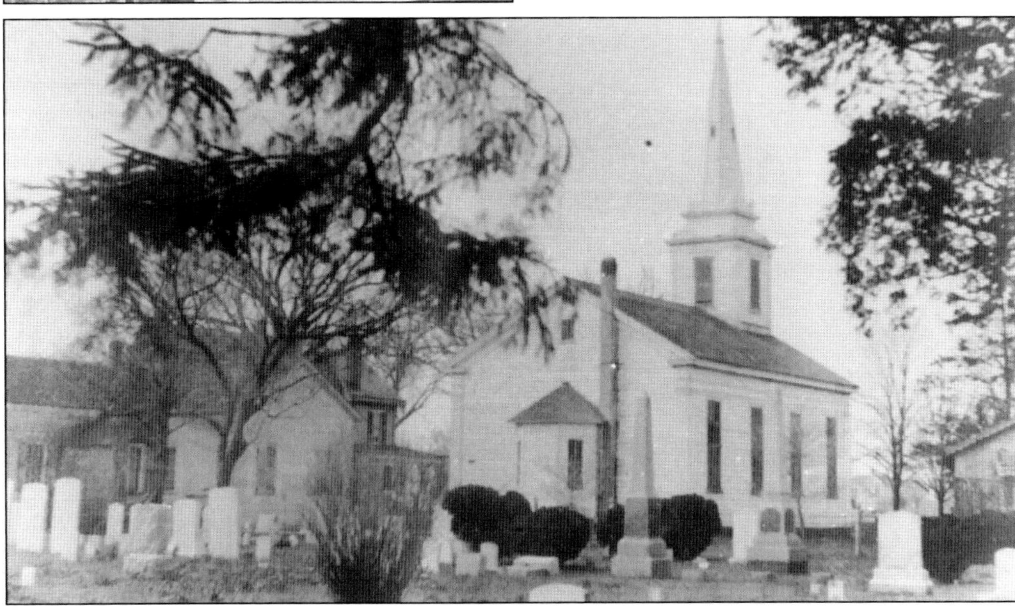

Established in 1848 by Presbyterians who built a larger church on Virginia Avenue in 1904, their house of worship was unused for some years before it became Holy Trinity Evangelical Church in 1914. The use of the site as a cemetery predates the construction of a church on Main Street and Osborn Avenue. Dr. John Morford, one of the borough's earliest physicians, who died on December 15, 1838, is buried in this cemetery.

The Shiloh Baptist Church on Union Avenue was started in 1905 by Jasper Morgan Sr. and his wife, Mattie. By 1909, a plot of land was purchased on Union Avenue, and meetings were held on the site in a tent. Also, meetings were held on the second floor of the Joseph Allen grocery store, 83 Main Street, until the sanctuary was built in 1913.

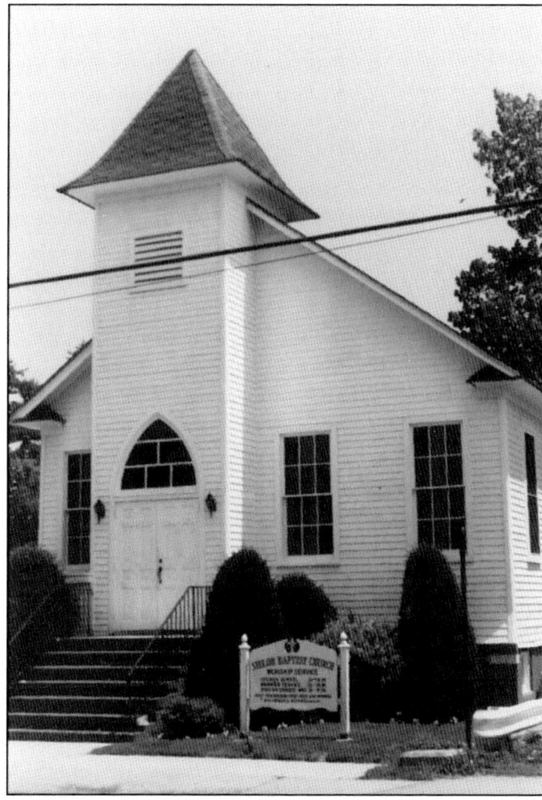

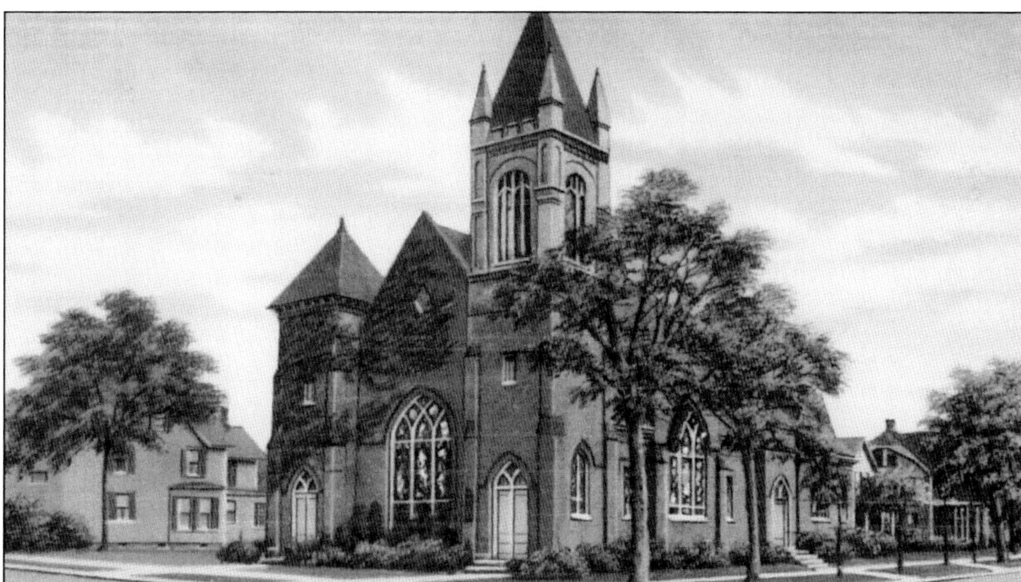

The Presbyterian Church of Squan Village was organized in 1848, with nine members. They established a church on Main Street. But by May 1903, the congregation had grown to 175 and parishioners voted to purchase property at the corner of South Street and Virginia Avenue to build a larger sanctuary. The church's name was changed to the First Presbyterian Church of Manasquan in November 1904.

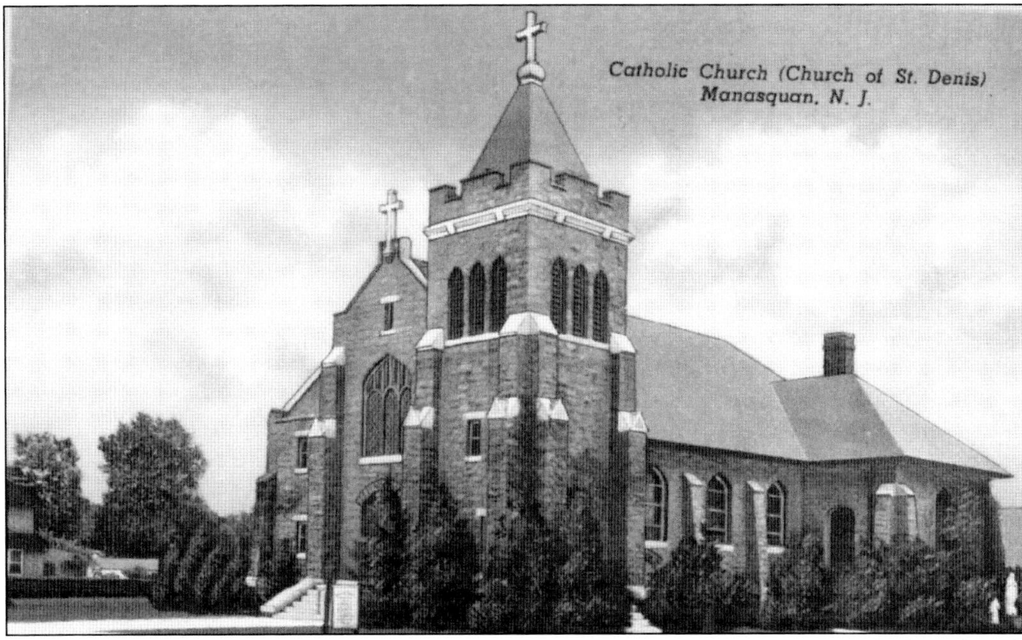

In April 1909, Dennis Sweeney, an original trustee of St. Denis Roman Catholic Church, donated the site on Union Avenue (Route 71) for the building of a church. By June 22, the Diocese of Trenton formed a church corporation titled "the Church of St. Denis, Manasquan, New Jersey." The name of the church honored St. Denis, a martyred bishop of France.

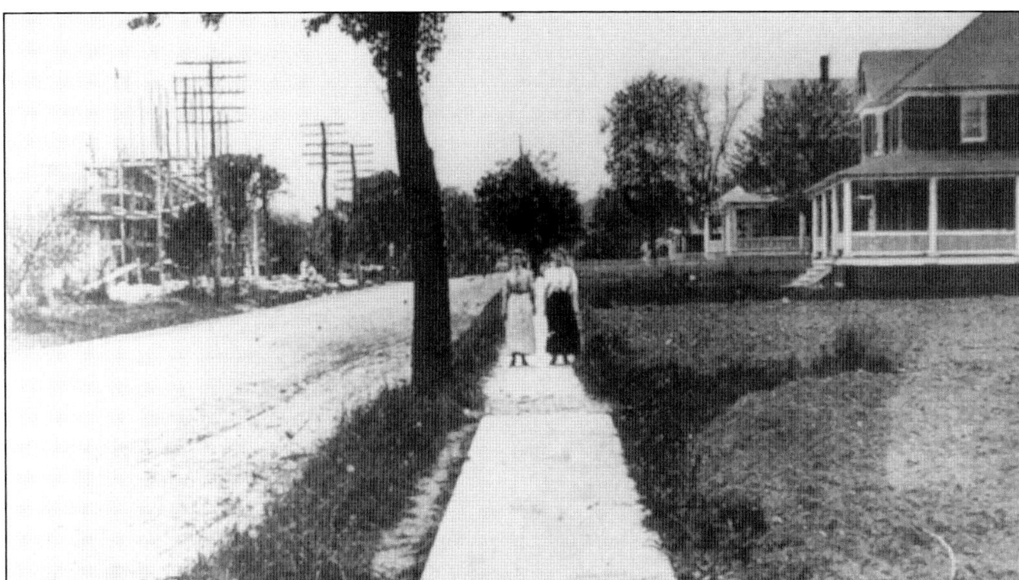

This view shows the construction of St. Denis Roman Catholic Church. The cornerstone for the church was laid on July 11, 1909, and the first Mass was offered in the church on October 15, 1911. On June 19, 1955, ground was broken to expand the church to accommodate 750 parishioners. Retaining the stone architecture of the building, the newly expanded church was dedicated on May 30, 1956.

Three

Around Town

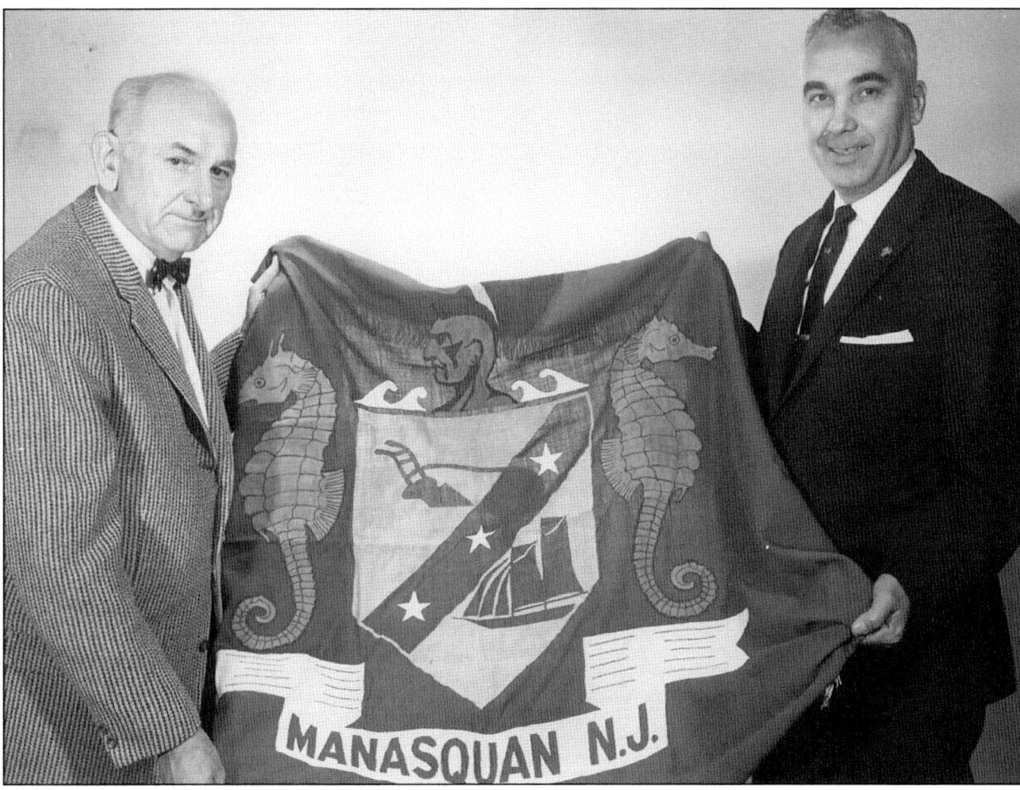

George R. Dempsey (right) presents a Manasquan flag to Mayor Robert E. Mount. The artwork for the bright blue flag was designed by I. Maurice Stokes of Manasquan, who won a competition in 1963 to create a town banner. The emblem shows the head of a Lenni Lenape Indian over a gold shield flanked by seahorses. On the shield, a plow recalls Manasquan's early farming days, a sailing ship depicts the borough's longtime link to seafaring activities, and three stars signify that New Jersey was the third state to ratify the U.S. Constitution.

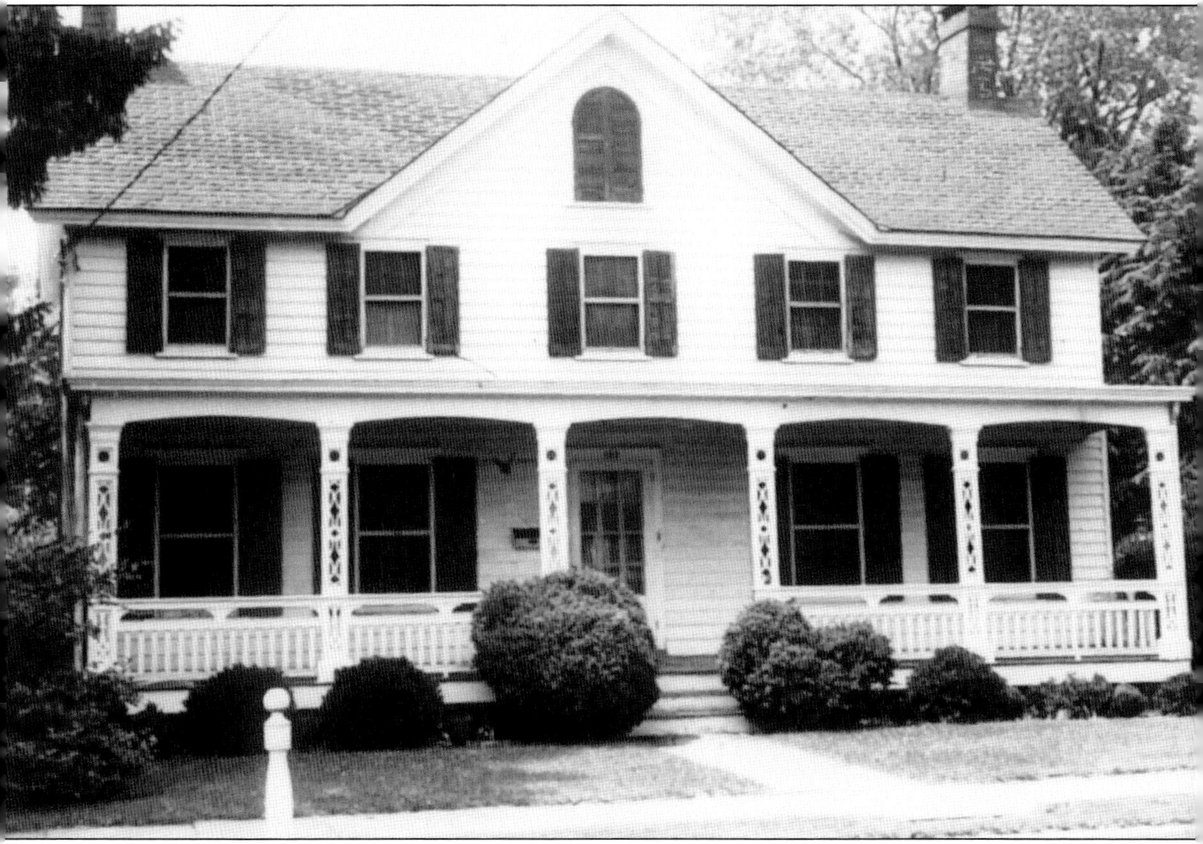

The Bailey-Reed House at 105 South Street was originally owned by John and Ann Bailey in 1812. The home is one of the original 37 dwellings built in the borough when it was known as Squan Village or Crabtown. According to Ernest Reed, the former owner, the carriage house on the property was constructed with floor joists that had once been ship's spars and parts of a mast of the *Thistle*, a ship wrecked off the Manasquan Inlet in 1811. In July 1997, the house was purchased by the Squan Village Historical Society to be used as its headquarters and museum.

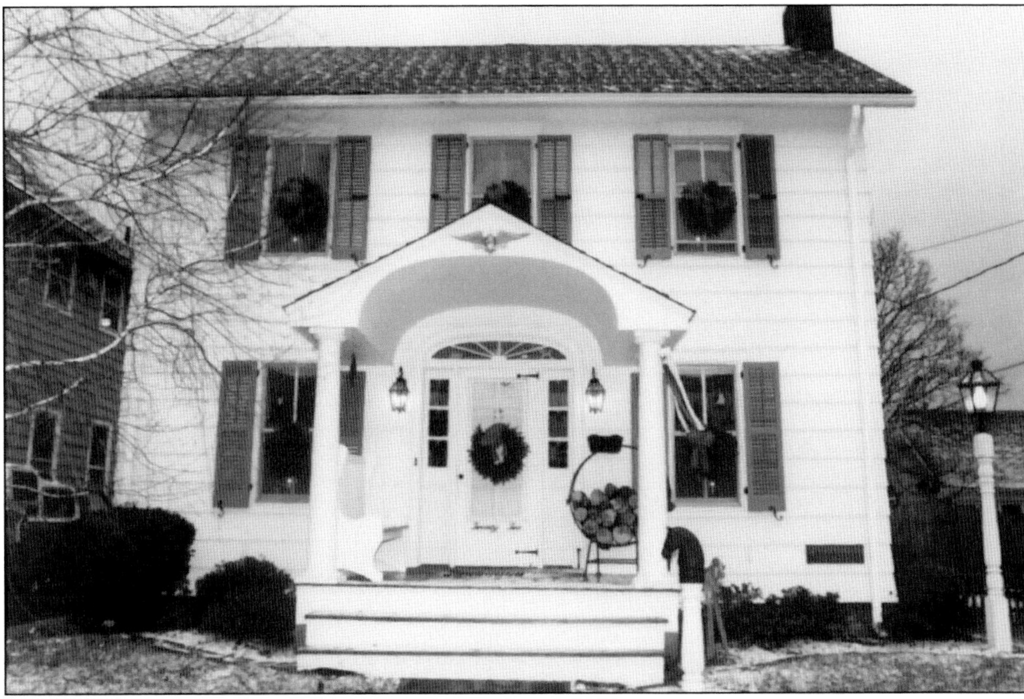

Osborn and Sarah Curtis were the first owners of the former wheat field which was located at 22 Curtis Avenue. The property was purchased by William P. and Catherine Reynolds on March 12, 1877, and a home was built shortly after the purchase. For more than 30 years, this Colonial-style farmhouse has been the home of Wesley V. Banse Sr. and his wife, Grace. From 1976 until December 31, 1997, Mr. Banse served as the Manasquan borough historian.

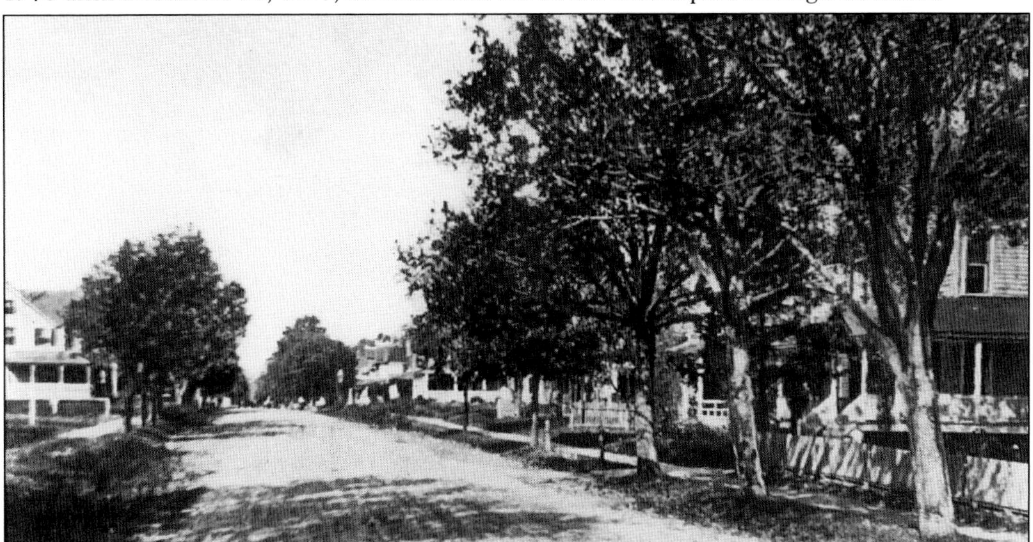

Looking west on Curtis Avenue, before the 1920s, this view of the street featured a gravel road and no curbs, but was well developed with houses. The street, named for local businessman Osborn Curtis, was home to sea captains and other businessmen. At one time, the Manasquan United Methodist Church parsonage was located at 18 Curtis Avenue, now the home of the Paslawsky family.

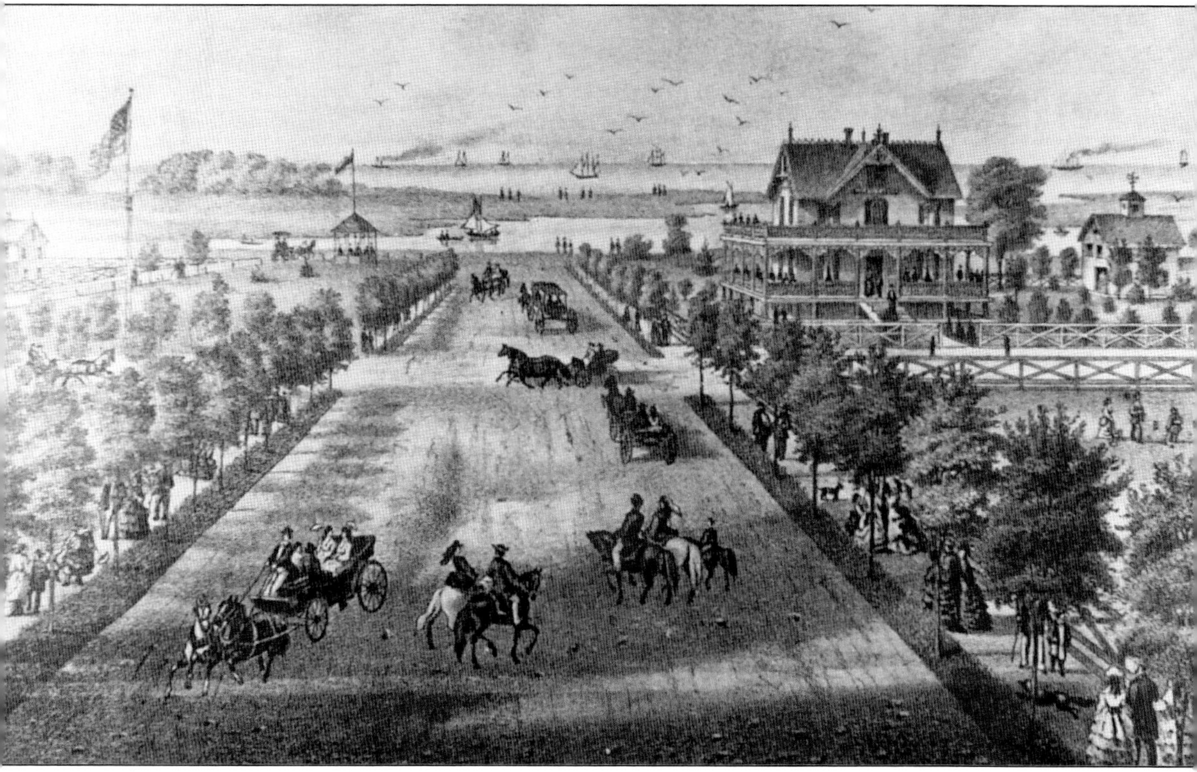

This sketch was the dream Nathaniel Wyckoff Morris had for his community Sea View—the tract of land located south of Squan Village bordered by Robert's Swamp Brook to its south and the Glimmer Glass to the east. In 1872, Mr. Morris purchased about 50 acres of farmland—known as the Marcellus tract—and records indicate that by April 1, 1876, the area had been named the Sea View Property and that 158 building lots, 50 by 125 feet, were established. In 1880, an editorial in the *Sea Side* reported that Sea View, although the most successful seaside resort along the New Jersey coast in recent years, would meet its demise with the extension of the Central Railroad of New Jersey. The extension crossed the property to Point Pleasant Beach, thus ruining the resort's main attraction—the waterfront. Within two years, at the age of 56, Mr. Morris died at his Sea View residence on June 30, 1882.

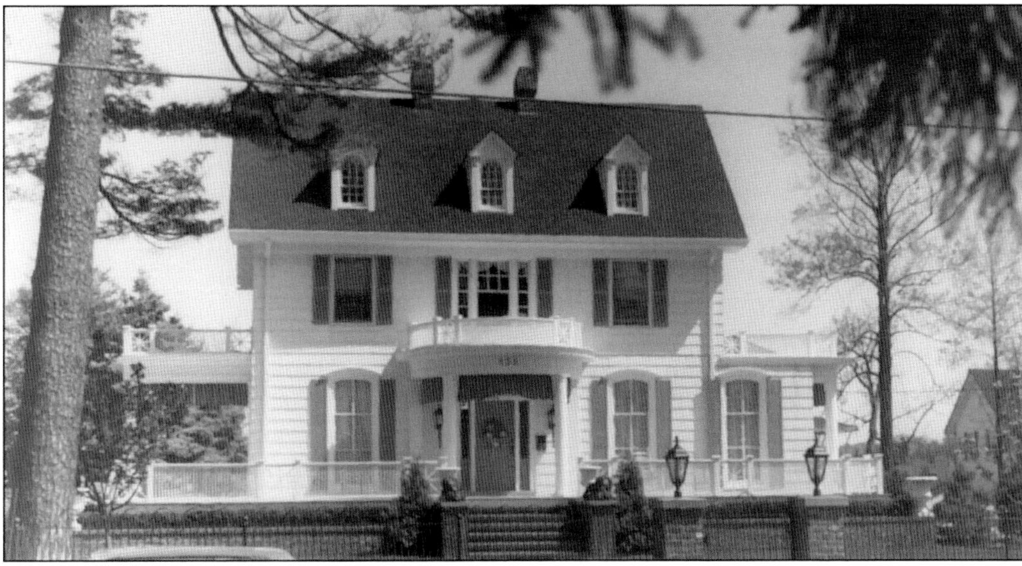

The Morris Villa located at 136 Union Avenue was once the grand residence of Nathaniel Wyckoff Morris, one of the earliest real estate developers in the Manasquan area. The waterfront home was designed with covered porches on two levels so that women visitors to the summer estate could always find a shady side to sit or an open porch with a breeze. The house also had grassy lands, flower gardens, and a safe swimming and boating area for children.

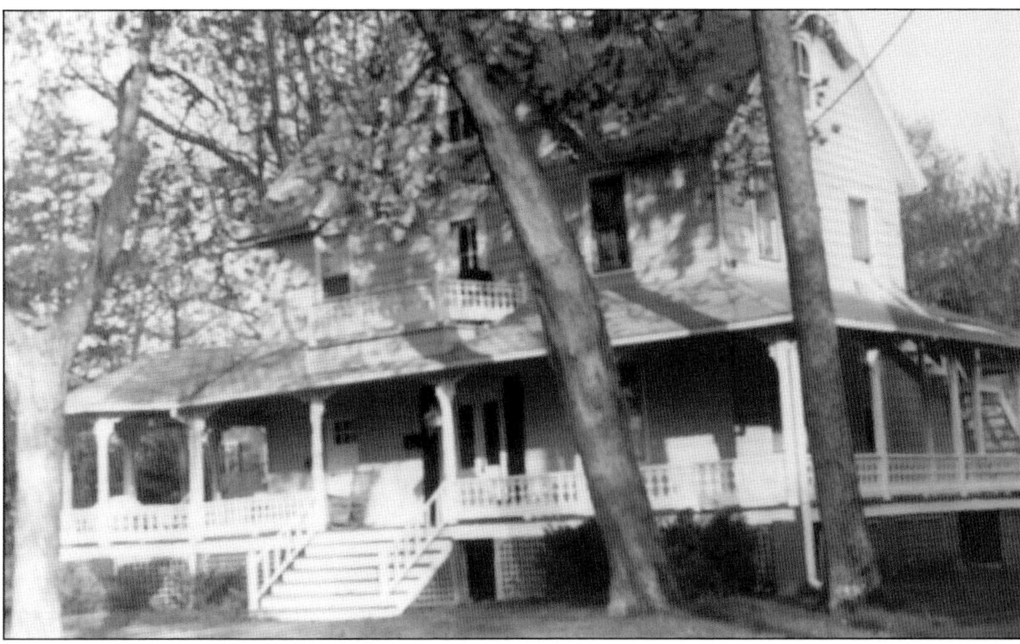

The Morris House, located at 131 Union Avenue, was identical to Morris Villa, 136 Union Avenue, which was also built and owned by Nathaniel Wyckoff Morris. Summer guests were invited to camp on the grassy lawns of the estate and enjoy meals at the house prepared by Captain John Willis, a well-known hotelier from Trenton. Mr. Morris, who was the postmaster for Manalapan and a horse and mule dealer, contracted to have Morris House and Morris Villa built.

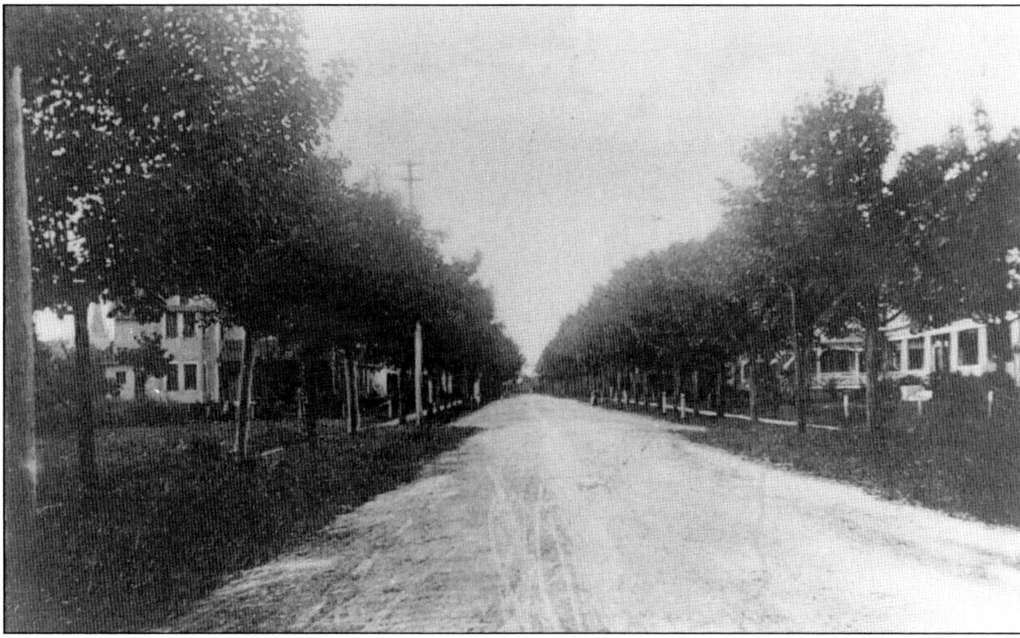

Many of the homes on Virginia Avenue are more than 100 years old. At the time this scene was photographed, the street was comprised of gravel. Dr. Harry Ruf, a local dentist, resided on Virginia Avenue. Records also indicate that Marvin Bailey, a sea captain, had resided on this street until he was lost at sea.

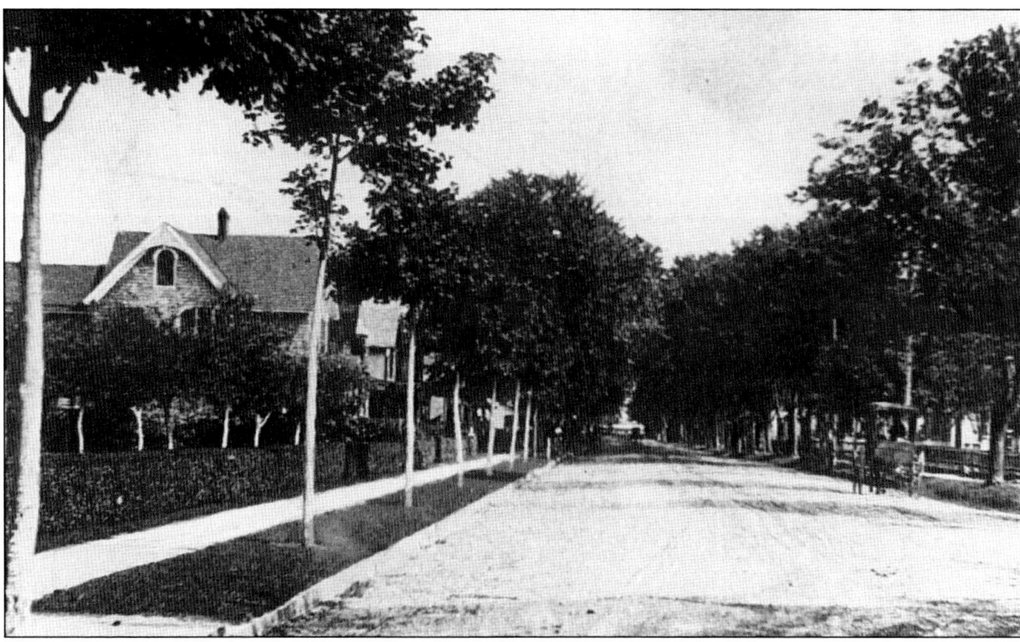

Newly planted trees line Morris Avenue in this image. In this 1920s view looking east from South Street, curbs and sidewalks have been installed. Morris Avenue is the last street south in Manasquan and is divided from neighboring Brielle by Robert's Swamp Brook. One of the oldest houses in the borough is located on the southeast corner of Morris Avenue and South Street.

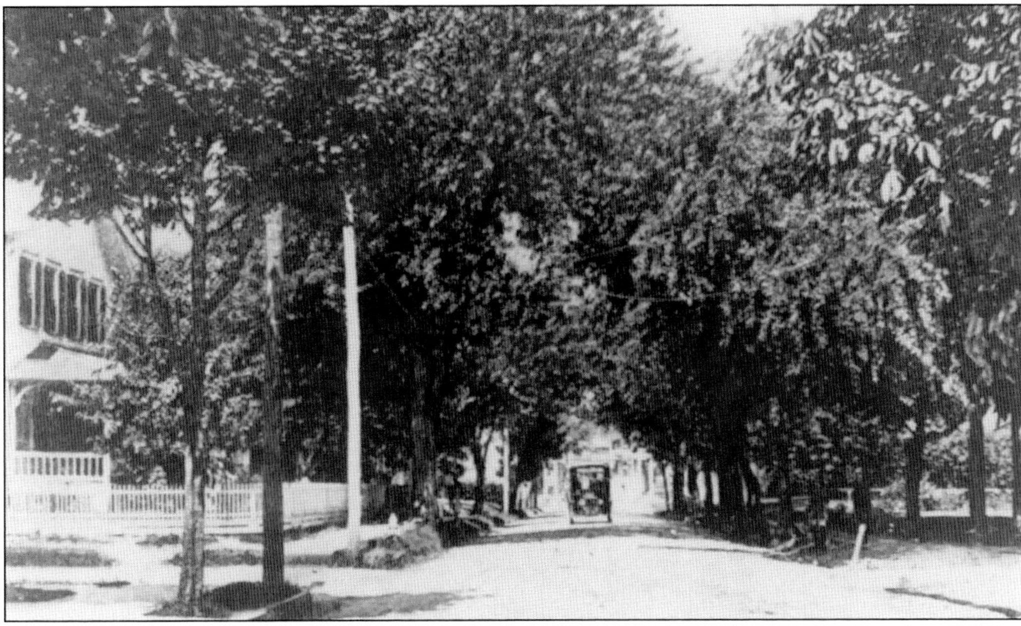

A vintage 1920 automobile makes its way along South Street, a newly paved major thoroughfare in the borough. This well-established street features some of Manasquan's oldest homes, including the Bailey-Reed House, owned by the Squan Village Historical Society. It is also home to most of the churches in the community.

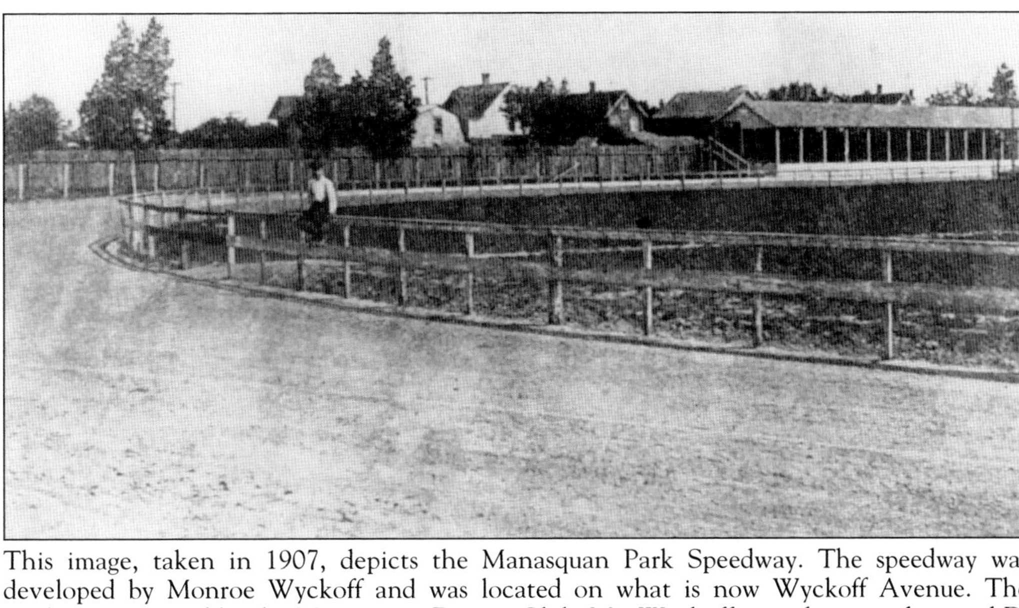

This image, taken in 1907, depicts the Manasquan Park Speedway. The speedway was developed by Monroe Wyckoff and was located on what is now Wyckoff Avenue. The track was operated by the Manasquan Drivers Club. Mr. Wyckoff served as president and D. Randolph Cook was secretary.

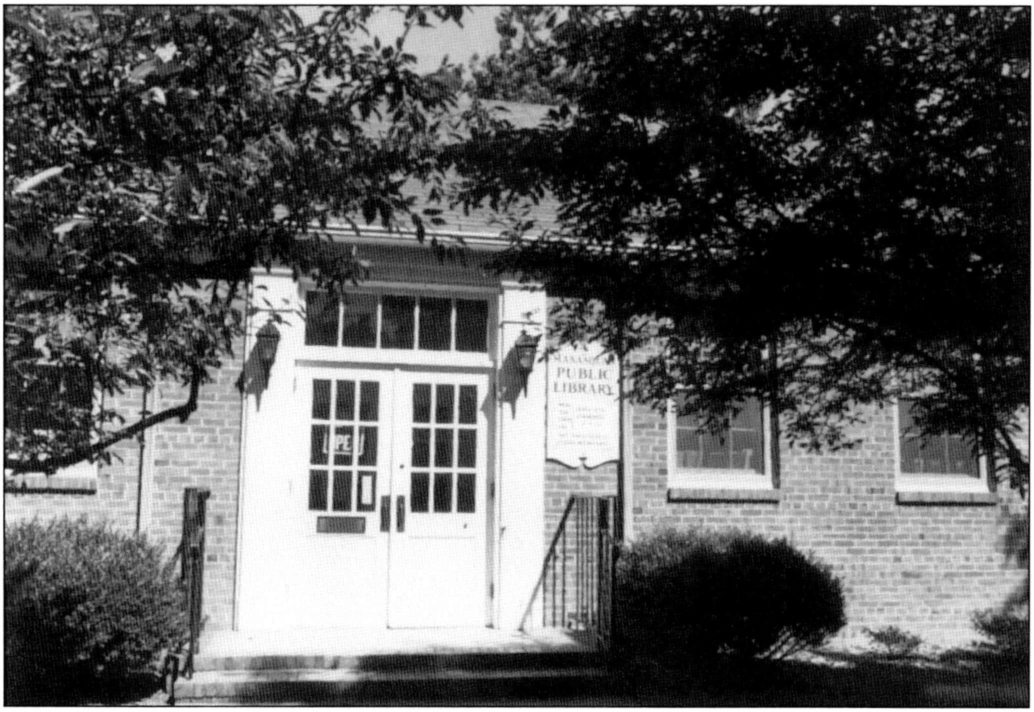

The front entrance to the Manasquan Public Library, 55 Broad Street, has remained the same since its construction in 1955. The first historical records of the library in Manasquan date from 1879, when it was reported that the library opened in a private home. Prior to the construction of the facility on Broad Street, the library also had been housed in homes, a church, a store, and Borough Hall.

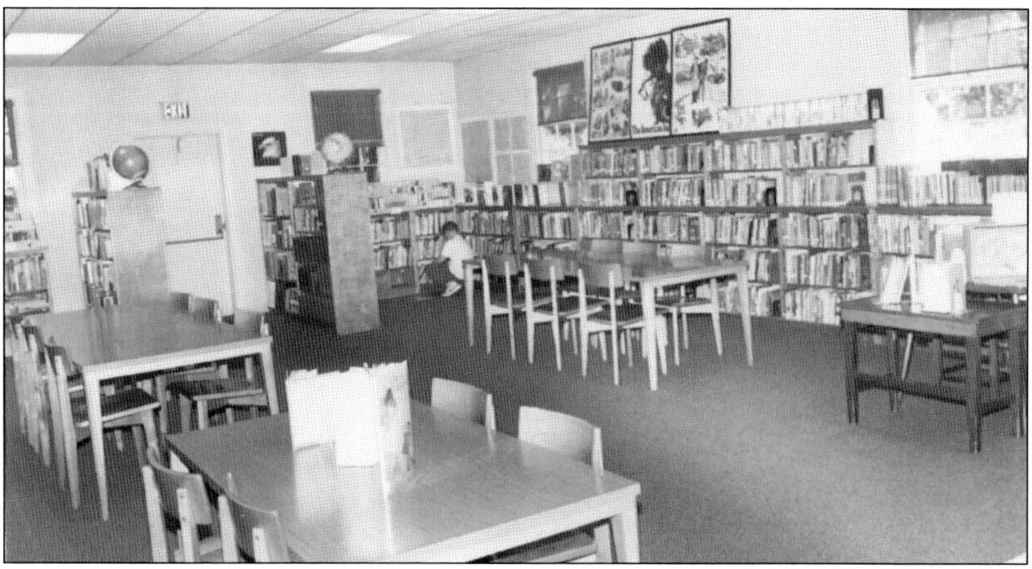

Space for reading, researching, and learning became plentiful when the 1989–90 addition of the F. Herbert Tiplin wing was constructed. Upon the death of Hallie D. Tiplin, a Wall Township resident, the library received a gift in memory of her husband. Mrs. Tiplin had noted that her husband, Herbert, who died in 1984, had always enjoyed reading.

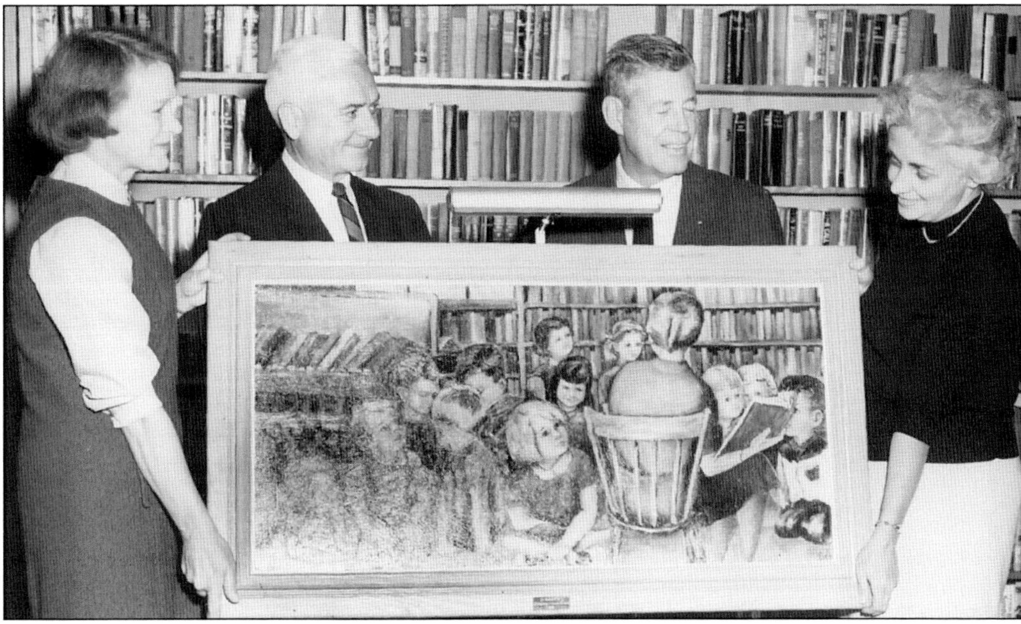

Mrs. Barbara DeFriest (at right), librarian of the Manasquan Public Library, accepts an oil painting in November 1965 from Mrs. Dale Wooley (left), a Manasquan artist, on behalf of the board of trustees of the library in memory of Mrs. Florence Fields Siver, while Fred Beam (second from left), board president, and Richard W. Siver, Mrs. Siver's husband, look on. Today, the painting, which depicts the library's story hour for children, hangs in the children's wing.

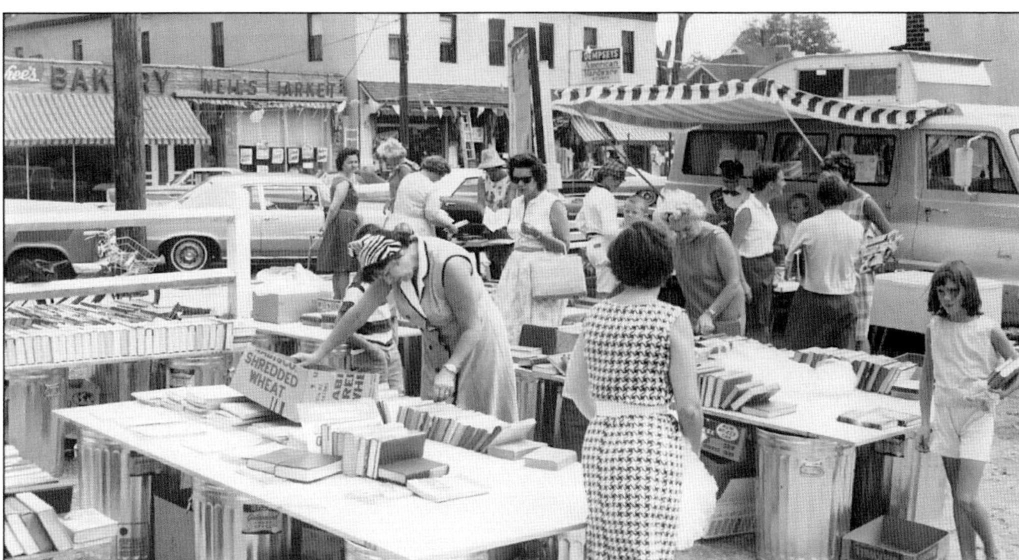

Members of the Ladies Auxiliary of the Manasquan Public Library hold a book fair and bake sale in August 1966 on a vacant Main Street lot in the downtown area of the borough. The auxiliary was established with the special purpose of extending interest and understanding of the library and to secure money to expand the children's wing. The empty lot was located between the former Ralph's Market and the former site of the Acme store.

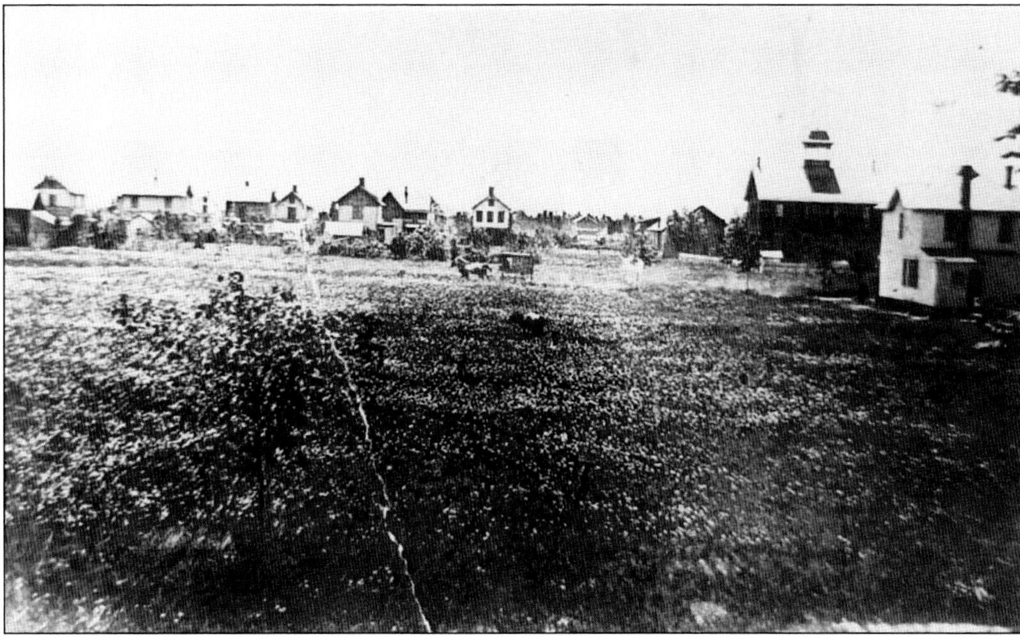

The structure in this view, looking east from what is now Pearce Avenue, is Manasquan School on Taylor Avenue (Route 71). The image was taken about 1880—just after the facility was built. Elementary school–age children attended classes on the first floor and high school–age students on the second. (Note that Parker Avenue is just a field.)

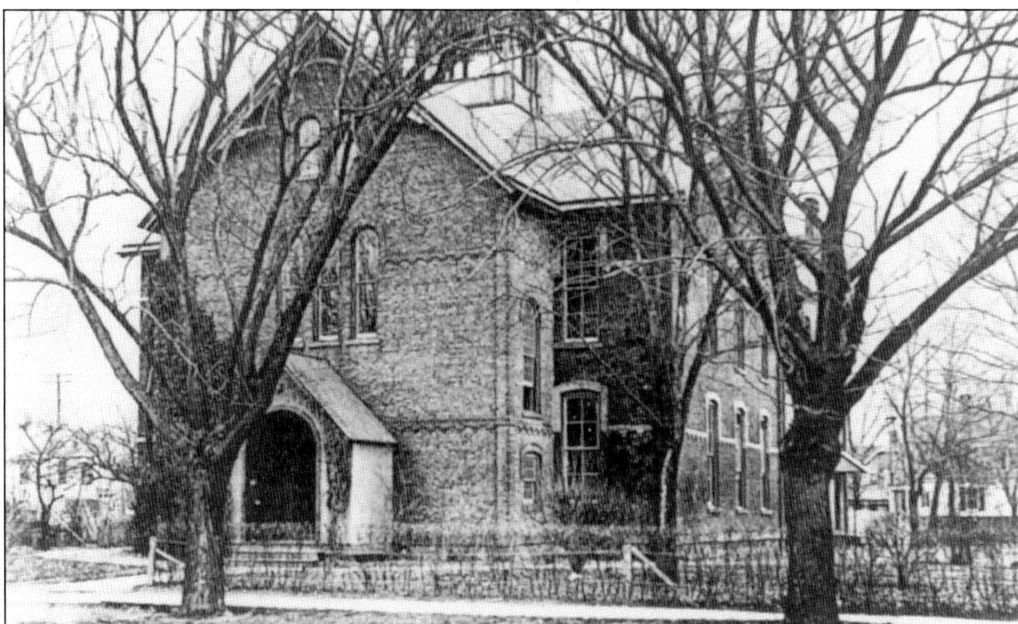

The students attending this new, brick building had been moved from the original wooden borough school that was located on Main Street. The new school, located on Taylor Avenue, was used for all children in the borough until 1914, when a building for high school students was built adjacent to the north side of this school. This building was deeded in 1933 to the Borough and is currently Manasquan Borough Hall.

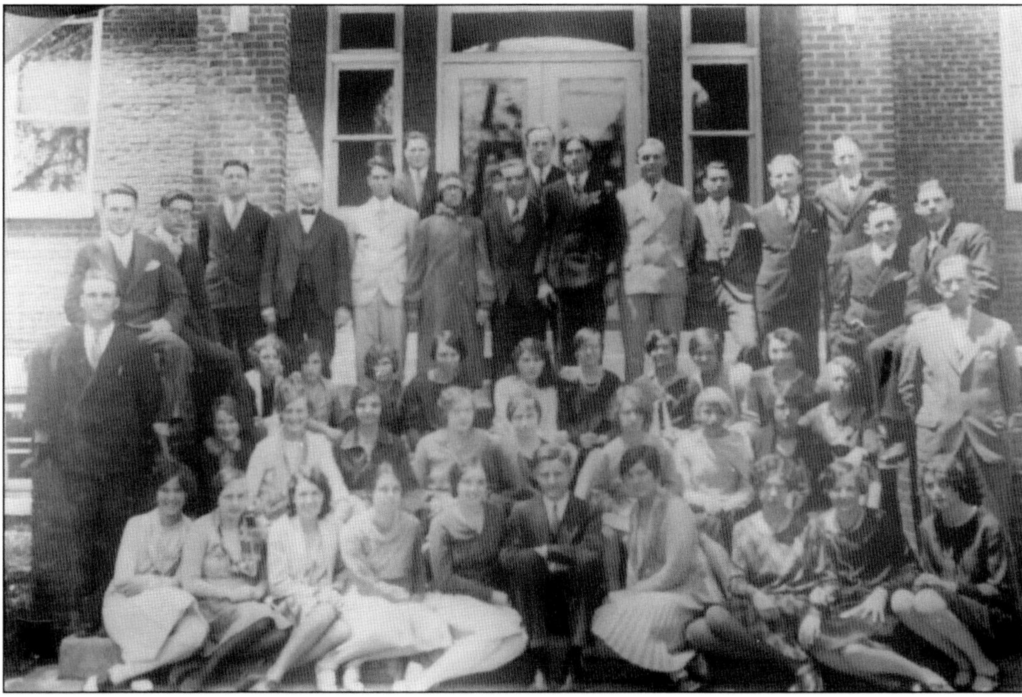

As the community grew, so did the population of its public school system. This graduating class in the late 1920s was one of the last classes before a larger, more modern educational facility was built in 1931–32 on Broad Street. The class of 1931 was the last class to graduate from the Taylor Avenue facility, although the Broad Street school was not fully operational as a junior-senior high school until 1933.

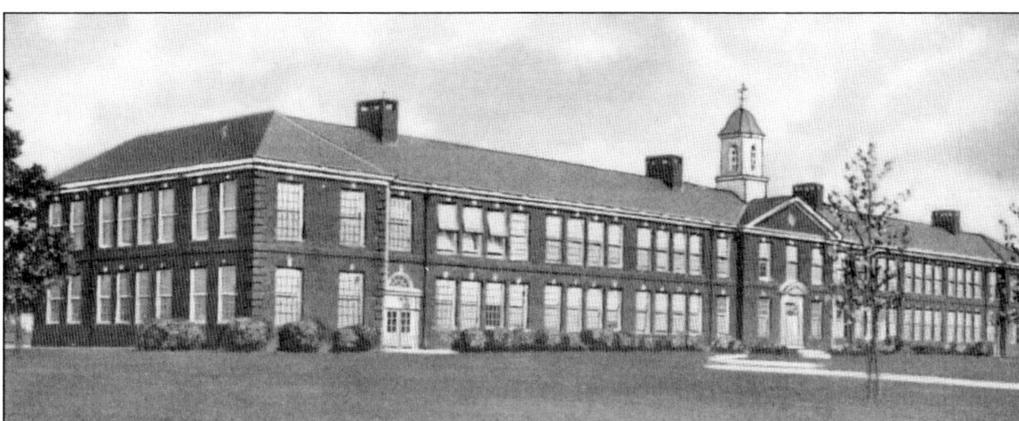

Manasquan High School—located on the west side of Broad Street—was built in the early 1930s to accommodate the district's ever-growing population. During the 1940s and 1950s, land adjacent to the high school was purchased because of continuing school needs. By 1962, an extensive addition including a gymnasium, science laboratory and classrooms, choral and music rooms, and modern food service facility was built.

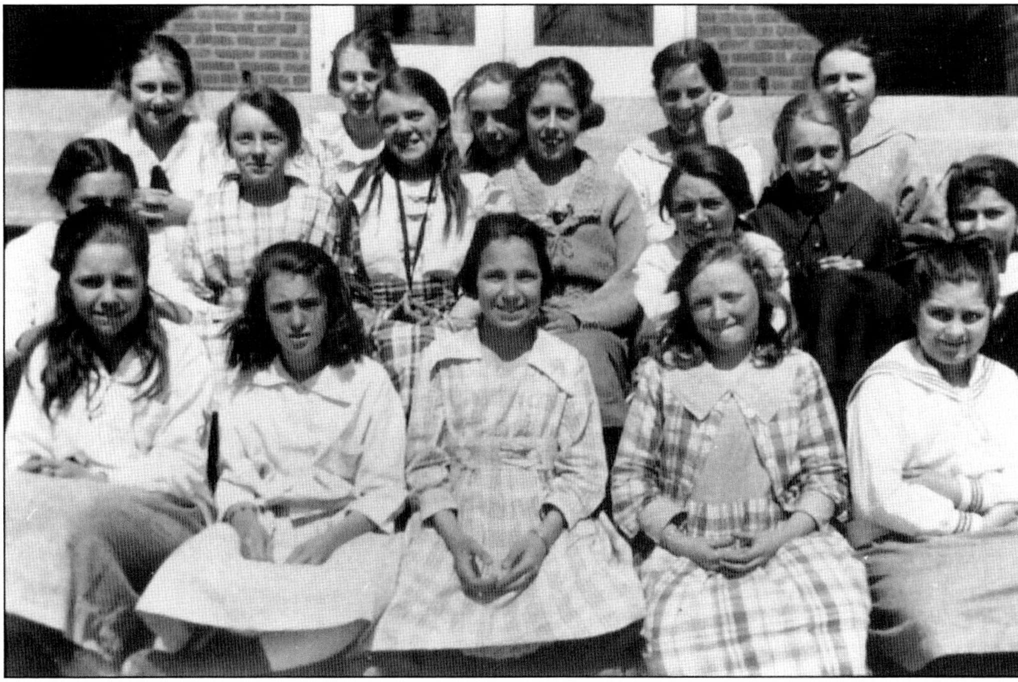

These fresh, happy faces show the girls' half of an eighth grade class entering Manasquan Elementary School on Taylor Avenue (Route 71) in the early 1930s wearing their best clothes: cotton dresses with dress socks and Mary Janes. (The boys are pictured separately, below). Although the photograph was taken some 60 years ago, these faces should look remarkably similar to any Manasquan parent attending "Back to School" night at Manasquan Elementary School on Broad Street.

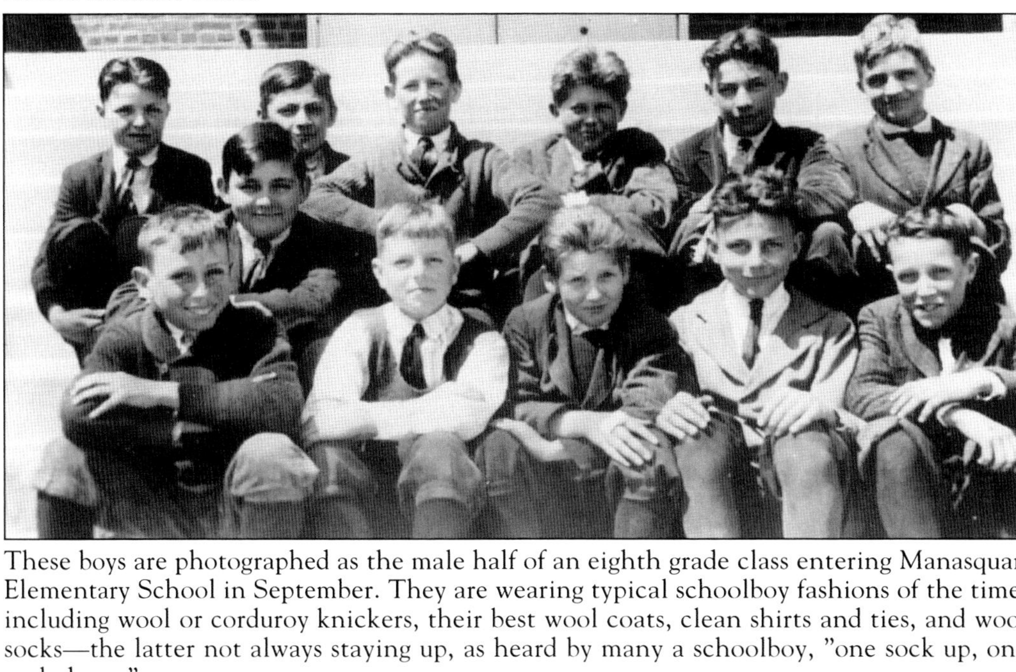

These boys are photographed as the male half of an eighth grade class entering Manasquan Elementary School in September. They are wearing typical schoolboy fashions of the time, including wool or corduroy knickers, their best wool coats, clean shirts and ties, and wool socks—the latter not always staying up, as heard by many a schoolboy, "one sock up, one sock down."

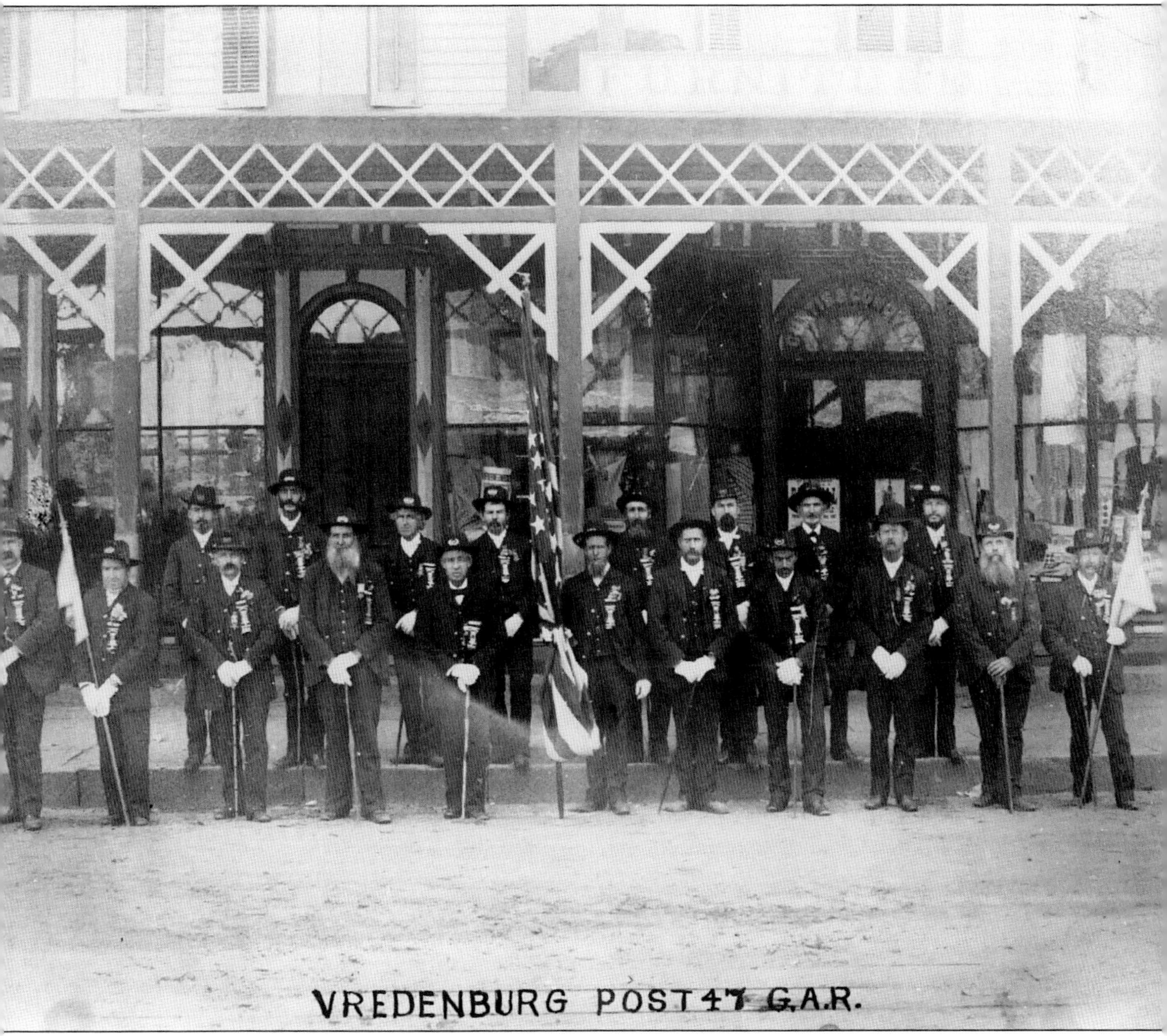

Research indicates that 94 men from the area fought in the Civil War. In this photograph, members of the Vredenburg Post 47 Grand Army of the Republic—"Damn Yankees"— retain their Union Army pride in the early 1880s. The veterans—many of whom had joined New Jersey's 14th Infantry Regiment—are in front of the Curtis and Davison general store on Main and South Streets.

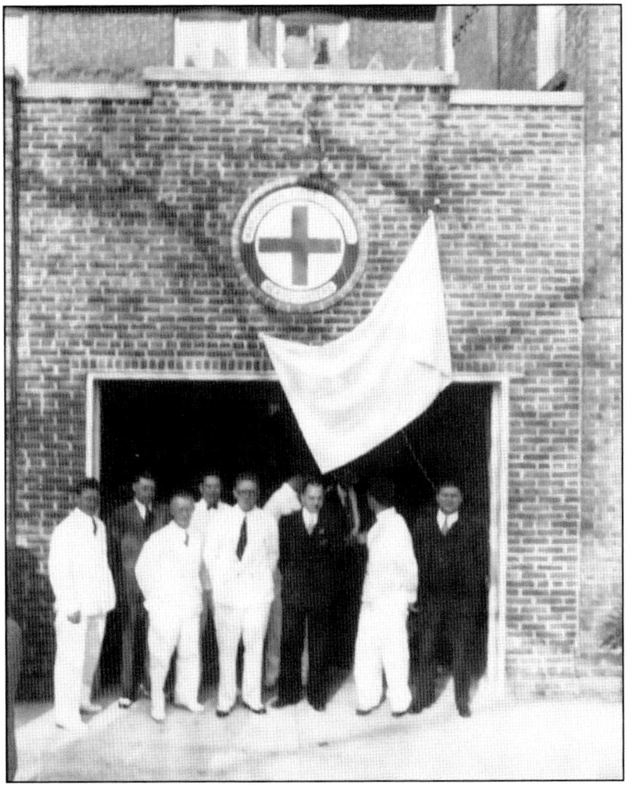

Members of the Dr. C.A. Norris First Aid Emergency Squad proudly gather at the headquarters located at the rear of Borough Hall on Taylor Avenue (Route 71.) Volunteer firefighters from Manasquan Engine Co. No. 2 established the squad in 1929 in response to the statewide need for such an emergency rescue organization.

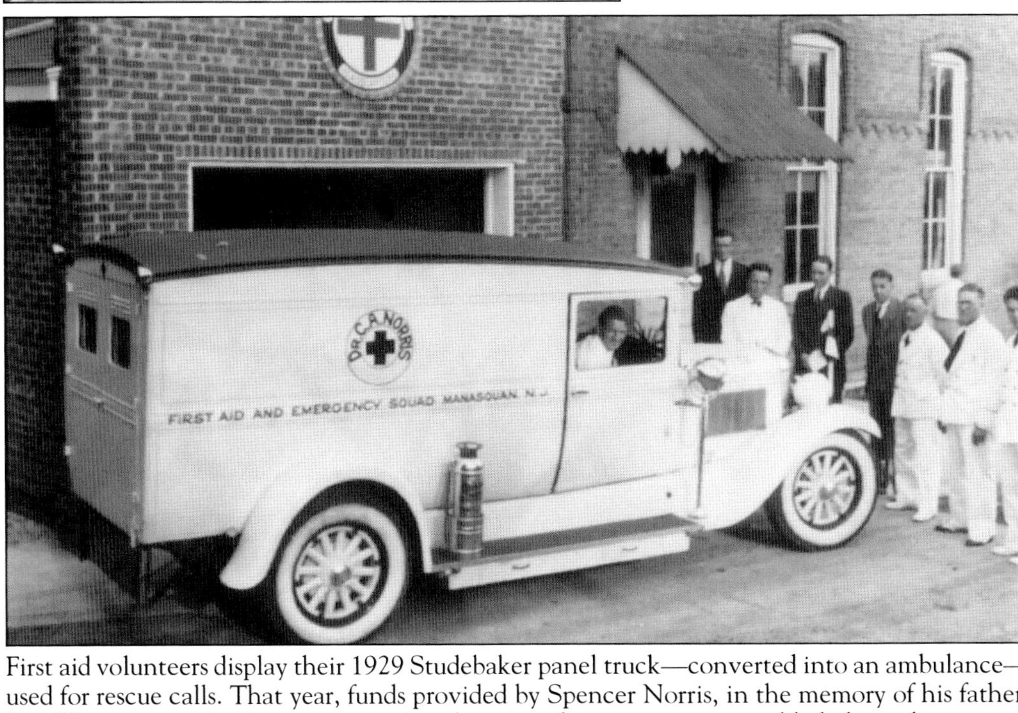

First aid volunteers display their 1929 Studebaker panel truck—converted into an ambulance—used for rescue calls. That year, funds provided by Spencer Norris, in the memory of his father, Dr. Clarence A. Norris, a community physician for many years, enabled the volunteers to purchase the rescue vehicle.

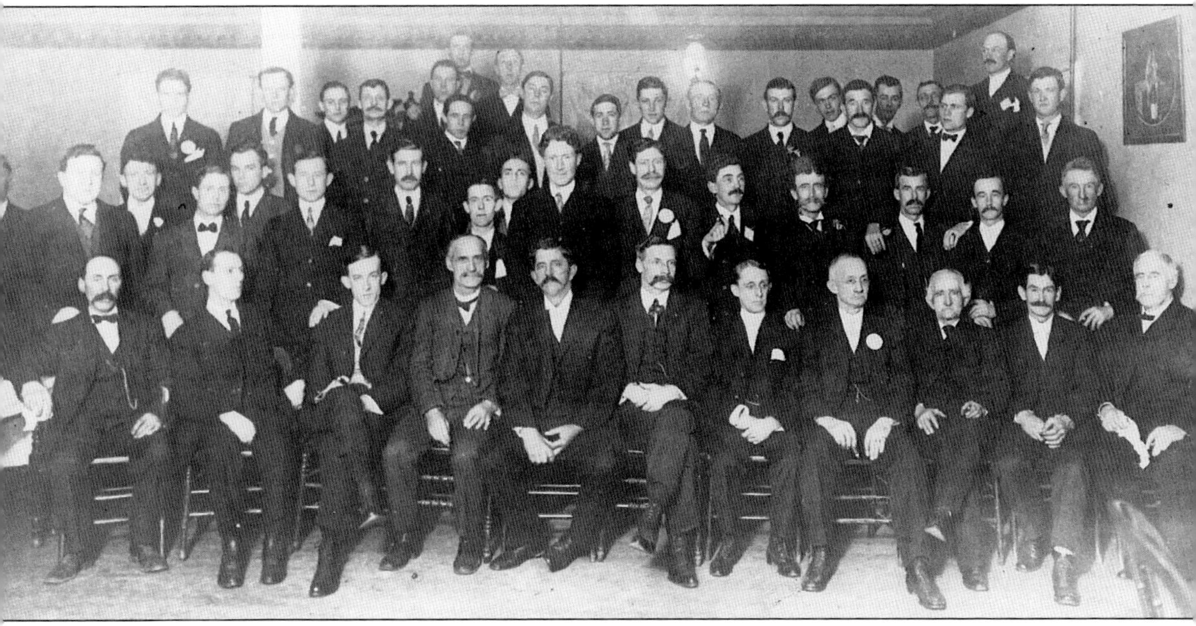

Firemen from Manasquan Hook & Ladder Company No. 1 and Engine Company No. 2, Manasquan, gather in 1908 for a banquet held in the Osborn House, well known in the region for its wonderful food. The banquet's menu no doubt featured the finest from the area's rich bounty, including oysters and crabs, fish and game, fresh produce, homemade ale, fruit pies, and other local goods. The photograph was taken by Sol P. Lewis.

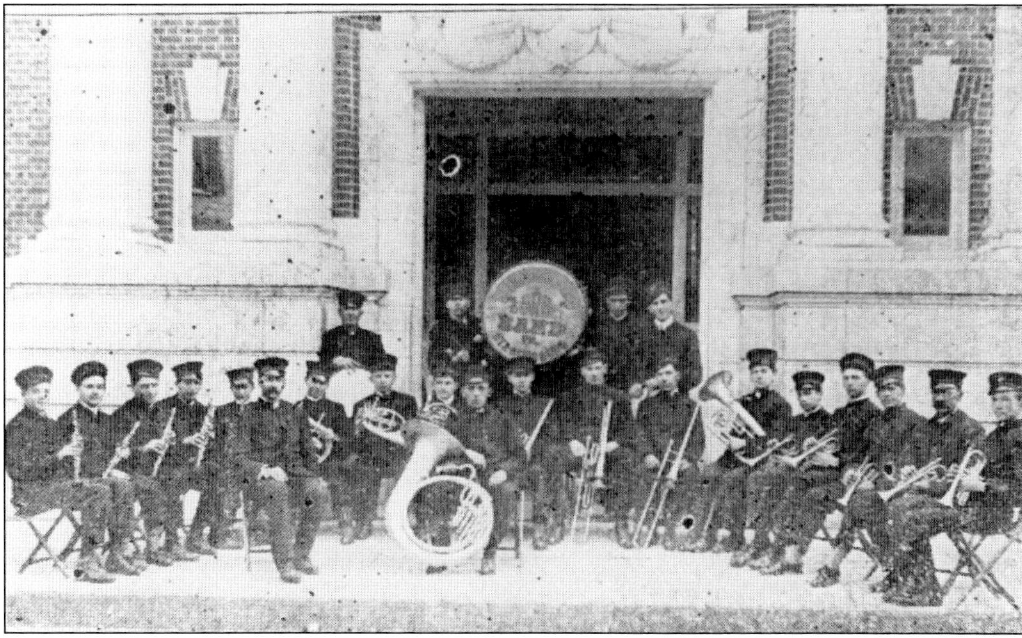

Members of the Carlisle (Pennsylvania) Indian School Band perform in front of the First National Bank of Manasquan on Main Street. During the summer months, bands were invited to the community to entertain shoppers in the business district as well as tourists in the beach area. This tradition continues today with regular evening band concerts at the beach during the summer months.

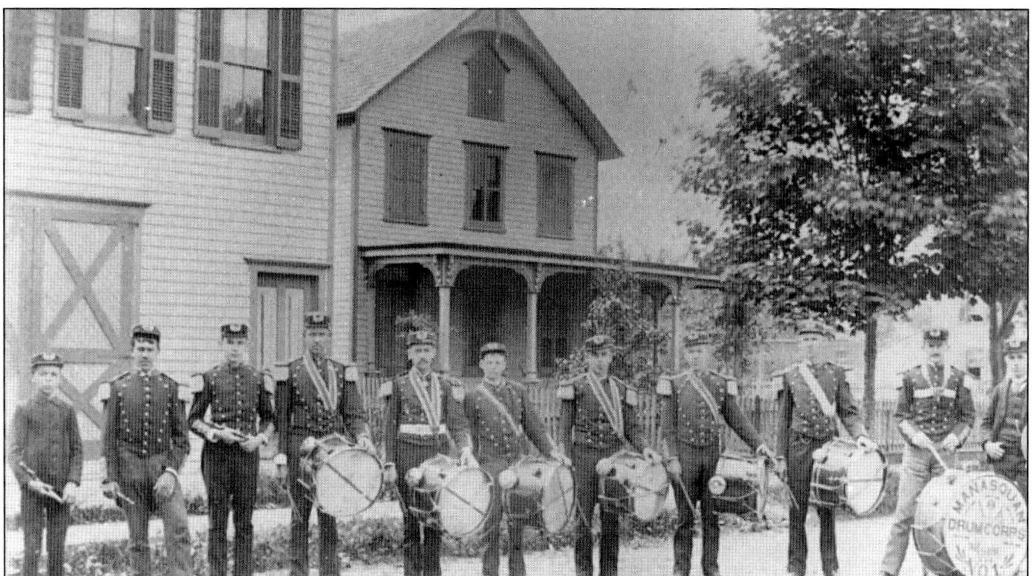

Members of the Manasquan Drum Corps formed by Manasquan Hook & Ladder Co. No. 1 volunteer firemen pose before a concert in front of Broad Street headquarters in this *c.* 1895 photograph. Responding to a need in the Shore Area, the fire company was established in 1884—prior to the incorporation of the Borough of Manasquan—and was officially registered in Freehold on March 21, 1887, just months before the borough was incorporated.

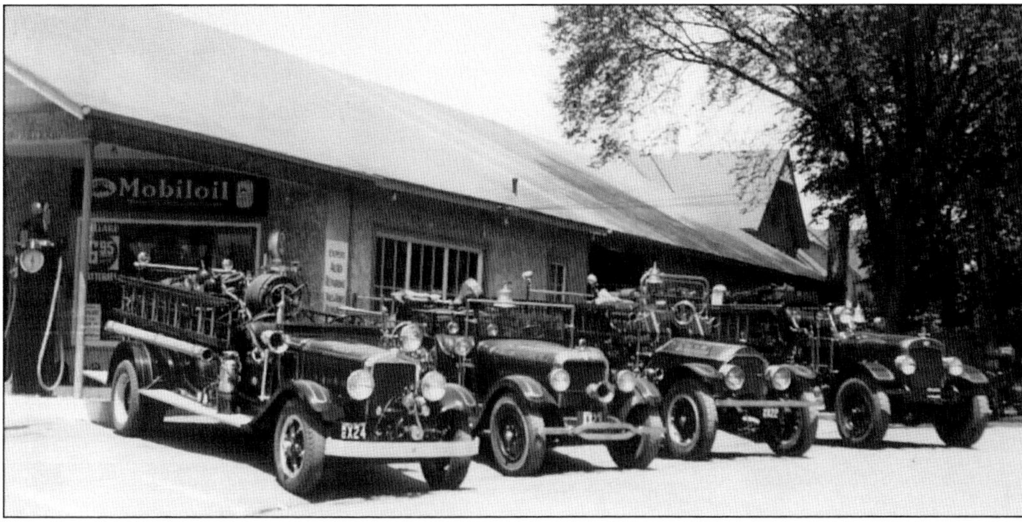

Engines from Manasquan Hook & Ladder Co No. 1 and Engine Co. No. 2, Manasquan, appear together in this early-1930s photograph taken at the Mobiloil gas and service station on the corner of Main Street and Pearce Avenue. The station, owned by John R. Morris, later became Case Buick, and today, it is Manasquan Lighting.

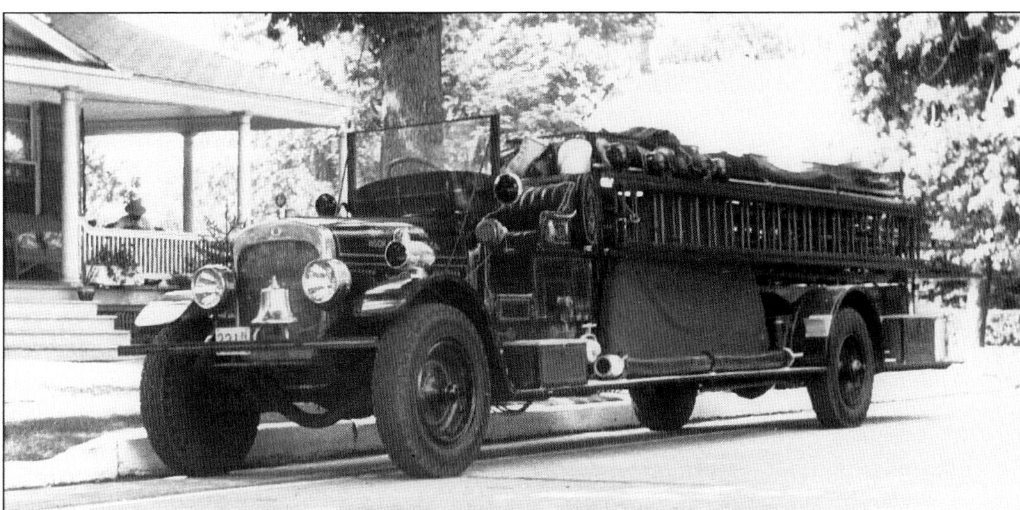

This 1927 Manasquan Hook & Ladder Co. No. 1 Seagrave 750-gallon pumper per minute is equipped with 1,000 feet of 2-1/2-inch fire hose, 50- and 30-foot ladders, as well as smaller ones. This photograph was taken at 39 Broad Street—just opposite the firehouse—in the 1940s. Joseph Hancock recalls driving the truck for 18 years through all kinds of summer traffic and all kinds of winter weather answering fire calls.

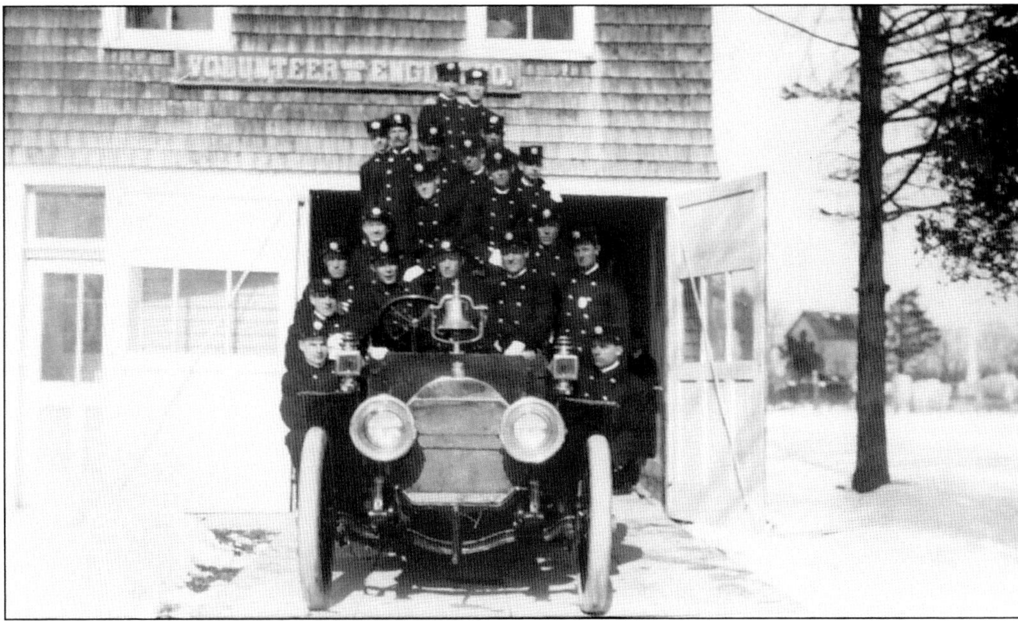

Members of Volunteer Engine Co. No. 2, Manasquan, make a pyramid on their fire engine at company headquarters on Osborn Avenue and Main Street. The fire company was established on November 15, 1894, with 29 charter members. The company headquarters were located on South Street, where the men met on the second floor of the R.T. Van Schoick sash and blind shop.

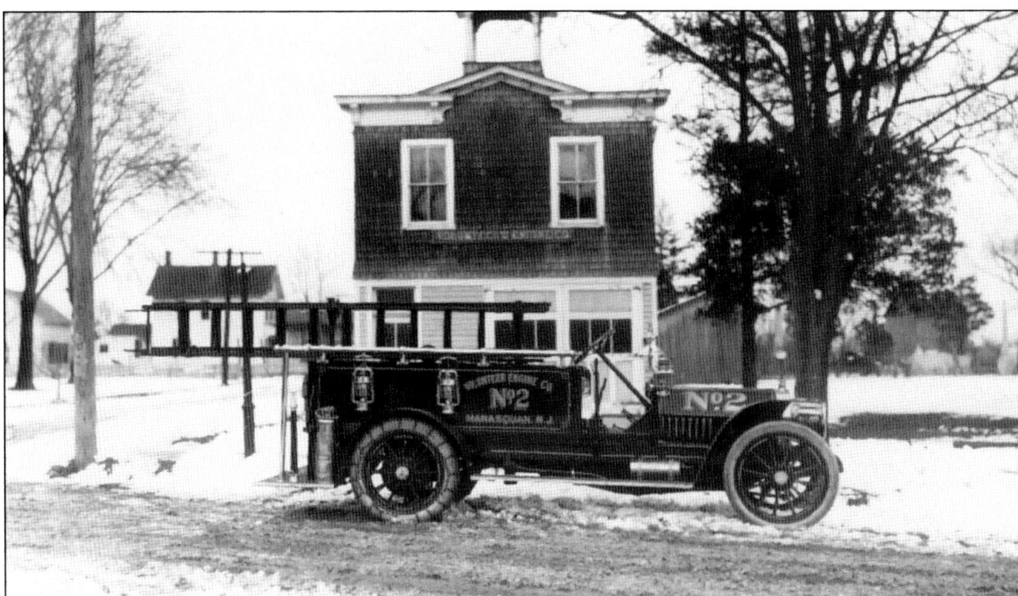

In 1902, the headquarters for Volunteer Engine Co. No. 2 fire was destroyed by fire, and the men relocated to a barn on the property of the Van Leer Lumber Company on South Street. On June 23, 1904, members the company moved to this location on Osborn Avenue and Main Street. In 1951, the company again moved, this time to its newly built headquarters on Parker Avenue.

Four

Railroading in Manasquan

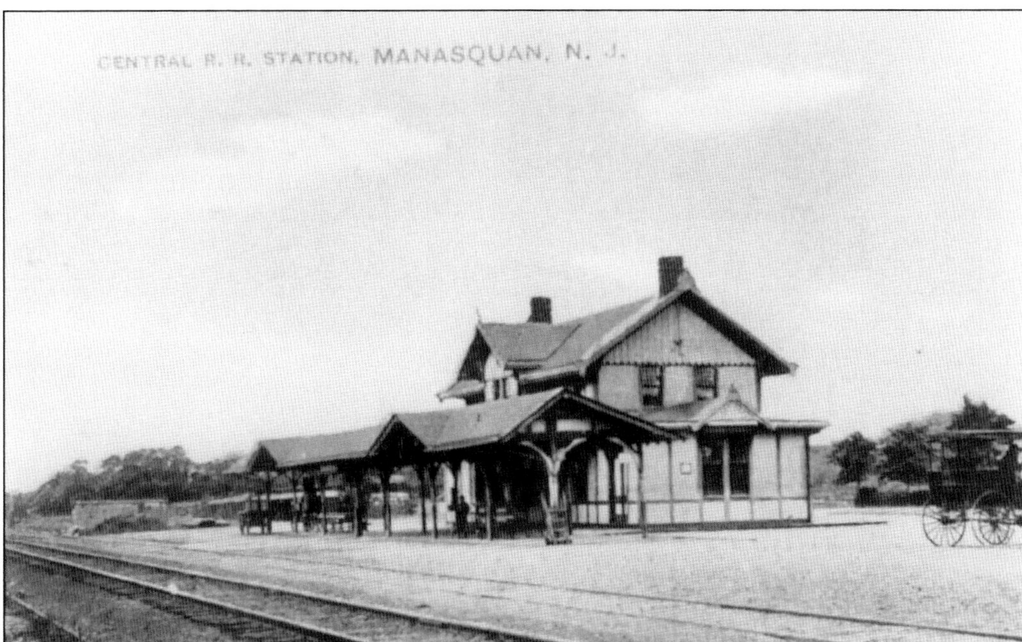

The Manasquan Railroad Station in 1885 had once been used as the Spring Lake Station. The rail depot was constructed with wood purchased by H.H. Yard, president of the American Timber Co., from the razed Agricultural Hall at the 1879 Philadelphia (Pennsylvania) Centennial Exposition. The first floor featured a ticket office, rest room, waiting room, and baggage area. Edward V. Patterson of Spring Lake served as stationmaster.

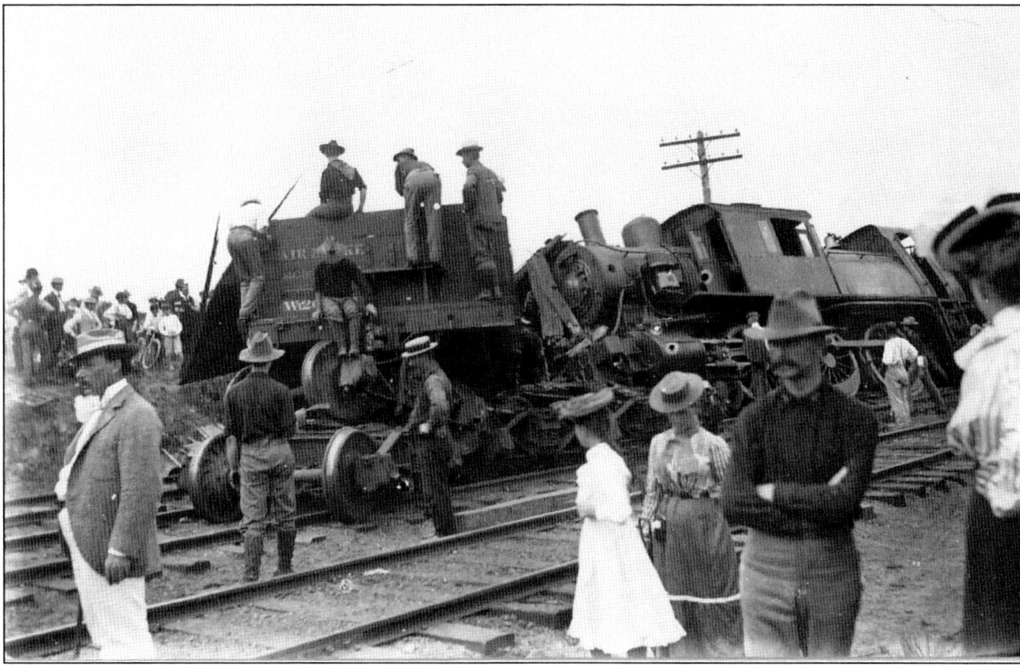

National Guard Cavalrymen assess damage and injuries following Central Railroad of New Jersey Engine 603 on the New York and Long Branch Railroad and Pennsylvania Railroad lines in Manasquan where the two lines merged near the present New Jersey National Guard Training Center, Sea Girt. The accident occurred about 1898 after the invention and use of air brakes for trains, but when engines were still steam driven and the cars were wooden.

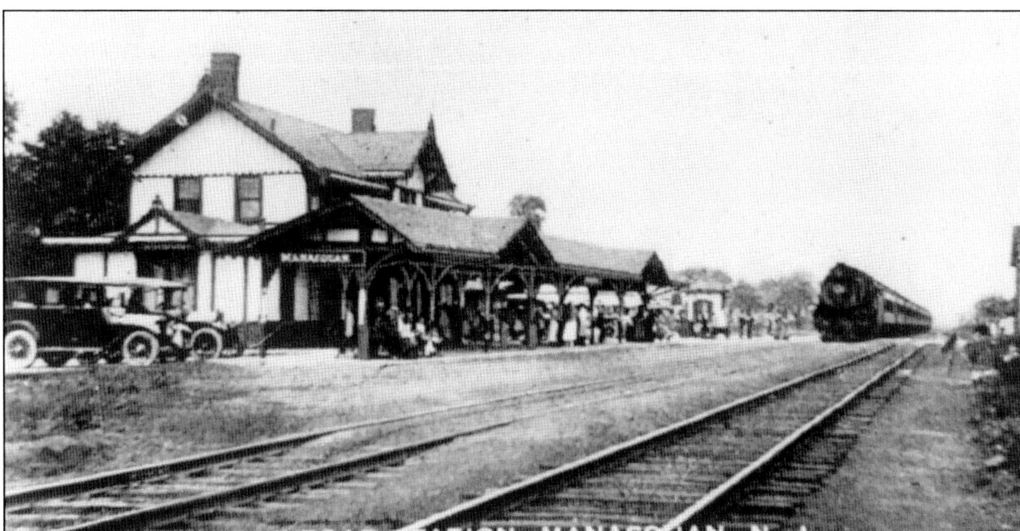

An automobile waits for a train—traveling south—to reach the rail depot. The rail line linked vacationers with the Jersey Shore and area residents with careers in North Jersey and New York City. After the station was relocated to Manasquan, the 120-foot canopy was added.

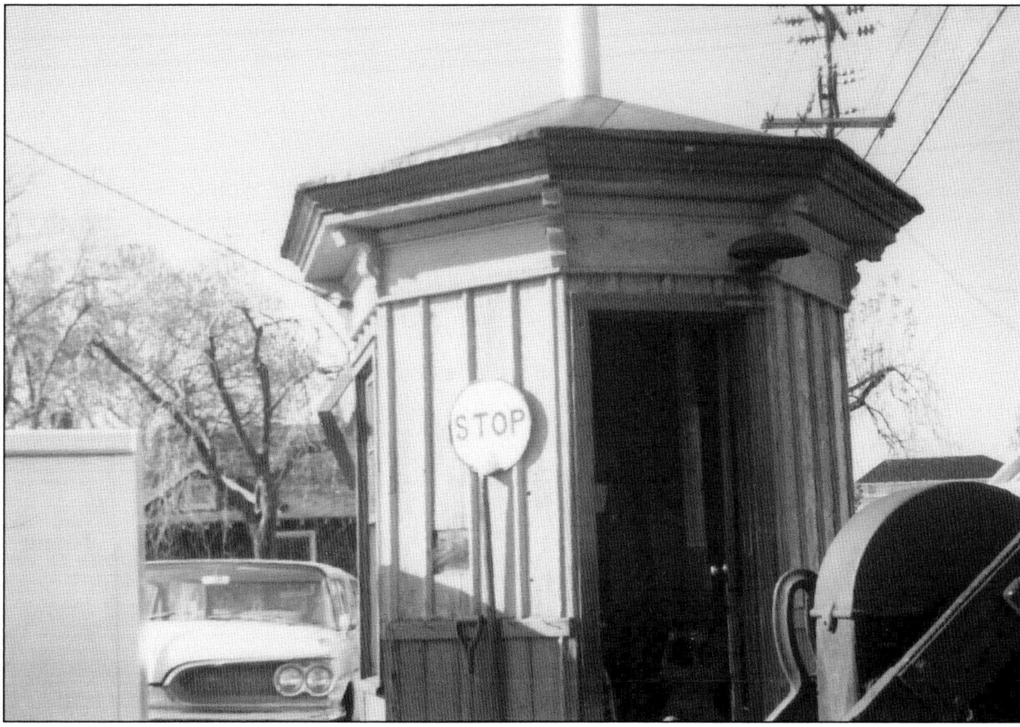

The crossing watchman's shanty was located at Main Street until 1962. The watchman was responsible for operating the hand cranks for the gates. Another duty he had was to clean the kerosene lanterns, which glowed red, warning motorists at night of train arrivals and departures. Inside the shanty, the watchman had a chair and a pot-belly stove.

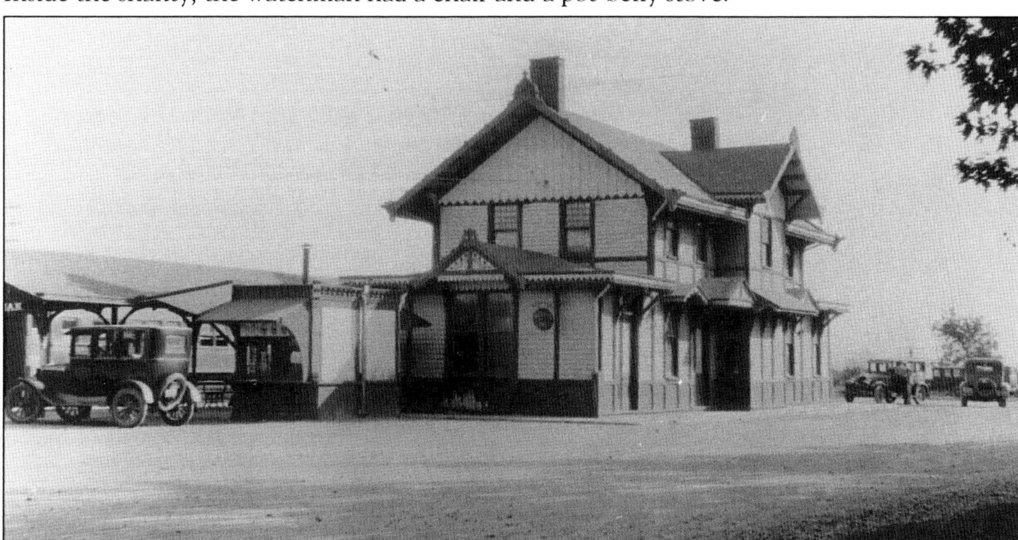

This 1920 view of the north and west sides of the Manasquan rail depot shows the baggage area of the station and the Union News stand. The newsstand sold newspapers, magazines, candy, gum, tobacco products, and other sundries. The newsstand and the Main Street crossing watchman's shanty now serve as part of the exhibit at the Pine Creek Railroad at Allaire State Park.

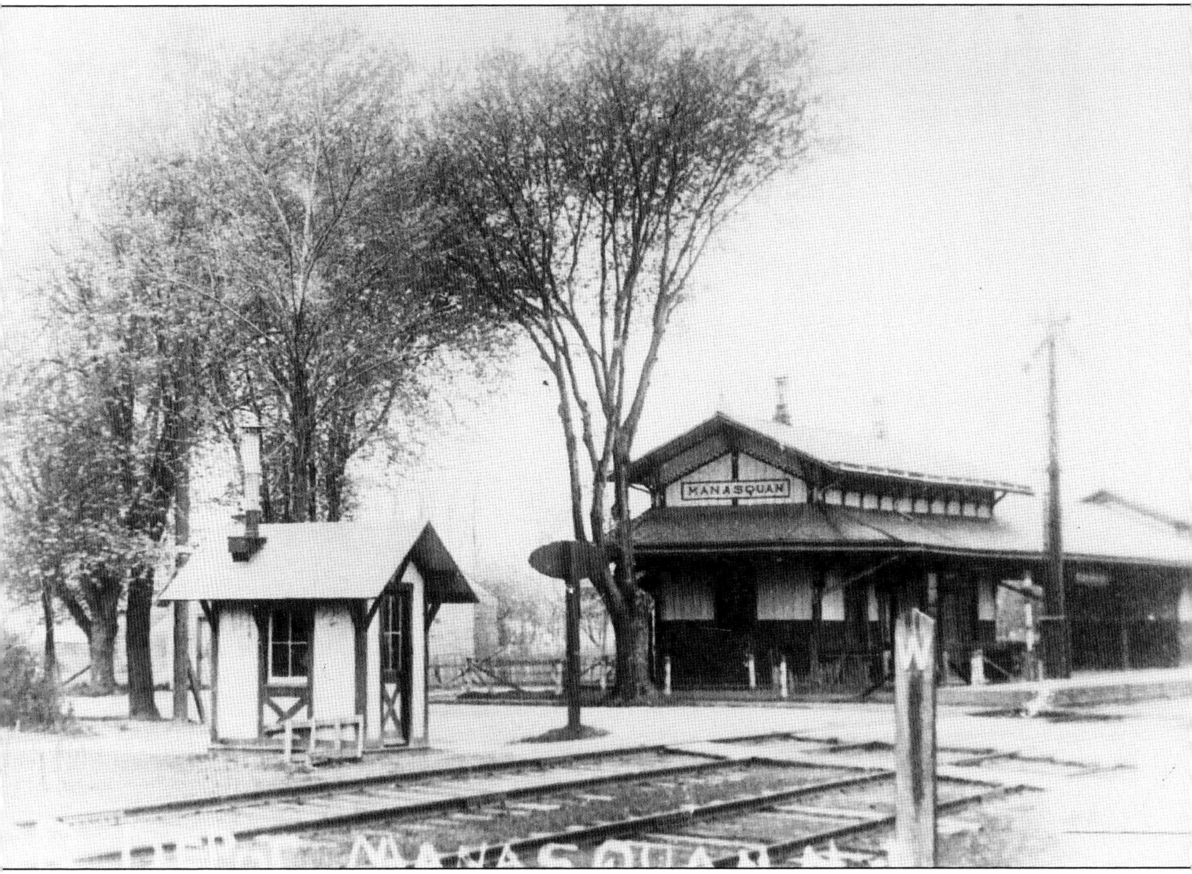

The Broad Street Station—built in 1881 and located on the southwest corner of Atlantic Avenue and Broad Street—was in use until 1962. The Freehold and Jamesburg Agricultural Railroad was the main line for presidents traveling to the summer White House in Long Branch. In 1912, it was from an observation car at this station that Theodore Roosevelt offered a campaign speech. The king and queen of England stopped at the station on June 10, 1939, during their Royal Tour. Today, the station and Route 71 overpass for the rail tracks are gone, but the train right-of-way is the Edgar J. Felix Bicycle Path.

Two area residents confer under a canopy outside the Manasquan Railroad Station prior to renovations completed by Save Our Station (SOS), a volunteer group established to restore the station. The train station had been in great disrepair in 1984 until SOS volunteers restored the exterior and interior of the rail depot.

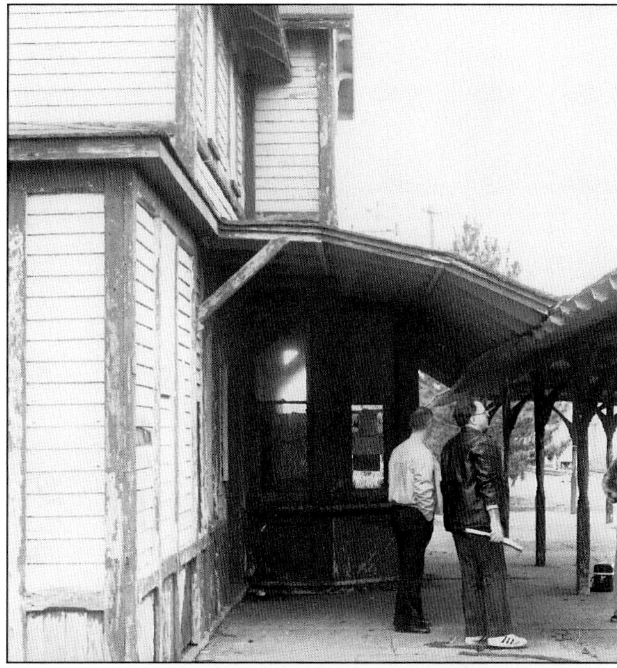

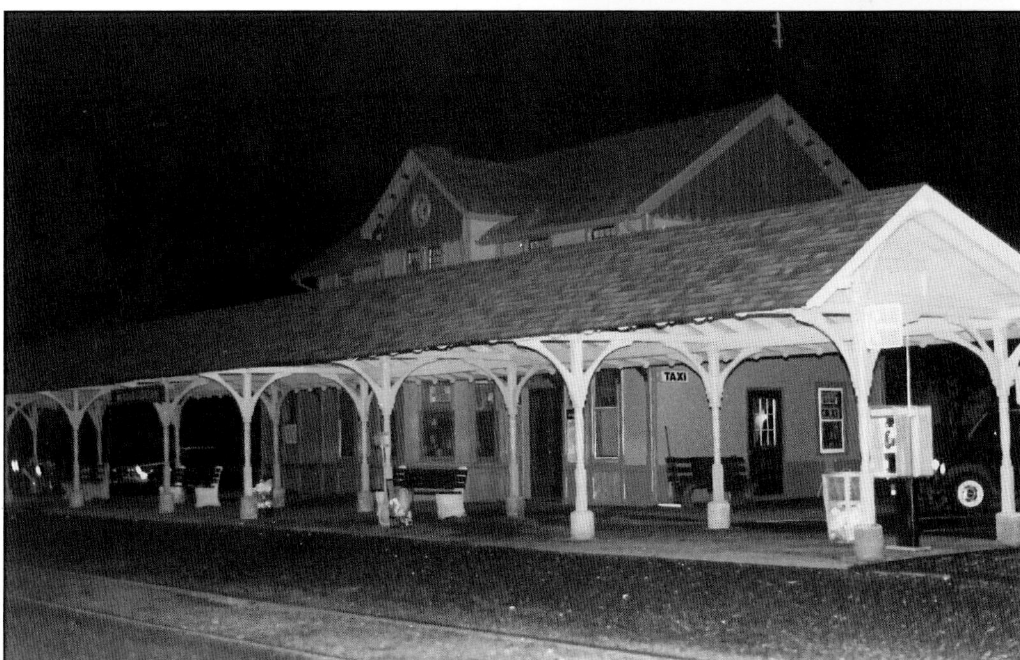

A volunteer organization, Save Our Station (SOS), established in 1984, restored the Manasquan Railroad Station to its original Victorian charm in time for the borough's Centennial celebration in October 1987. The group gained the support of its community, the Manasquan mayor, and council, as well as the New Jersey Transit. Upon completion, the first floor included a turn-of-the-century ticket booth and meeting area. The Squan Village Historical Society's museum was located on the second floor.

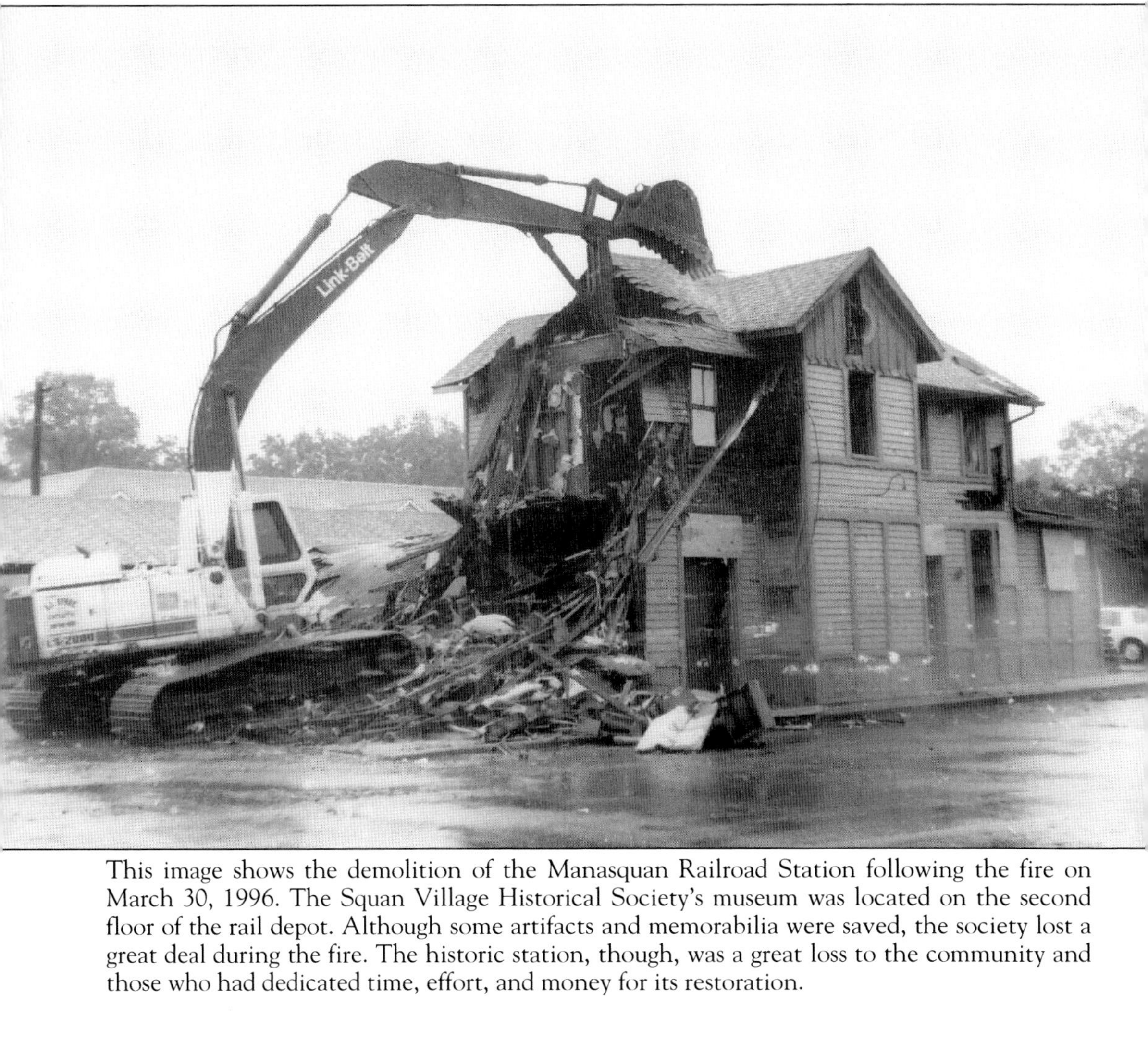

This image shows the demolition of the Manasquan Railroad Station following the fire on March 30, 1996. The Squan Village Historical Society's museum was located on the second floor of the rail depot. Although some artifacts and memorabilia were saved, the society lost a great deal during the fire. The historic station, though, was a great loss to the community and those who had dedicated time, effort, and money for its restoration.

Five

The Business District

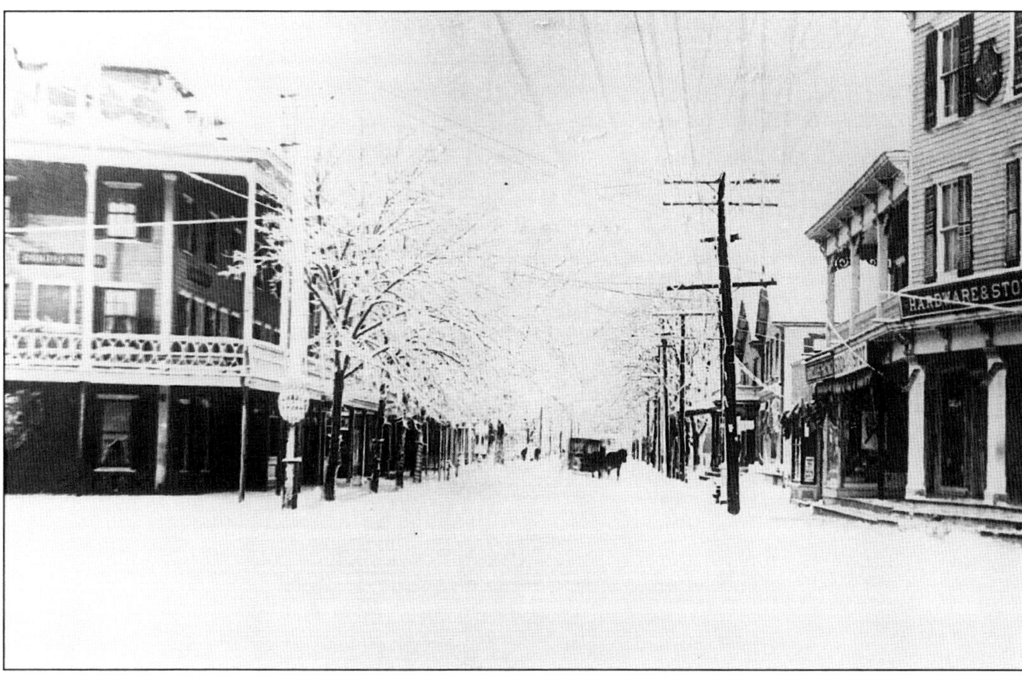

A horse and carriage makes its way through Main Street in this tranquil scene following a snowfall in 1877. The Osborn House, with dining room, palm room, and livery, is on the southwest corner of Main and South Streets. Records indicate that part of the Osborn House dated to 1808.

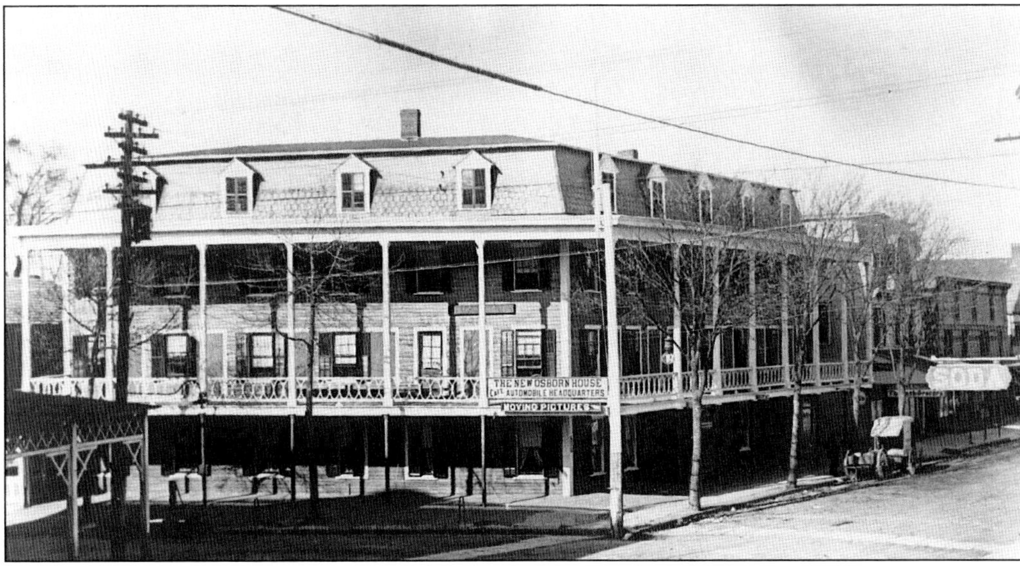

The Osborn House, located on the southwest corner of Main and South Streets, was one of the oldest buildings in Squan Village—and the state of New Jersey—until it was destroyed by fire on January 28, 1928. The hotel—which fronted on both streets with a porch extending around it—featured the stores of Charles Kurtz, the Candy Kitchen owned by James Dooros, Mickey's City Market, and Prown-Copper Five & Ten Cent Store.

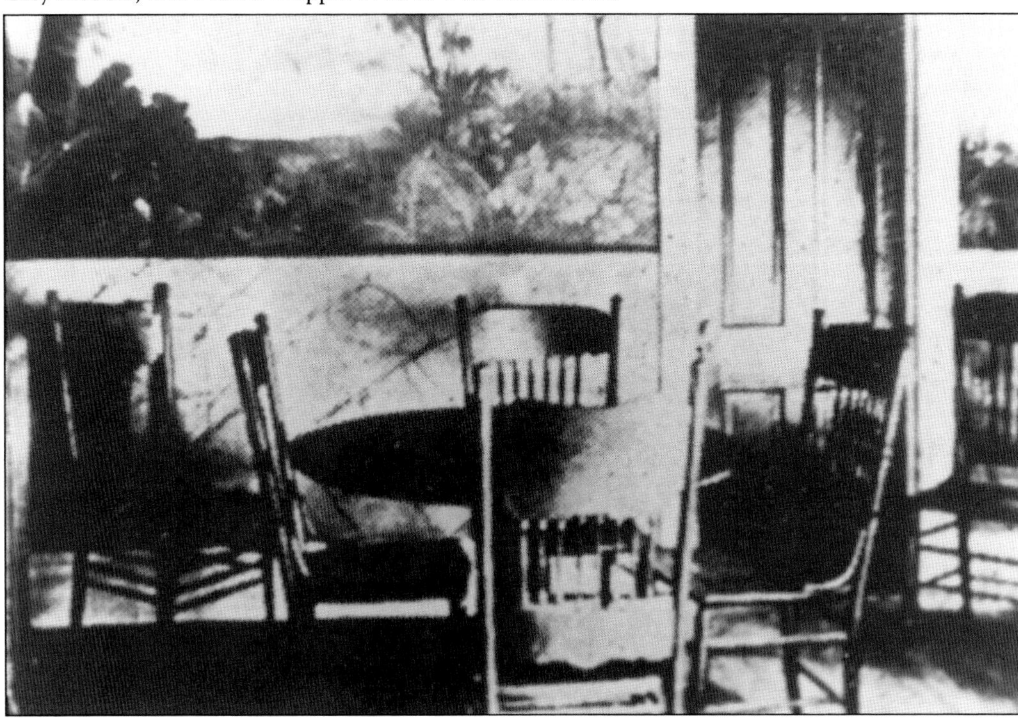

The Palm Room at the Osborn House was a sitting area. In 1877, the editor of the New York *Commercial Gazette* said, "At Manasquan there is a good hotel kept by Theodore Fields, where the summer idler will find good cheer. If we mistake not, there is the making of a large town out of Squan Village."

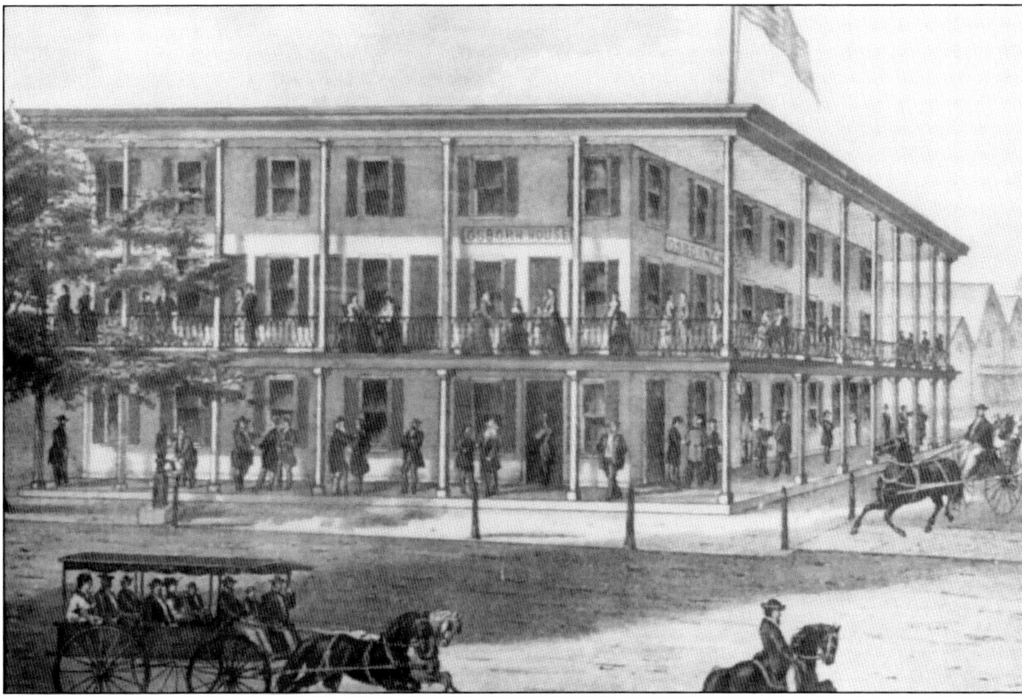

This artist's 1878 rendering depicts the popular Osborn House with visitors to the hotel on its wraparound porches. The building, originally a stagecoach stop, was a thriving establishment known throughout the state, as well as in Philadelphia and New York City, for its fine dining. The original proprietor was Col. James Osborn.

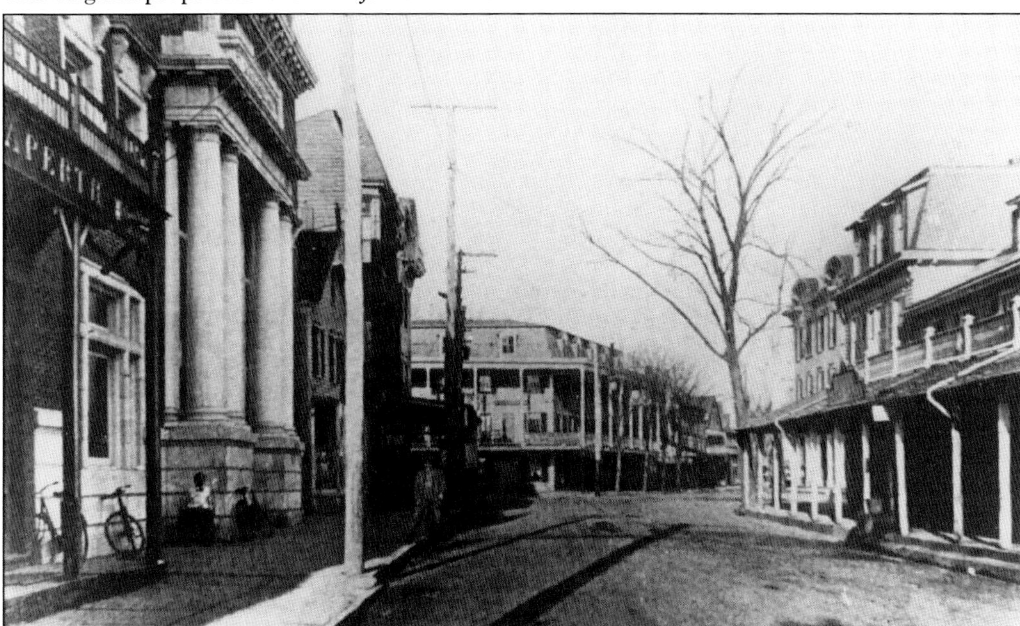

Main Street about 1910—looking west at the south side of the business district—was already developed with dry goods stores, a hotel, and a bank. The pillars of the borough's Manasquan National Bank—established in 1908—are visible adjacent to the Paperth Building to the east.

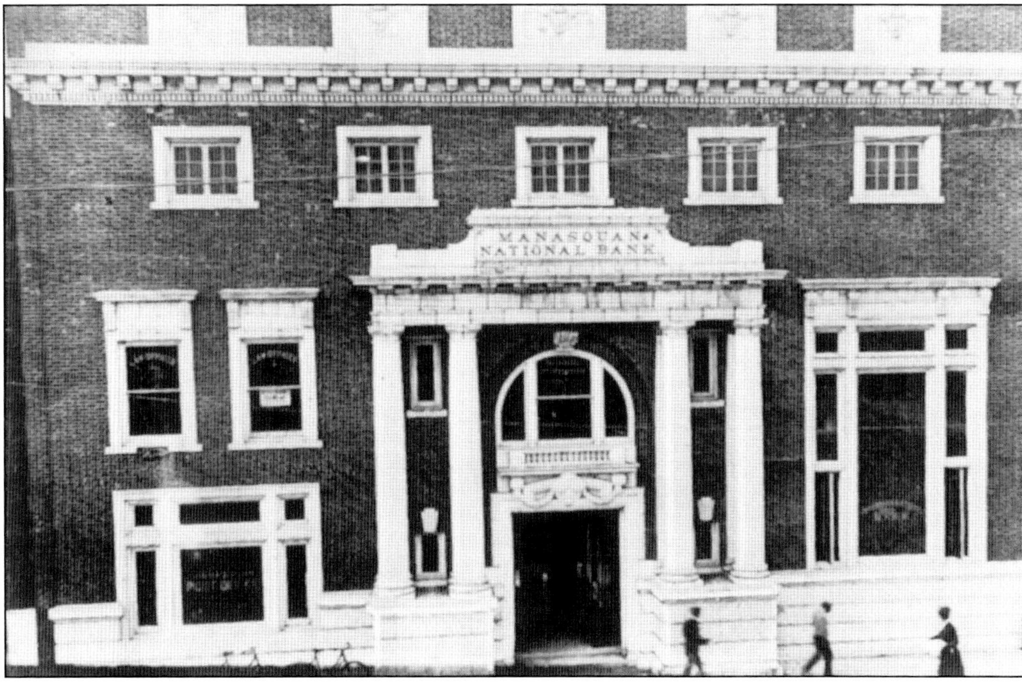

The Manasquan National Bank, located on the south side of Main Street, was founded in 1908. Prior to this banking institution, the First National Bank of Manasquan had been established at this location and served the community from 1883 until closing in 1908. When the bank reopened as the Manasquan National Bank, William P. Taylor served as its president.

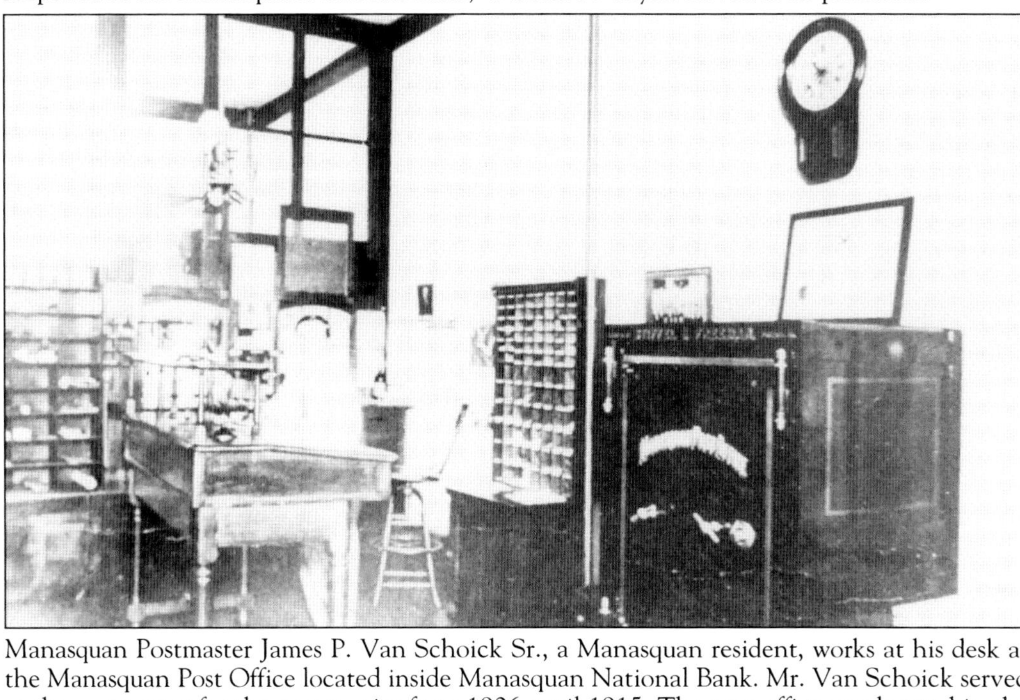

Manasquan Postmaster James P. Van Schoick Sr., a Manasquan resident, works at his desk at the Manasquan Post Office located inside Manasquan National Bank. Mr. Van Schoick served as the postmaster for the community from 1906 until 1915. The post office was located in the east half of the bank from 1906 until 1951.

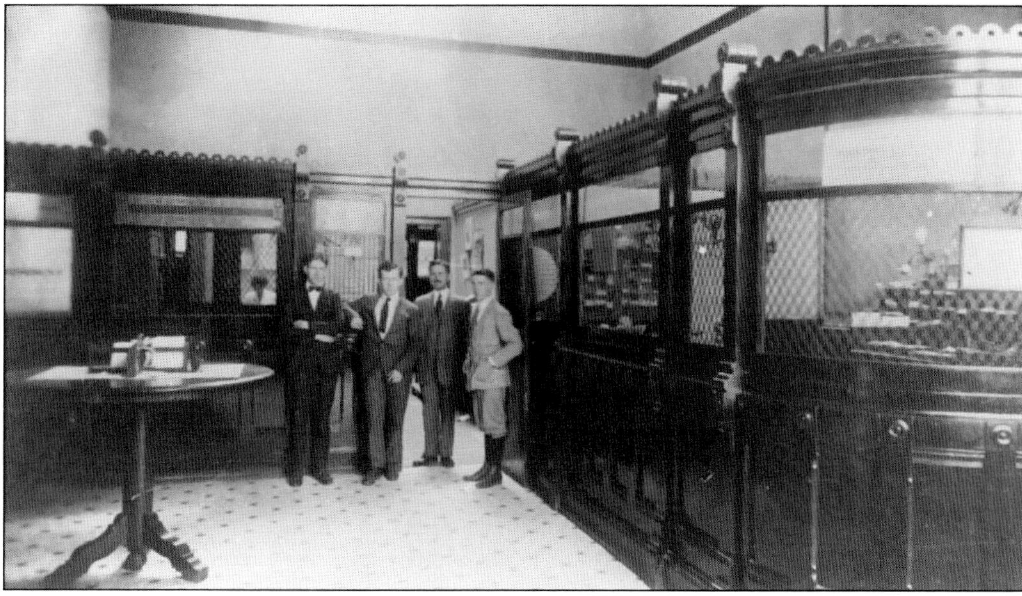

John W. Hulsart (third from left), president of Manasquan National Bank, stands with other bank executives in this *c.* 1929 image. Mr. Hulsart had served as assistant to the cashier of the bank when it opened in 1908. In this interior photograph of the facility a bank teller is visible.

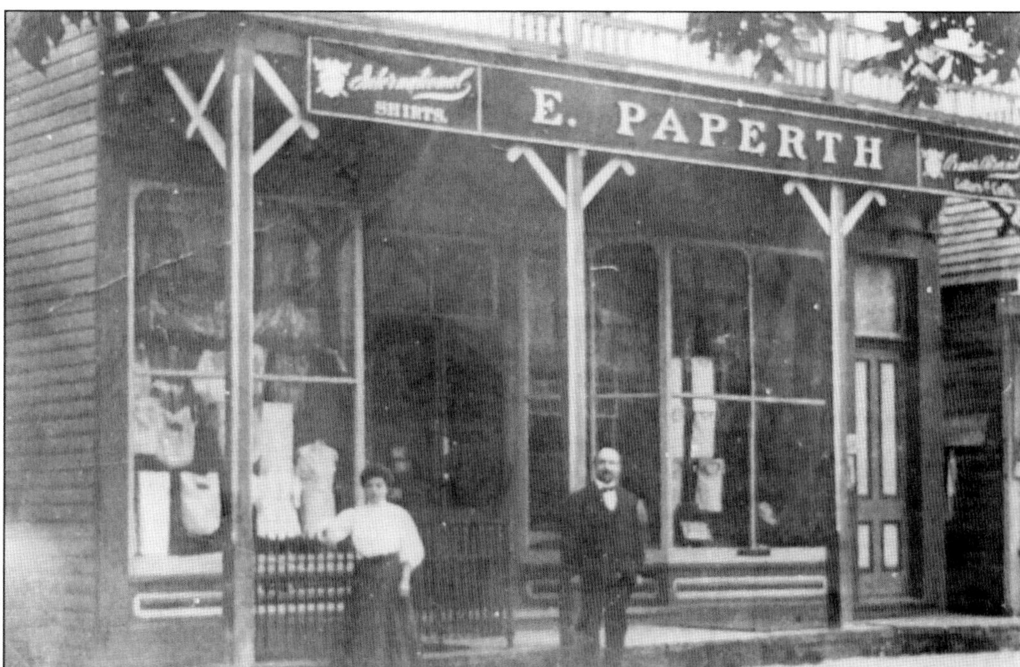

The building at 113 Main Street, now the Center Food Market, was built about 1865–1870. In 1904, under ownership of Ellis Paperth, the store carried general merchandise. His son, Dr. Milton Paperth, later operated a dental practice on the second floor, and his daughter, Mrs. Sally Paperth Yatter, updated the store's inventory to offer fashionable women's clothing and accessories. Mr. Paperth died in 1955 at age 93.

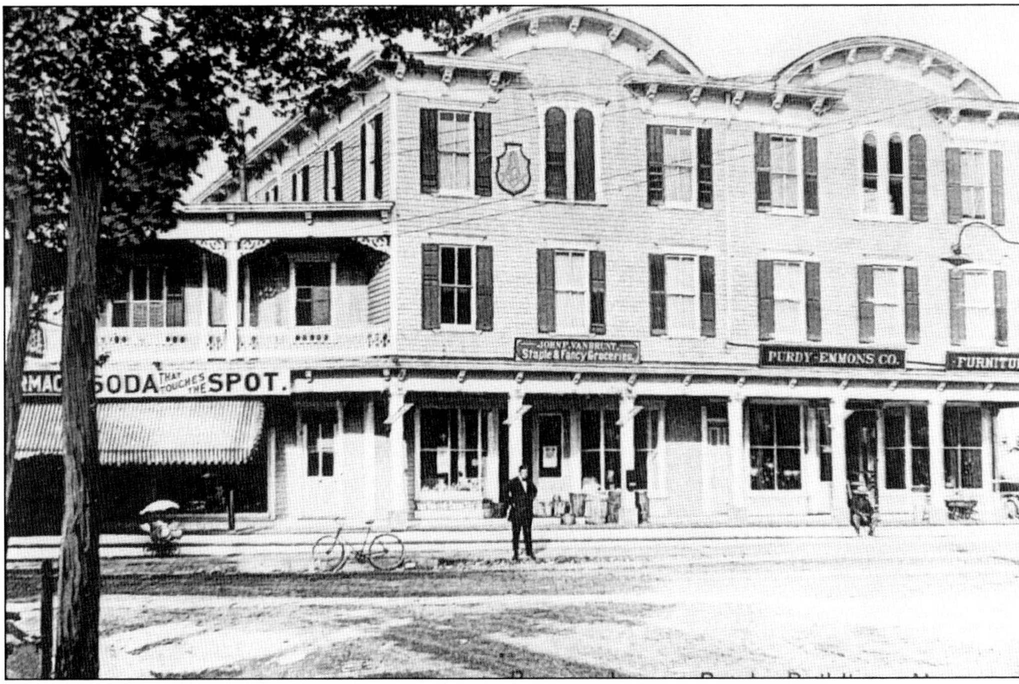

The Purdy-Burrough's Building (formerly the Wainwright & Errickson Building) on Main Street featured Burrough's Pharmacy, James P. Van Brunt's Staple & Fancy Groceries, and a furniture store in this 1920s scene. Located at the west end of the business district on the north side of Main Street, this structure featured a roof over the sidewalk to protect shoppers in all types of weather.

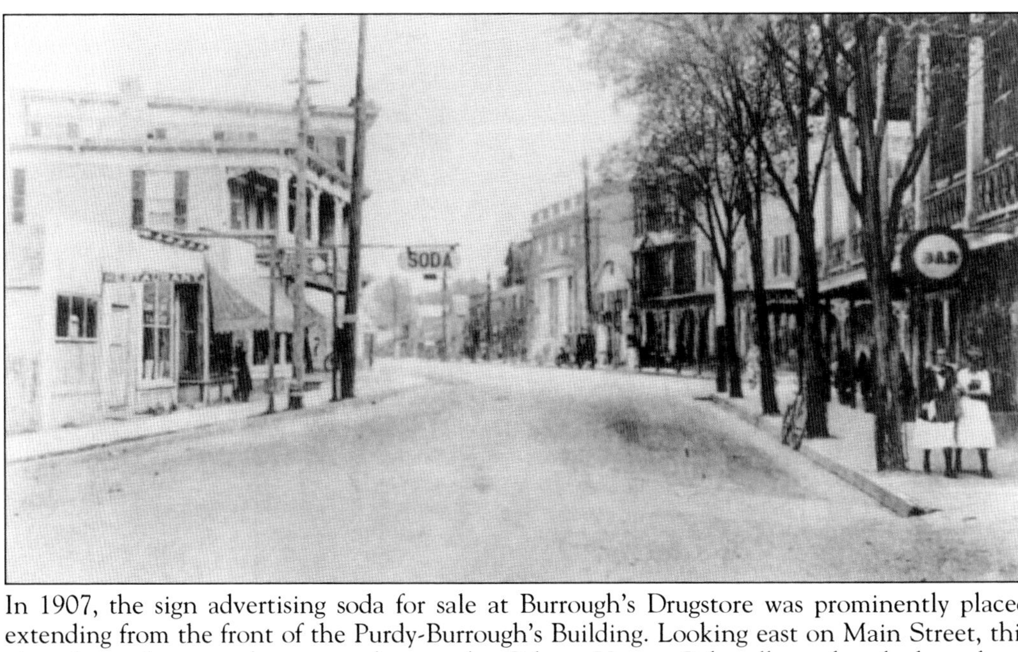

In 1907, the sign advertising soda for sale at Burrough's Drugstore was prominently placed extending from the front of the Purdy-Burrough's Building. Looking east on Main Street, this view shows the second-story porches on the Osborn House. Sidewalks and curbs have been installed, but the street still is dirt surfaced.

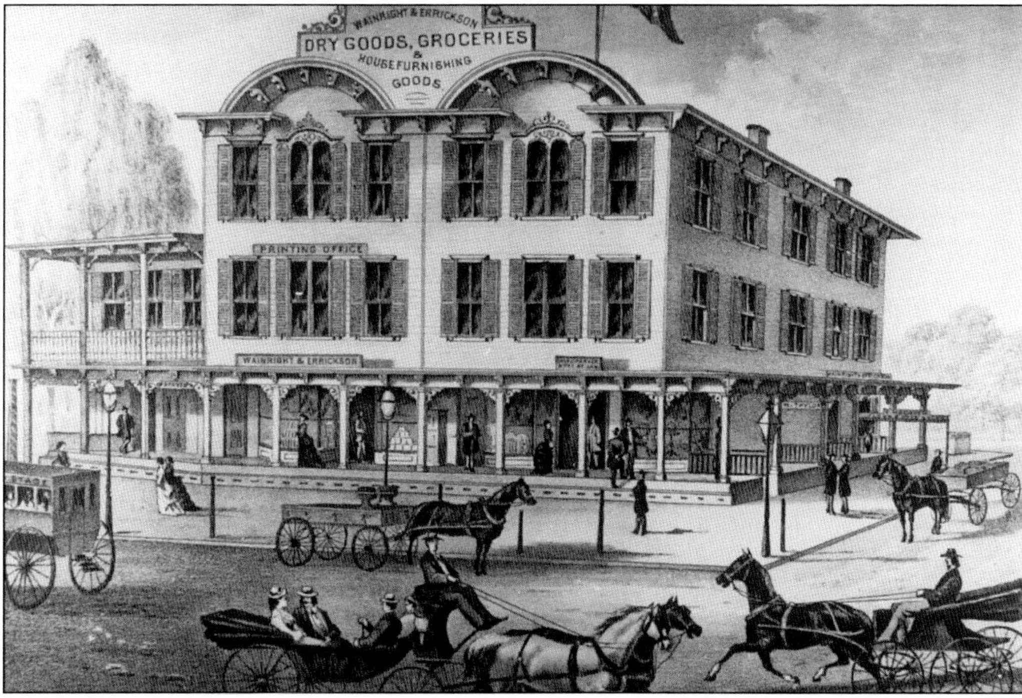

The Wainwright & Errickson Building on Main Street—before the turn of the century—advertised dry goods, groceries, and house furnishings, as well as professional offices for local businessmen. The center portion of this building—later known at the Purdy-Burrough's Building—was more than 100 years old when it was razed in 1946.

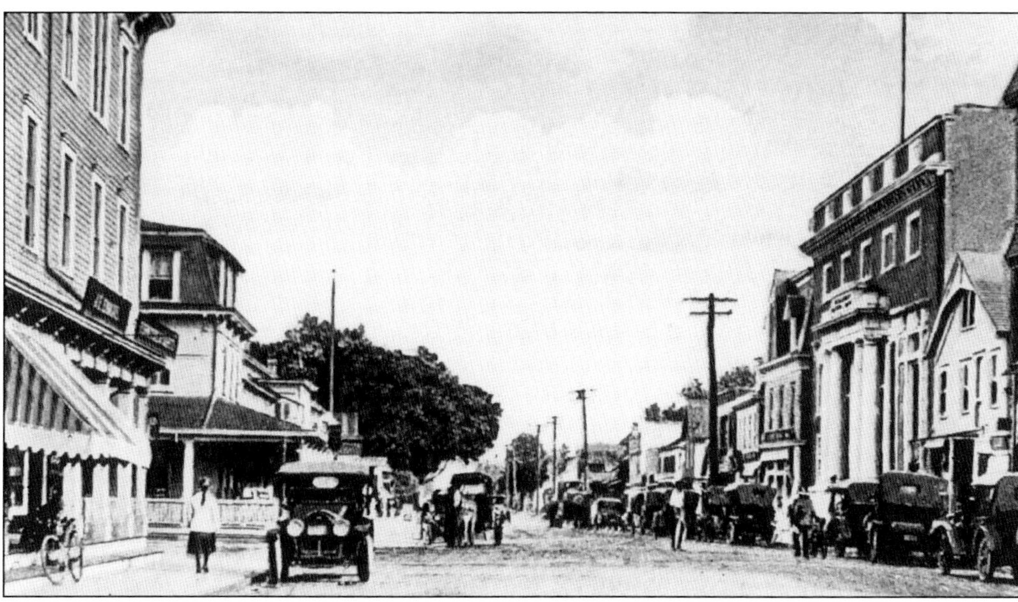

A horse and carriage is seen in the shopping district along with automobiles during the early part of the century. In a view looking east on Main Street, the Borden Building—just visible in the corner of the photograph on the south side—has been restored today to its Victorian appearance.

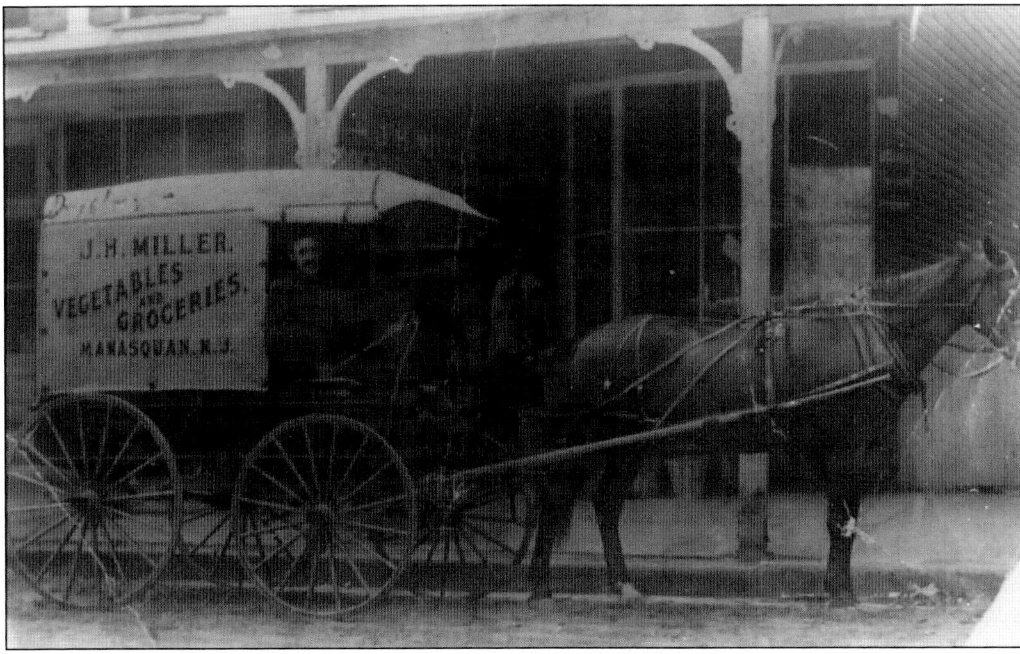

"Staple and Fancy Groceries, Fruits, Vegetables, and Seeds" were available from J. Howard Miller, who is seen perched in the carriage of his delivery wagon. Advertisements for the business, which was located at 12 South Street, continued through the early decades of the 1900s. His store is visible in the background.

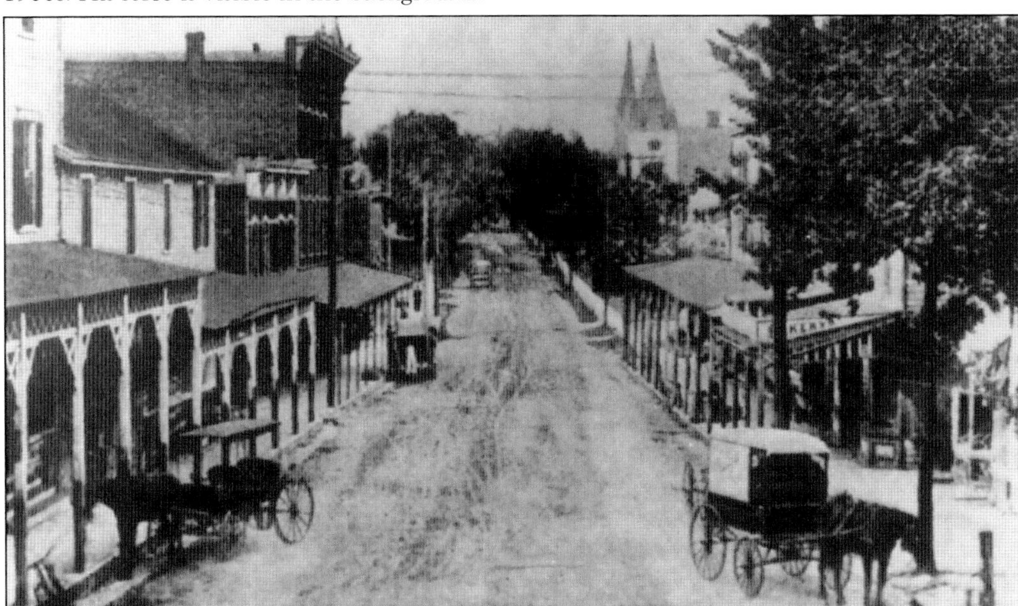

Captured in the view of the much-developed business district on South Street in 1914, the spires of the Manasquan First Baptist Church are visible in the distance. In 1899, the clock in the north tower of the church was installed. For years, it was known as the town clock. Canopies covered the paved walkways to make shopping in the business area more comfortable in sun, rain, or snow.

The Borden Building at 97–99 Main Street was built in 1896 by John W. Borden, a Manasquan entrepreneur who resided in Brielle. Mr. Borden died in 1909, and the Hanover Fire Insurance Co., which he had begun, continued under direction of Ralph D. Bush. Other businesses through the years located in the building were the *Coast Star* and the Manasquan Pharmacy.

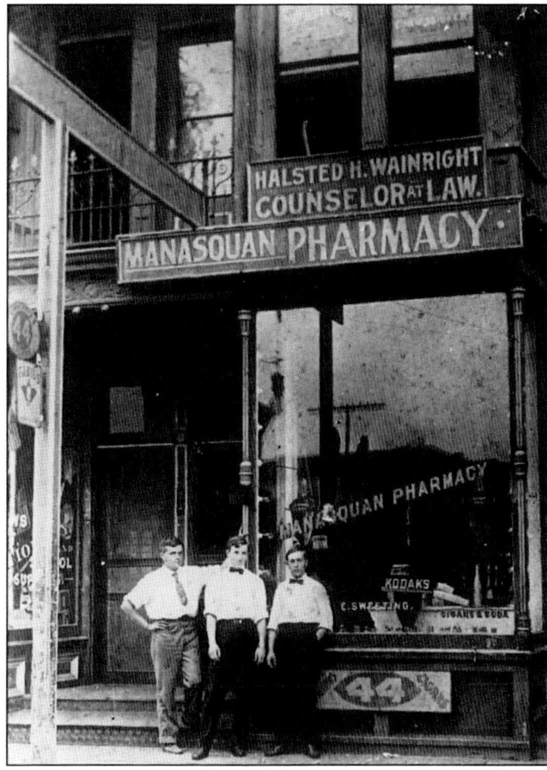

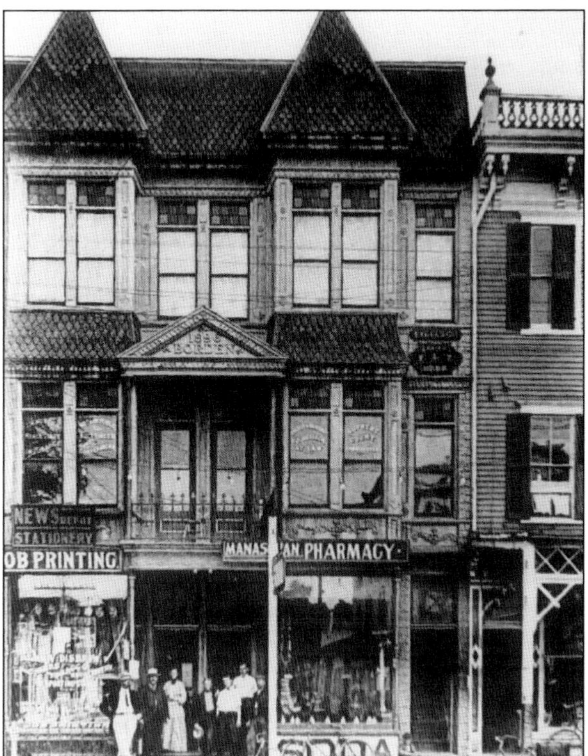

This full-view photograph of the Borden Building—taken in early 1920s—is an excellent example of the intricate gingerbread and Victorian architecture used throughout the older section of the community. In 1987, William and Richard Wight purchased the building from Irving Kirsch and restored it to its Victorian charm. They said that after seeing old pictures of the building, coupled with their pride in Manasquan, they had to preserve it. The building is currently owned by Lawrence Dunning.

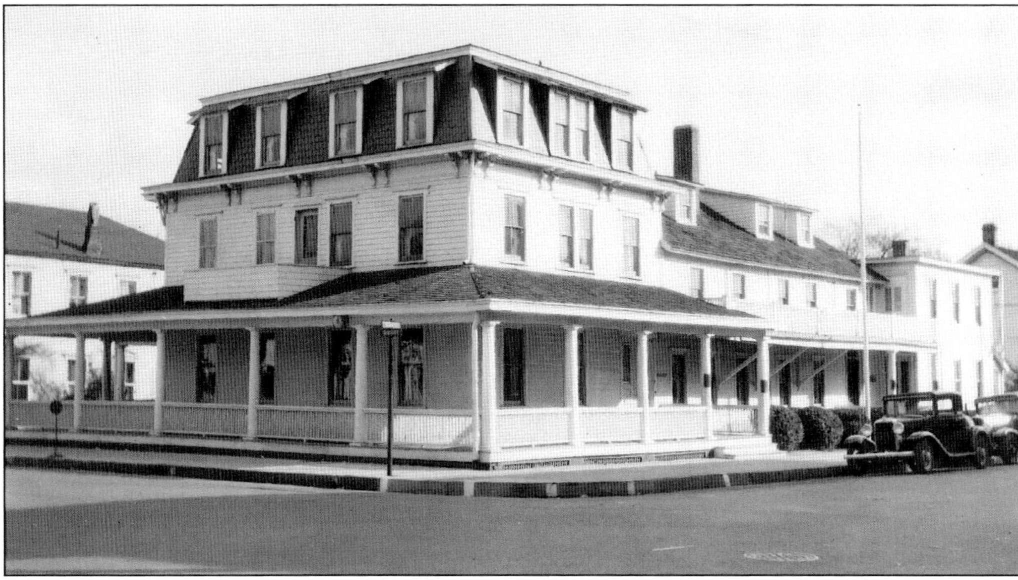

The Squan House at the corner of Main and Broad Streets was originally the home of the Huntzinger family. In 1879, John H. Davison purchased the house, rebuilt part of it, and hung a sign calling it the "Squan House." Within a few years, the establishment was well known from New York City to Philadelphia, Pennsylvania. According to historical records, the structure was razed in 1946 "to make way for more modern buildings."

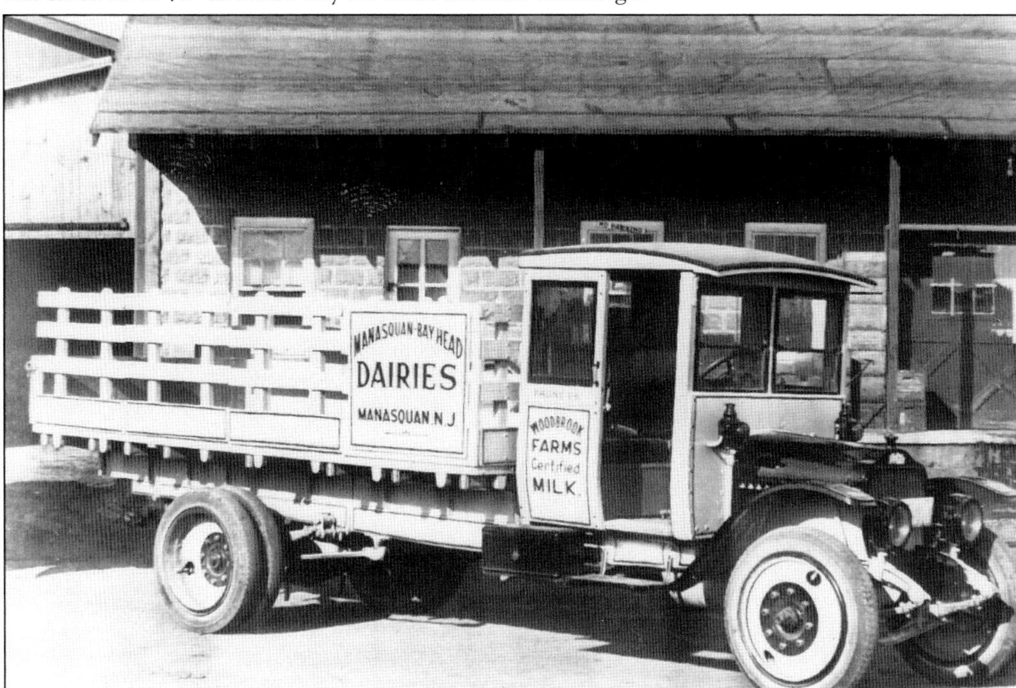

This truck was one of the fleet owned by the Manasquan-Bay Head Dairies, which was located on Colby Avenue in the borough. Adjacent to the dairy was the Block Ice and Cold Storage Co. J. Milton Cook and Richard F. Applegate, a brother of Mr. Cook's wife, operated the dairy from 1923 until 1941, at which time Mr. Cook sold his half of the partnership.

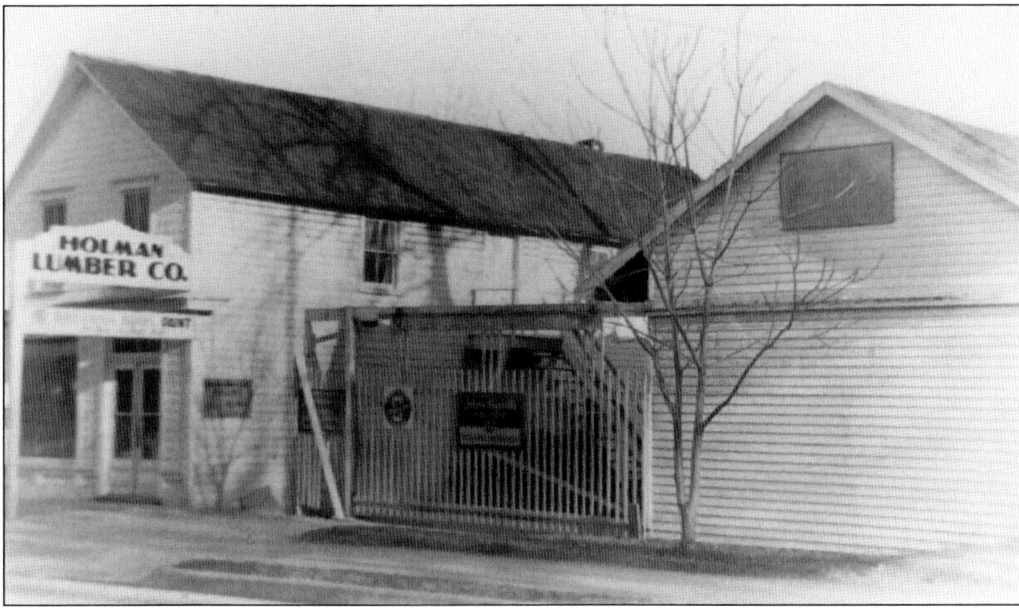

Chauncey Holman acquired the Van Leer Lumber Company and changed its named to Holman Lumber Company. In the 1930s, Mr. Holman provided the wide molding for the ceiling of the sanctuary of the Manasquan First Baptist Church, which was situated across the street from the lumber company.

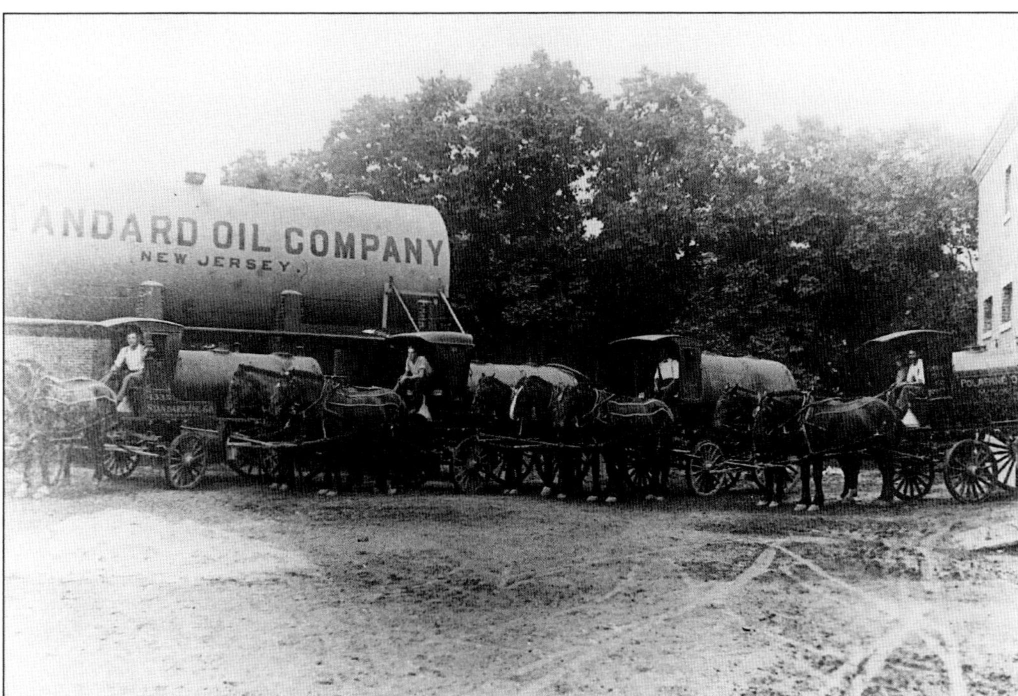

Men operating horse-drawn carriages are working at Standard Oil Company in this picture. The oil business was located where Mount Lane and Euclid Avenue meet. The company's oil storage tanks were situated south of the rail depot.

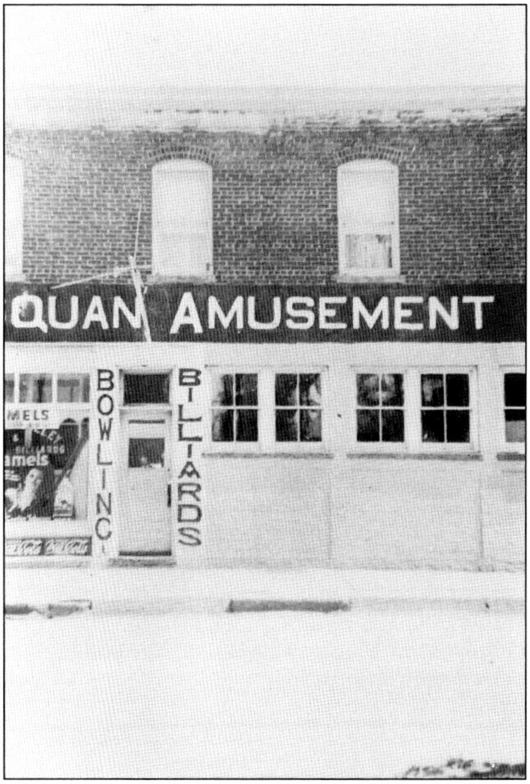

The Manasquan Amusement Palace on the east side of South Street, owned by Peter J. and Despina Skokos, featured four bowling alleys, two pool tables, and a billiard table. The Skokos family lived on the second floor with their children, George and Alice. The family operated the business for about 30 years until 1941, when Mr. Skokos purchased and renamed a luncheonette in Point Pleasant Beach, Peter Skokos Drive-in, which is still owned and operated by the family.

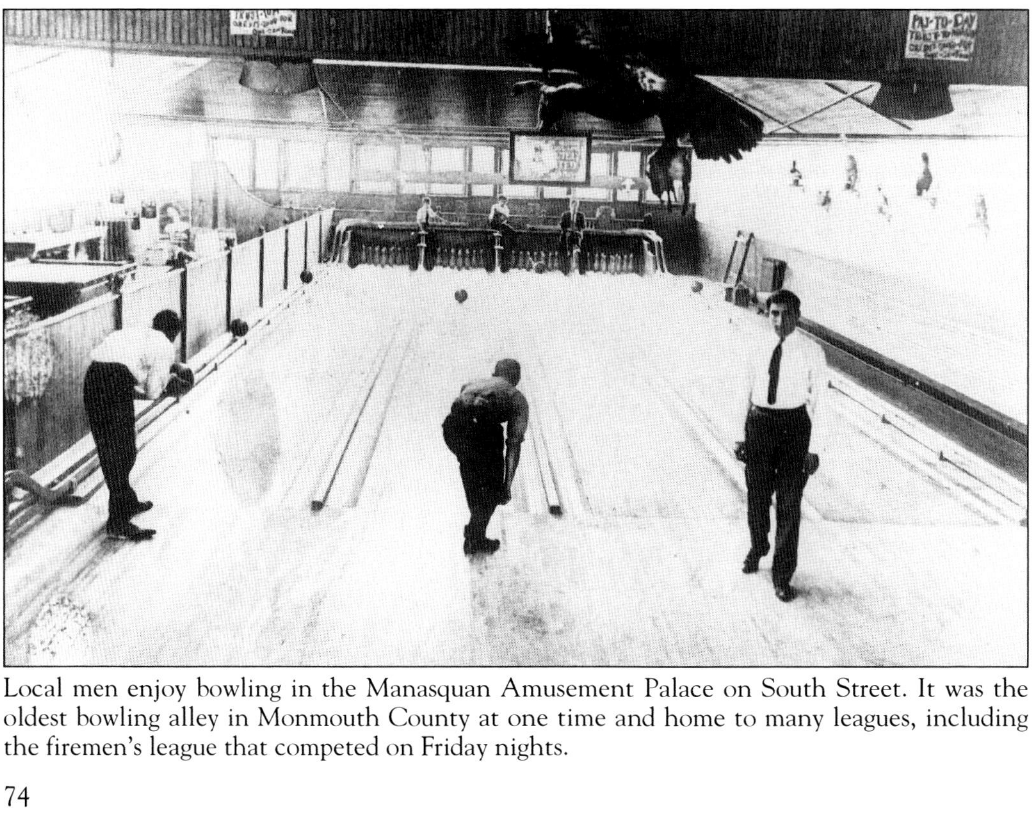

Local men enjoy bowling in the Manasquan Amusement Palace on South Street. It was the oldest bowling alley in Monmouth County at one time and home to many leagues, including the firemen's league that competed on Friday nights.

The Arcadia Theatre was located on the west side of South Street opposite the Manasquan Amusement Palace. Prior to this structure, Parker Hall, a two-story theater, was located on the site until it was destroyed by fire in 1915.

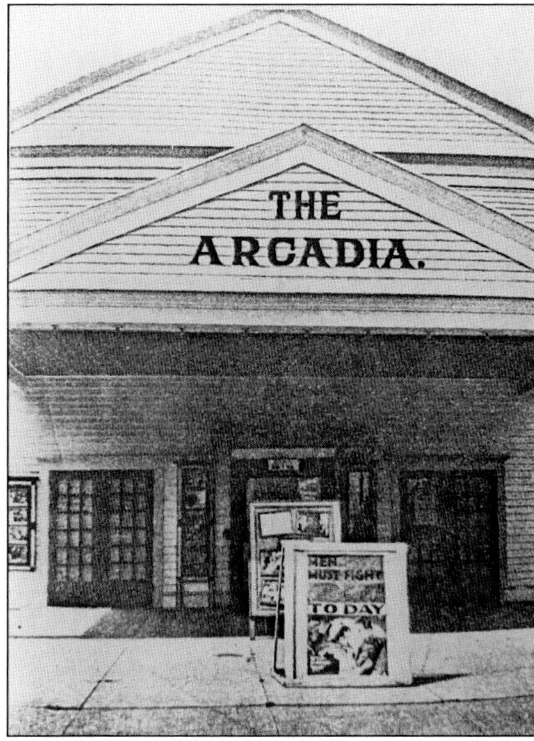

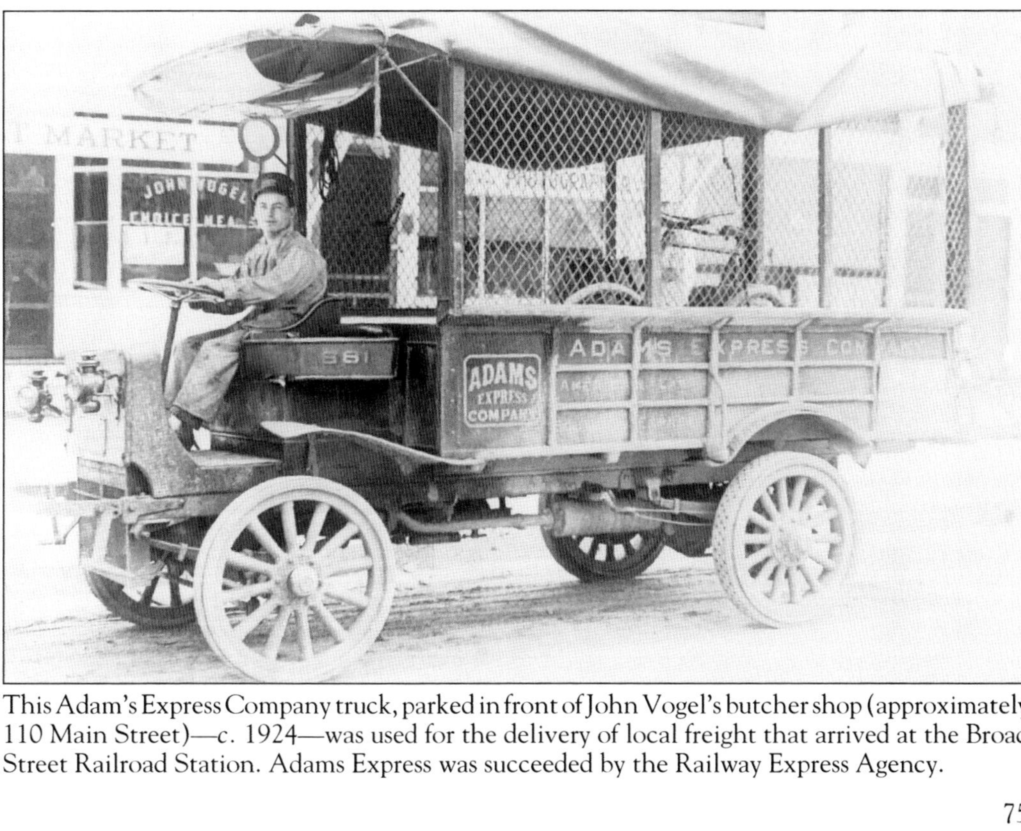

This Adam's Express Company truck, parked in front of John Vogel's butcher shop (approximately 110 Main Street)—*c.* 1924—was used for the delivery of local freight that arrived at the Broad Street Railroad Station. Adams Express was succeeded by the Railway Express Agency.

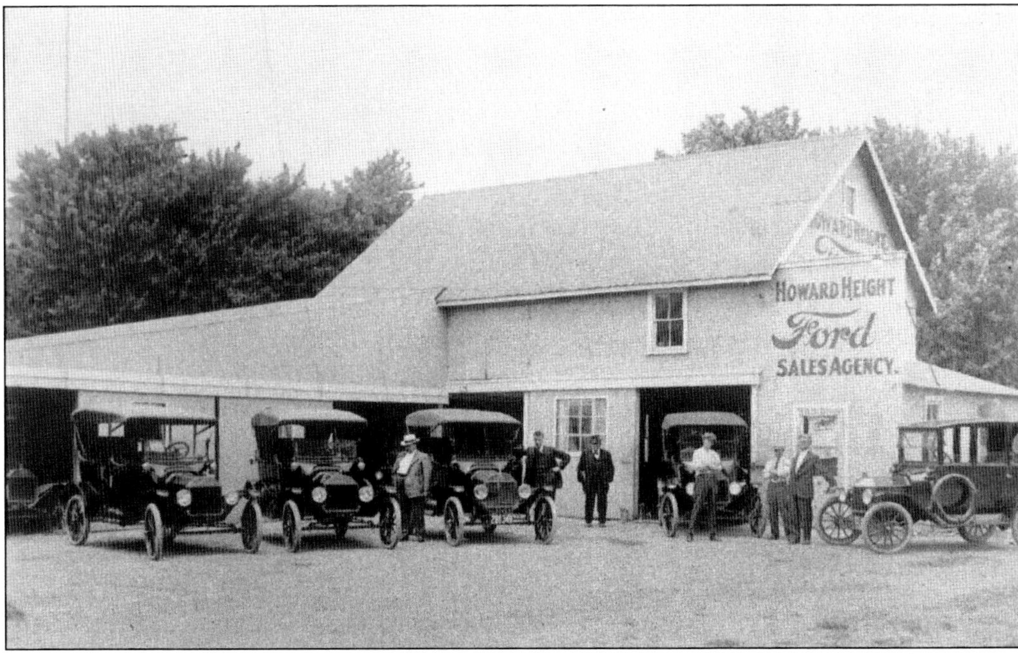

Staff members at Howard Height Ford Sales Agency display 1912 models—with a list price of $395—at the business located on the northeast corner of Taylor Avenue (Route 71) and Main Street. Howard Height Sr., a former Wall Township farmer, opened the first Ford dealership in Monmouth County in a converted barn. Mr. Height was born in 1881 and died in 1942.

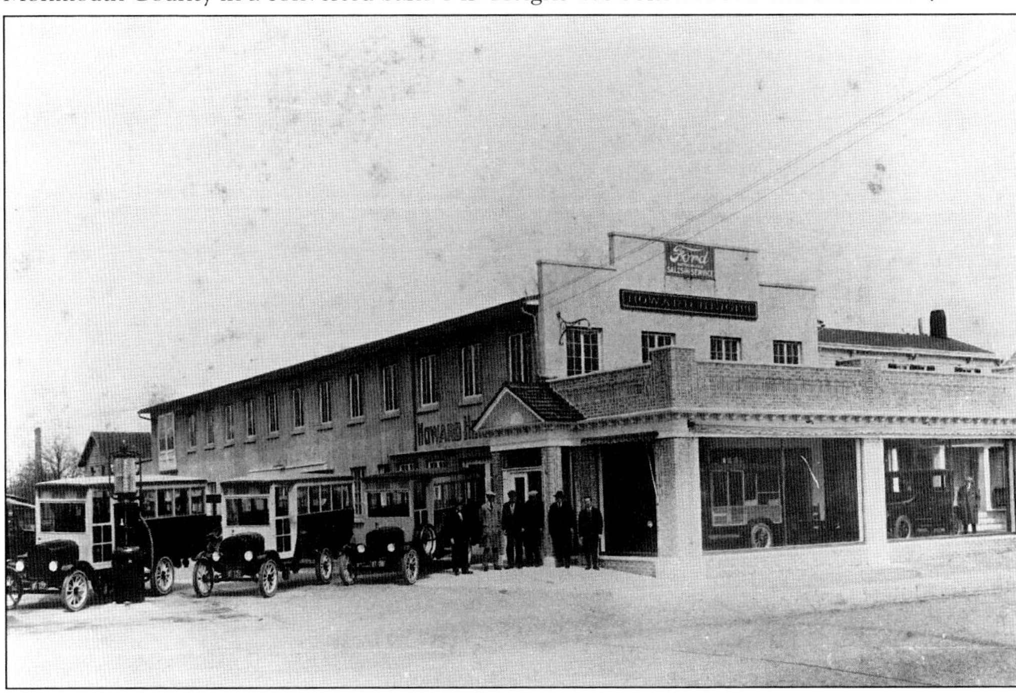

Later, following the death of his father in 1942, Howard Height Jr. assumed ownership of the Ford Agency founded by his father. Expansion of the business had taken place prior to this photograph. The 1920s vehicles on display are part of a fleet of new school buses.

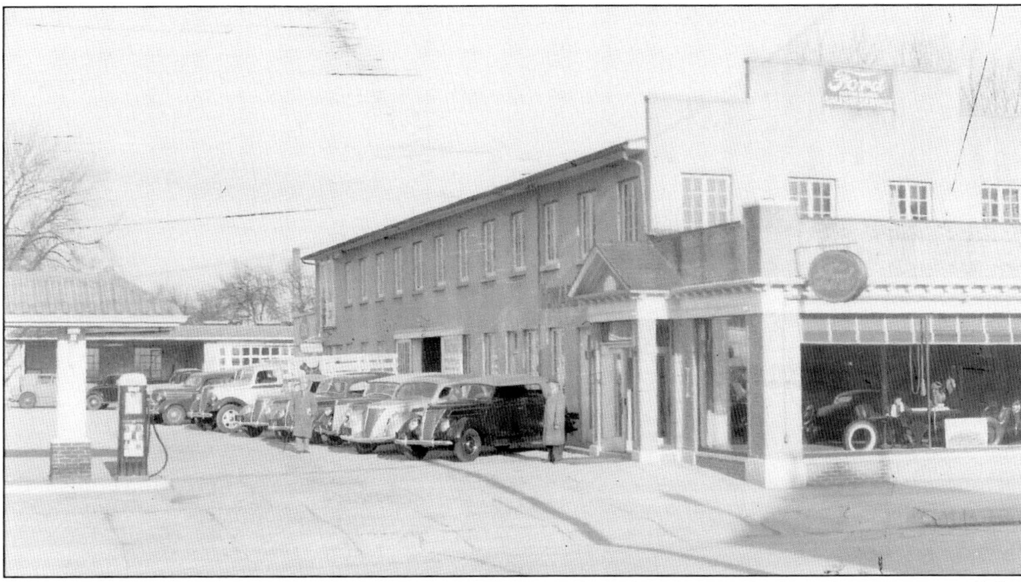

The agency expanded with the times and growing needs of families with these larger automobiles. In 1965, the agency was again expanded and moved to Route 35 in Wall Township. That location was closed in 1981, and all business activity was completed at the company's final location in Point Pleasant.

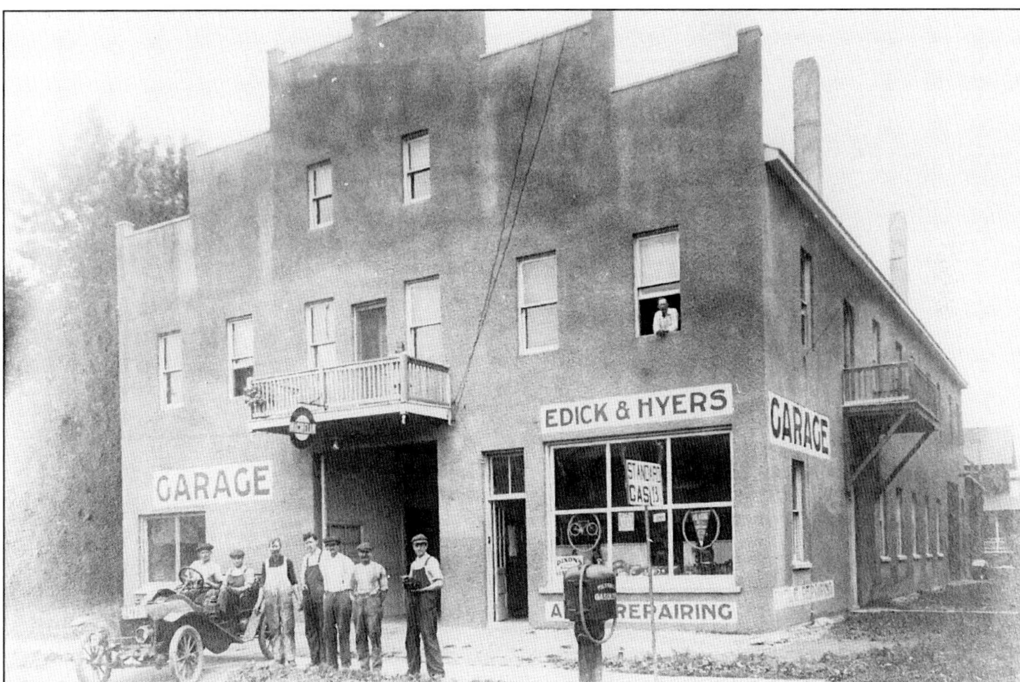

Local men gather in front of Edick & Hyers Garage in this early-1900s photograph. The building at 140 Main Street later became the hardware store of John French. In 1944 the Wright Company hardware chain purchased the site and opened a hardware store. George R. Demspey Sr. served as manager of the store until 1953, when he purchased the business and opened Dempsey's Hardware store.

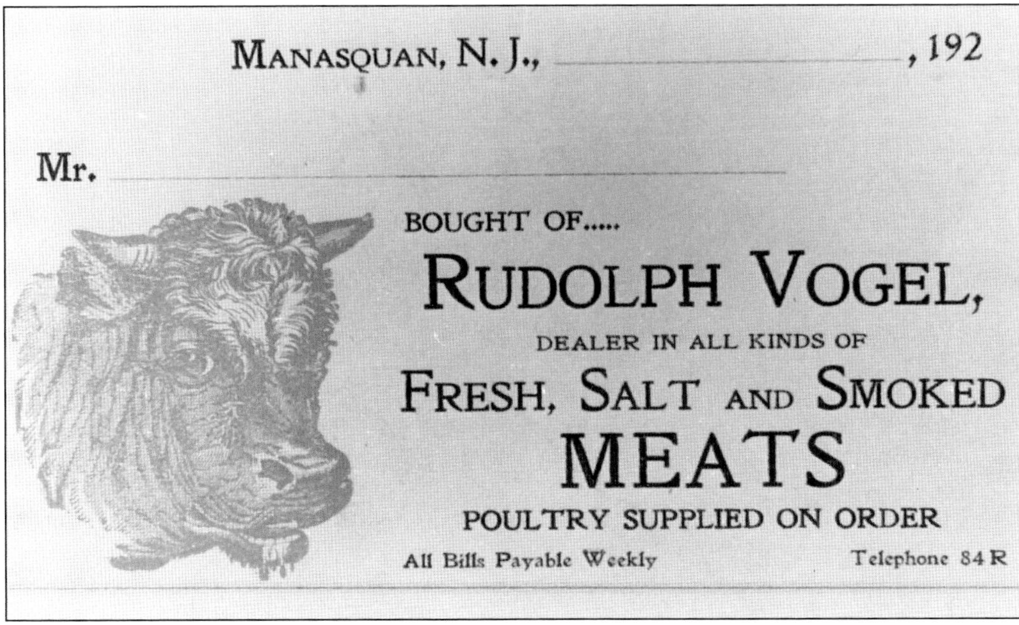

MANASQUAN, N. J., ______________, 192

Mr. ______________________________

BOUGHT OF.....

RUDOLPH VOGEL,

DEALER IN ALL KINDS OF

FRESH, SALT AND SMOKED

MEATS

POULTRY SUPPLIED ON ORDER

All Bills Payable Weekly — Telephone 84 R

This sales receipt is from Rudolph Vogel's meat business. Rudolph, a Swiss slaughterhouse man, operated an establishment specializing in fresh, salted, and smoked meats on South Street, while his brother, John Vogel, operated a specialty meats store on Main Street. Although Rudolph's business eventually closed, John's business later became Thompson's Meat Market.

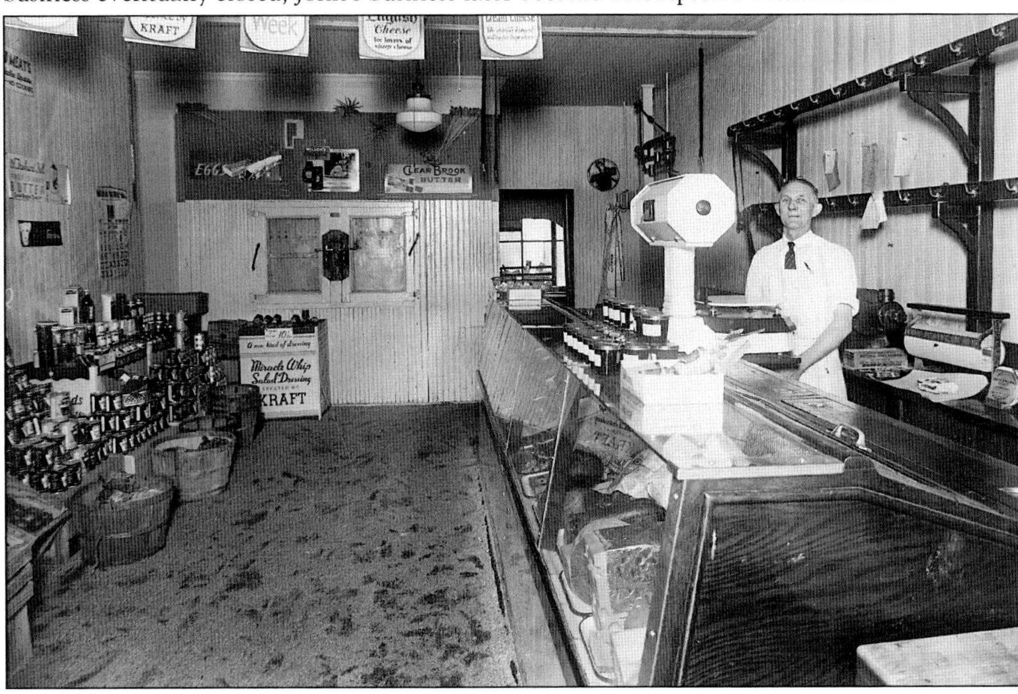

A. Eugene Thompson stands behind the counter in his 114 Main Street meat market in the late 1930s. Thompson's Meat Market featured prime cuts of meat, Kraft products, pickles, and specialty delicatessen items. Local residents note that during World War II they remember waiting outside the store for it to open so that they could purchase their meat rations.

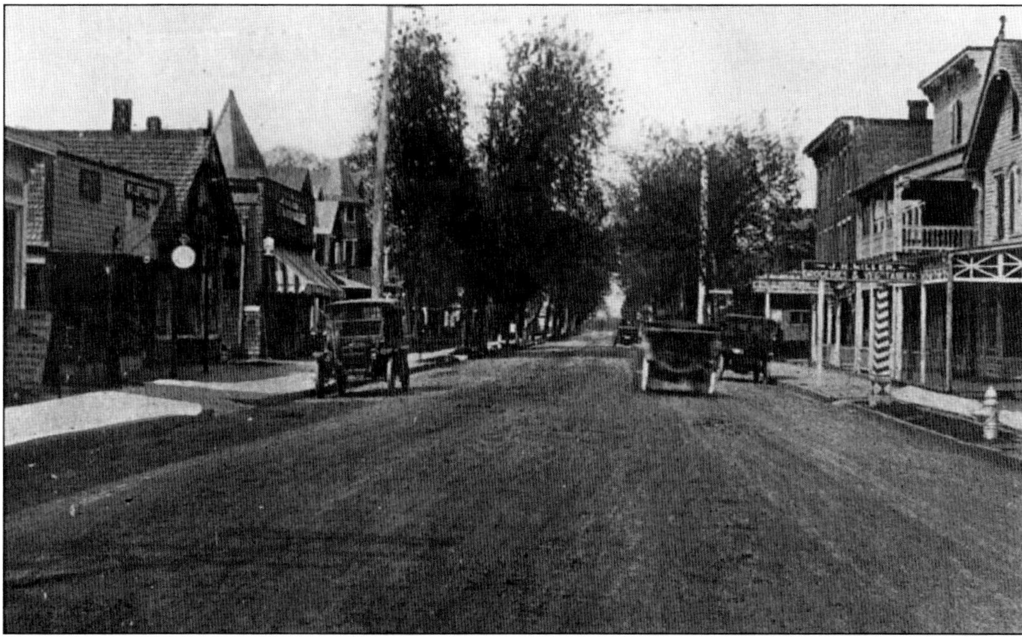

Broad Street in Manasquan was an integral part of the business district as early as the turn of the century. In this early-1900s photograph, J.H. Miller Groceries & Vegetables store is visible on the east side of the street, in a this view looking north.

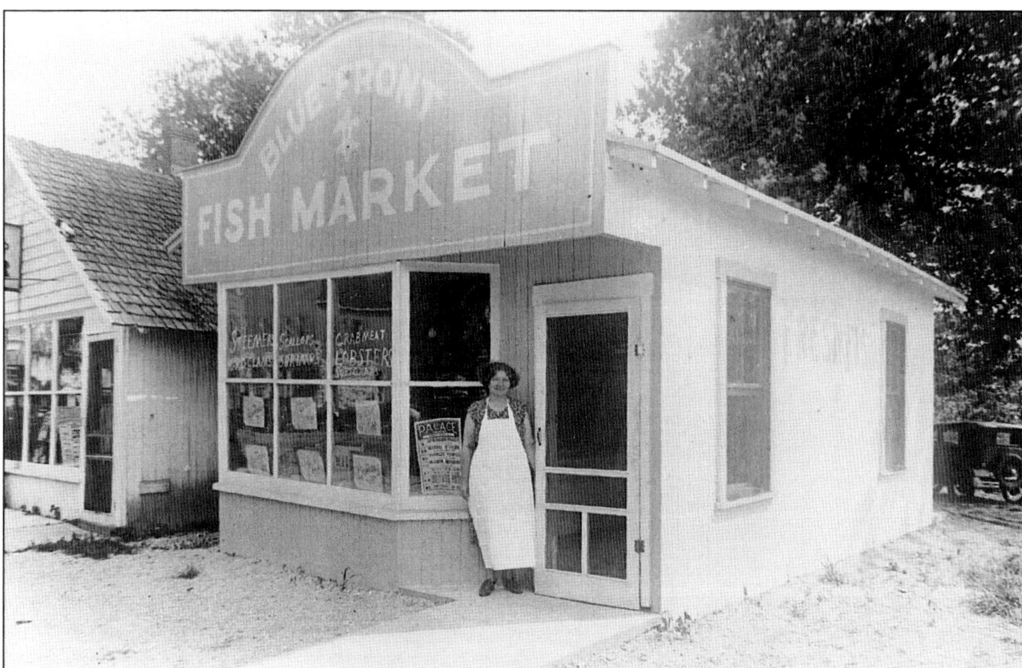

Theresa Carlson stands outside the Blue Front Fish Market on the south side on Main Street. Mrs. Carlson and her husband, Axel Carlson Sr., had operated the business until the 1930s. Mr. Carlson was one of the first to operate fishing boats out of the Manasquan Inlet.

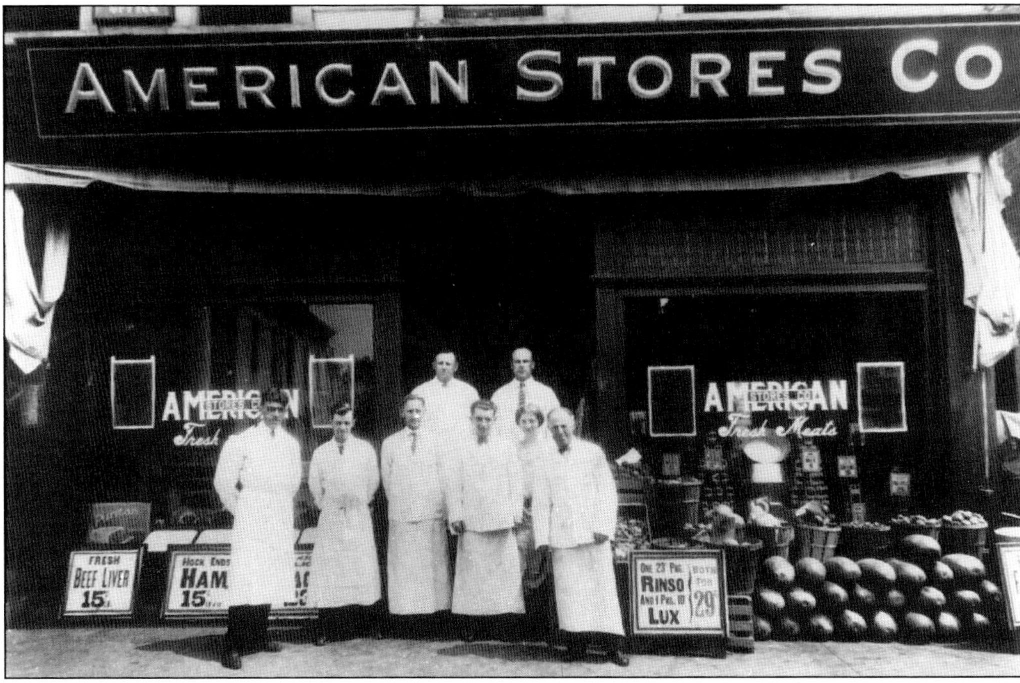

American Stores Company, the forerunner of Acme Stores, was located at 108 Main Street. Ralph Hartranft served as manager of the business until it was closed and reopened on the south side of the street as an Acme. At that time, Mr. Hartranft opened Ralph's, a specialty store, that was adjacent to the food store.

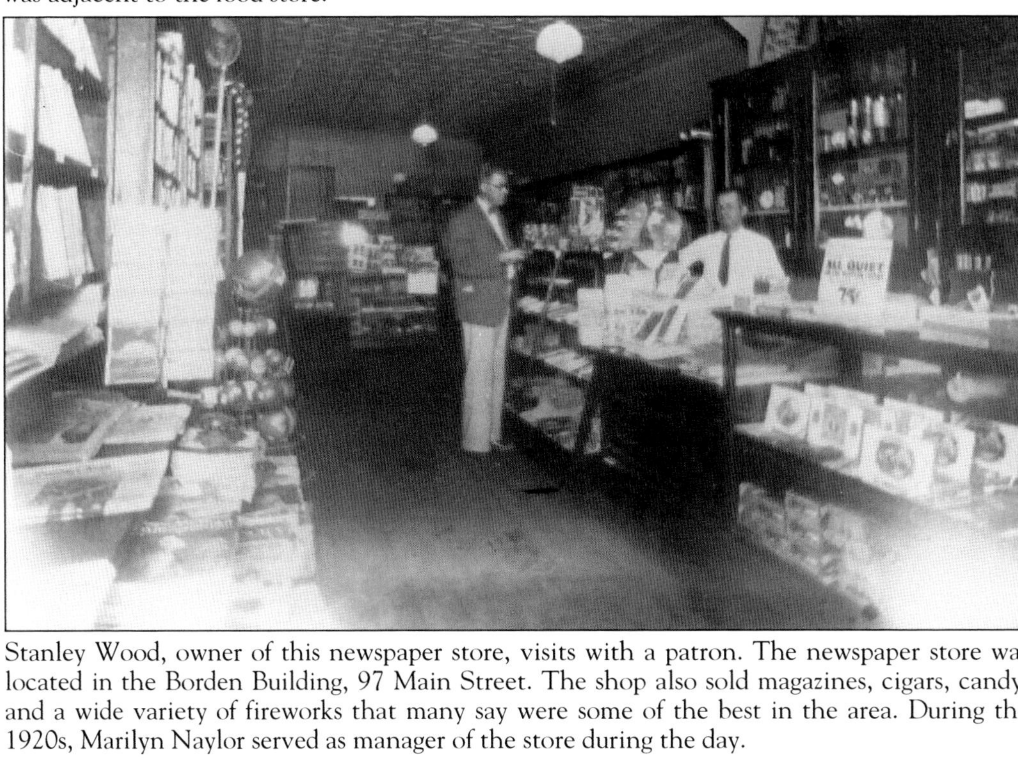

Stanley Wood, owner of this newspaper store, visits with a patron. The newspaper store was located in the Borden Building, 97 Main Street. The shop also sold magazines, cigars, candy, and a wide variety of fireworks that many say were some of the best in the area. During the 1920s, Marilyn Naylor served as manager of the store during the day.

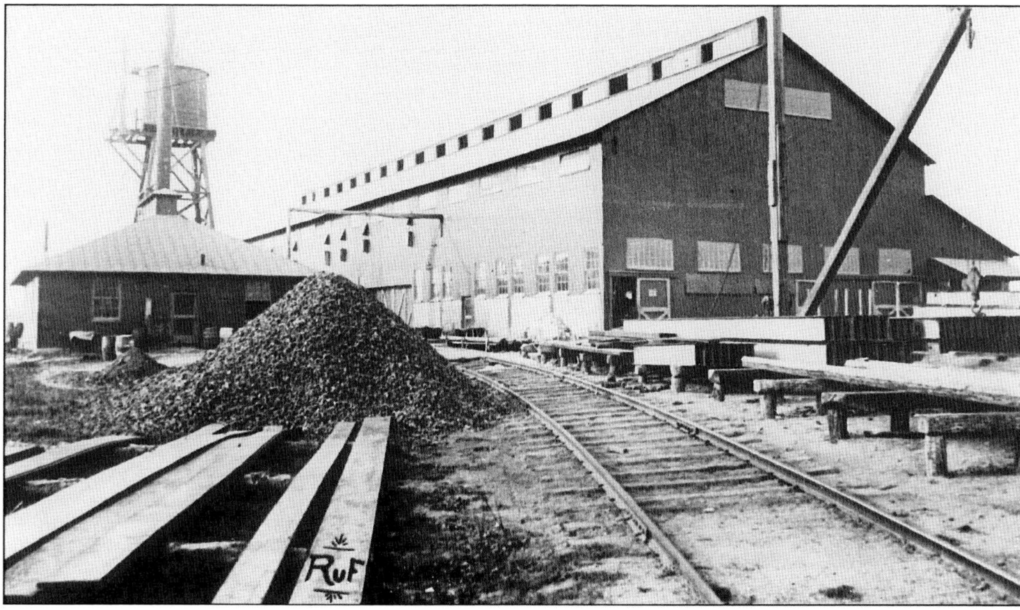

The New Jersey Bridge Company was located on the north side of Atlantic Avenue not far from the current location of Manasquan High School. History records indicate that the firm—in service from 1890 to 1907—was probably the largest individual manufacturing facility to have operated in Manasquan, employing 120 persons in its 100-by-300-foot plant.

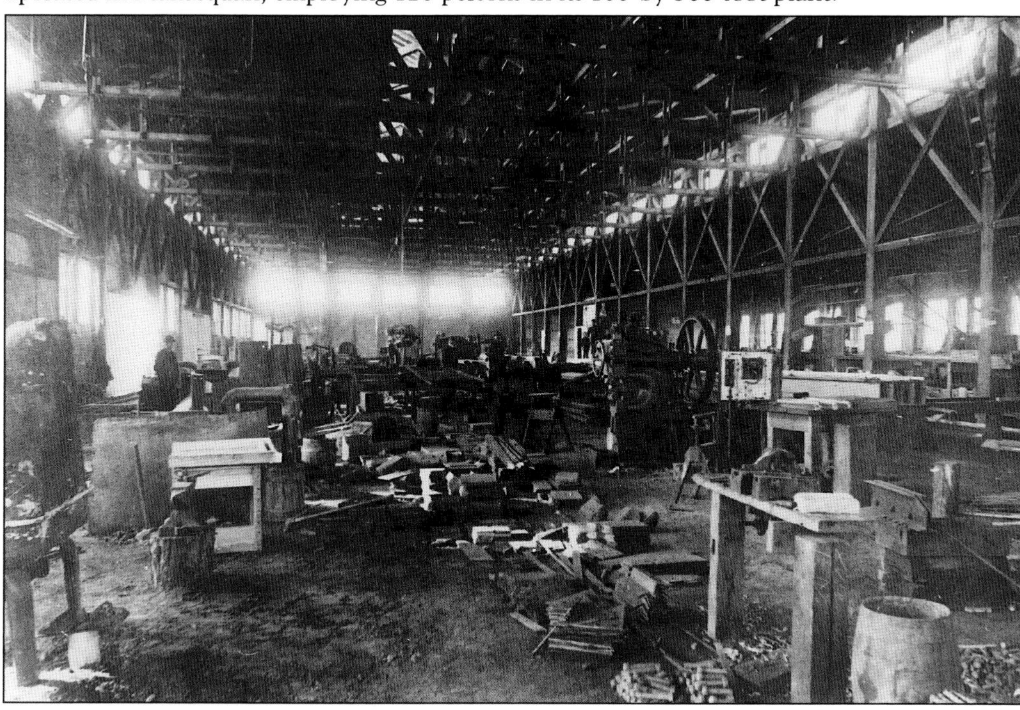

This interior view of the New Jersey Bridge Company illustrates its magnitude. The company was responsible for building several steel bridges used in highway construction throughout the state. The plant was closed following financial difficulties resulting from a bridge contract with a firm in Portland, Maine.

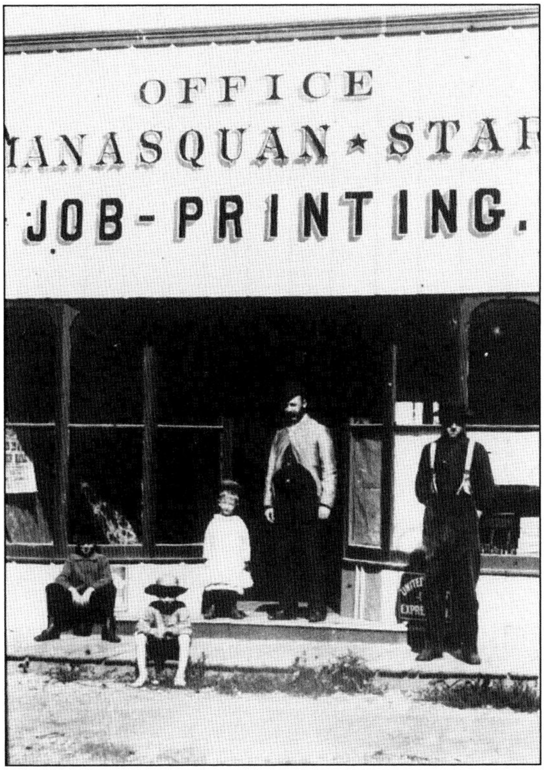

The forerunner of the *Coast Star*, the *Manasquan Star* was located at 13 Broad Street. Local residents believe that the man standing in the doorway of the building is Tracy M. Hoskins, the owner of the newspaper, and that his sister, Gertrude, is standing just to his right. In 1909, Wilmer E. Hoskins gave ownership of the newspaper to his son.

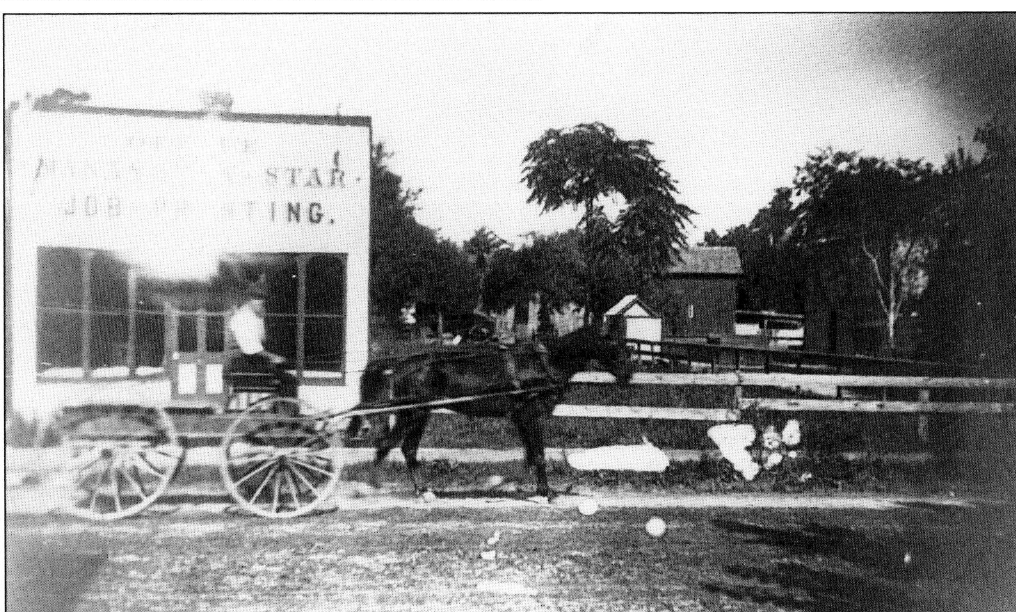

In this 1890s photograph, a man travels along Broad Street. In view is the office of the *Manasquan Star*. Prior to this building's use as the offices of the weekly newspaper, it had been the Manasquan Billiard Parlor and Bailey's cigar store. Tracy M. Hoskins served as editor and publisher of the newspaper—later named the *Coast Star*—for 50 years until his death in 1959, when his sister, Gertrude S. Hoskins, assumed ownership.

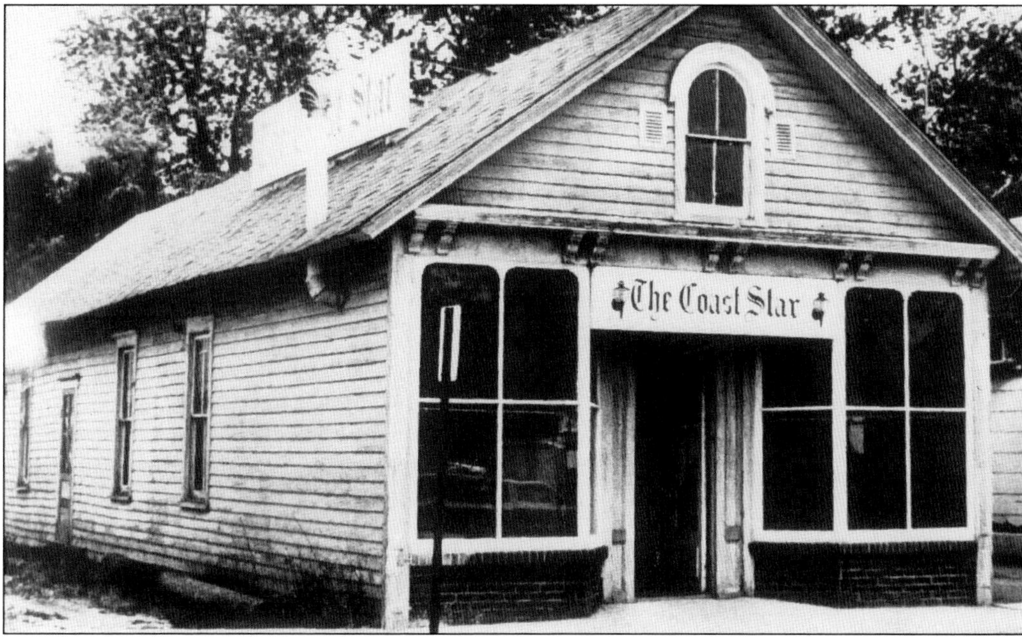

Thomas S. Birckhead Jr., a native of Manasquan, purchased the *Coast Star*, a weekly newspaper serving the borough, Brielle, and Sea Girt, from Miss Gertrude S. Hoskins, also of Manasquan, on July 1, 1961. Mr. Birckhead's first renovations to the structure at 13 Broad Street were to add the signs on the top of the building as well as to the front above the door. The plate-glass windows were removed later in the decade.

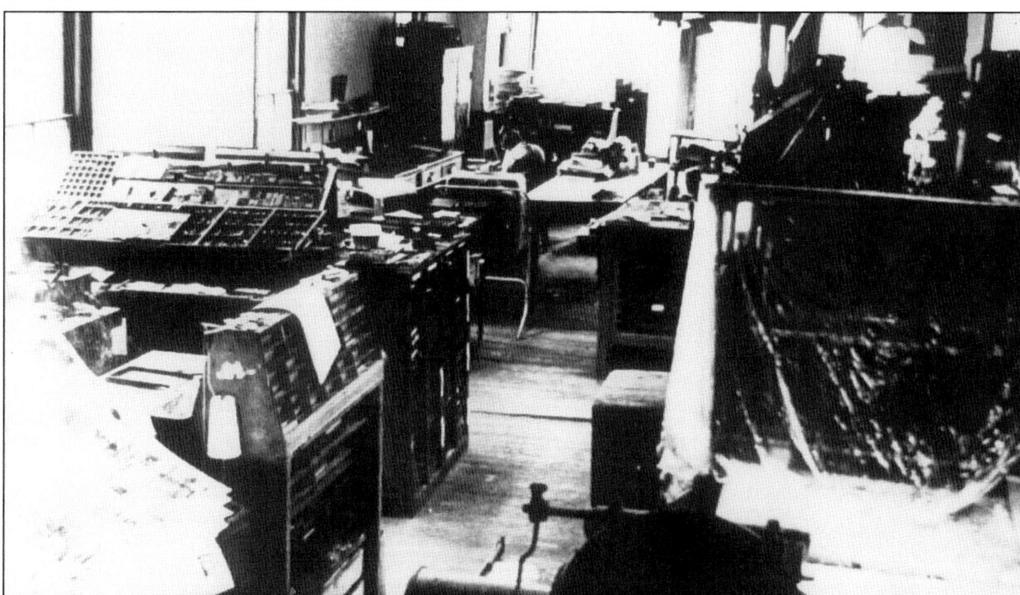

Inside of the offices of the *Coast Star* in the summer of 1961, this view depicts the publishing of a newspaper using letterpress style. Miss Susan Jordan, daughter of Dr. and Mrs. Joseph Jordan of Manasquan, writes an article at the rolltop desk surrounded by typecases and hand-fed presses. Miss Jordan was employed as a reporter for the newspaper while on summer break from Wilson College in Chambersburg, Pennsylvania.

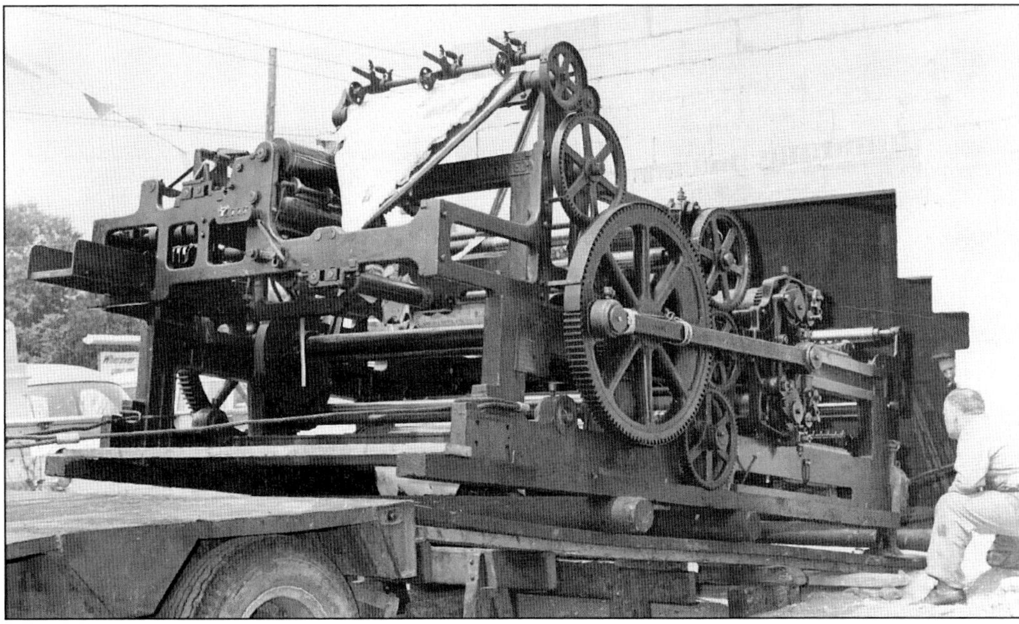

In 1964, a 9-ton rotary press replaced the hand-fed press at the *Coast Star* to make the process of printing the newspaper faster. The reconditioned press was purchased from Universal Printing Equipment in Lyndhurst and had originally been used at the *Courier* in Toms River. The addition to the newspaper offices was under construction at the time the press arrived. Sam Puntolillo, owner of the equipment company, directed delivery of the press to its new home.

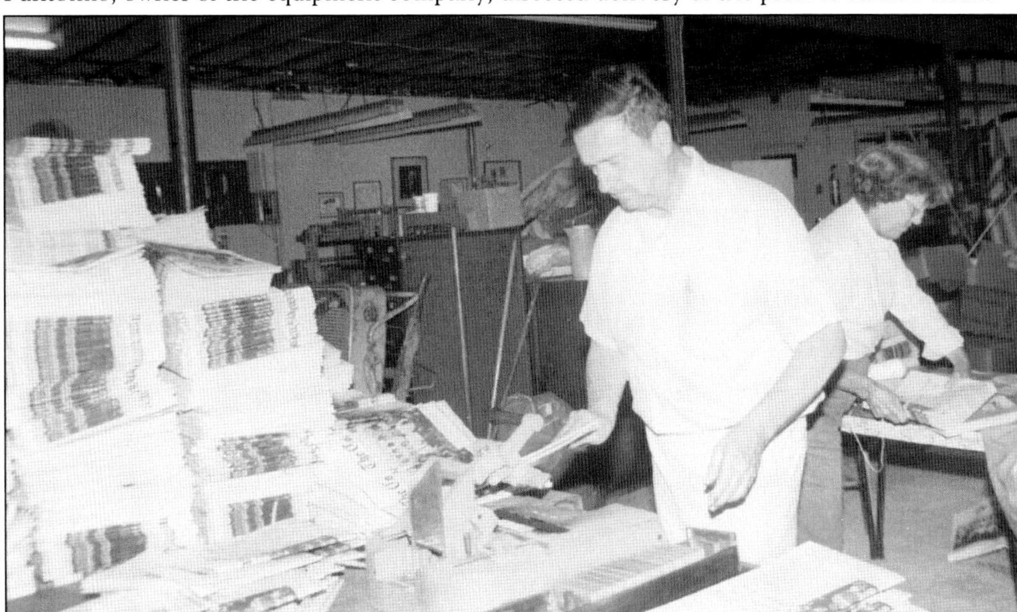

Thomas S. Birckhead Jr. and his wife, Virginia, address and bundle the weekly Thursday edition of the *Coast Star* during the overnight prior to delivery of the newspaper to area post offices and newsstands. For 28 years, the Manasquan couple worked side-by-side with staff members during this weekly process. Mr. and Mrs. Birckhead sold the newspaper in 1989 to James M. Manser of Allenwood.

Six

Fishing

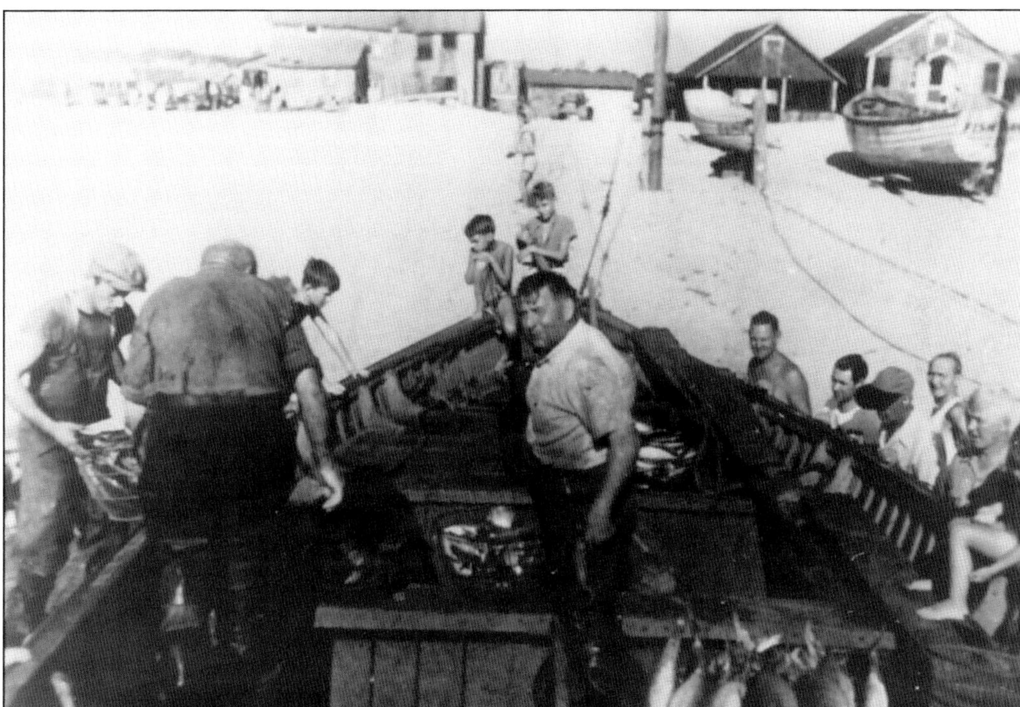

This view of a pound boat illustrates its massive size and construction. These 30- to 40-foot-long boats were built locally by Charles Hankins in Lavallette, among others, of white pine wood, and these vessels carried a captain and about six men and up to 5,000 pounds of fish. Fish pounds offshore consisted of three parts—a weir, forebay, and pocket—and were constructed using poles, nets, rope, and chain.

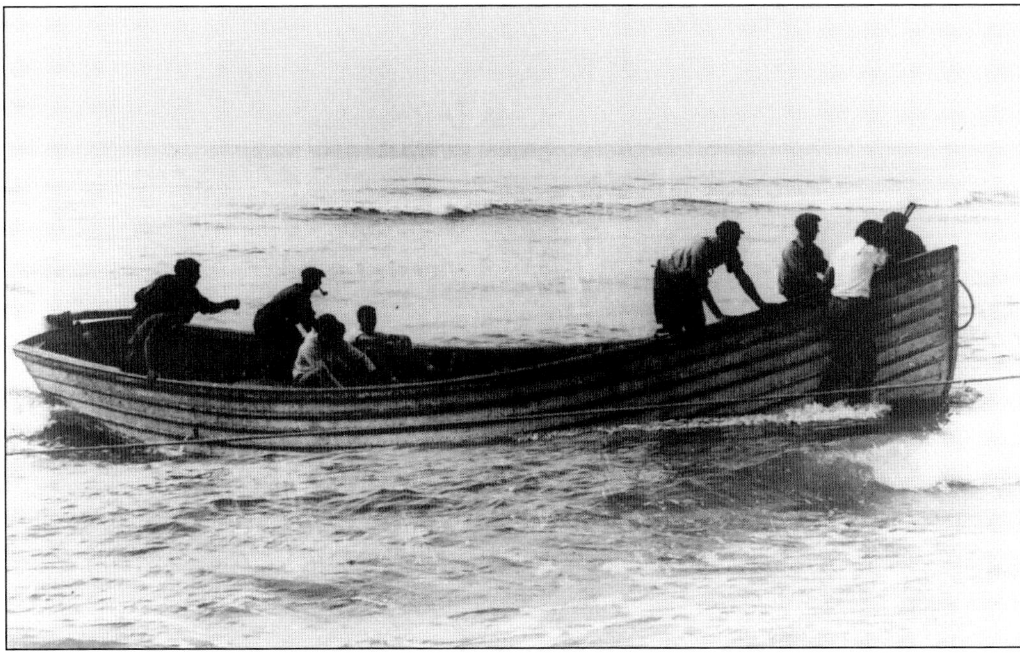

The pounds were an ingenious means of trapping huge quantities of local fish—whiting, mackerel, fluke, weakfish, porgies, croaker, sea robins, skates, butterfish, bluefish, and others. Most New Jersey coastal communities were home to one or more pound fisheries, which employed seasonal workers who settled locally, married, and raised families.

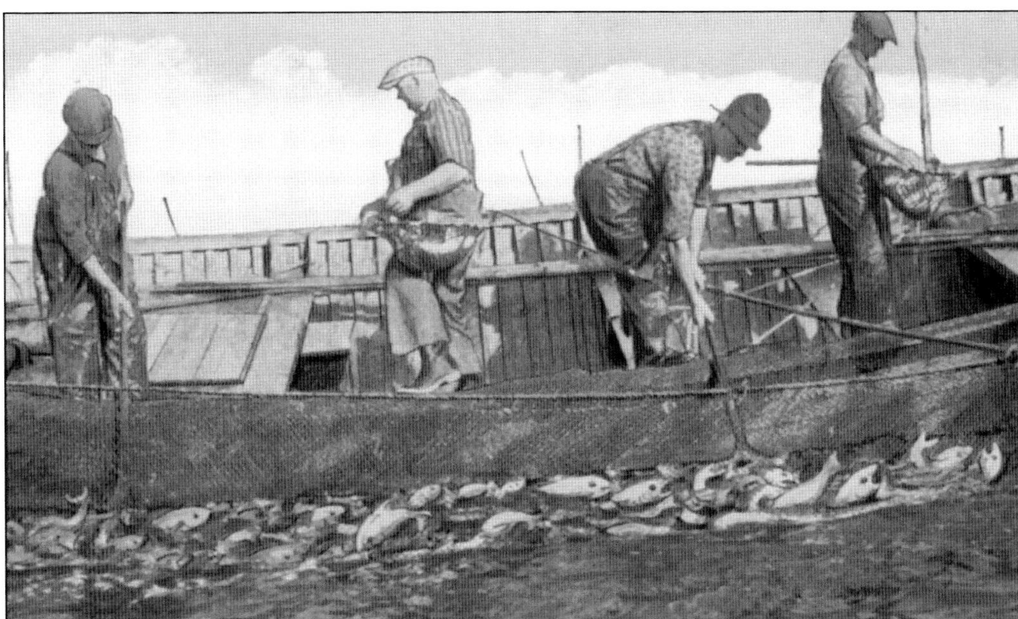

This image illustrates fishermen working the fish pounds. The pounds—comprised of poles (75 to 80 feet in length), nets, rope, and chain—were set up offshore (1 to 2 miles) in early spring (March). The nets were emptied every day except Sunday. This activity continued until cold weather in December.

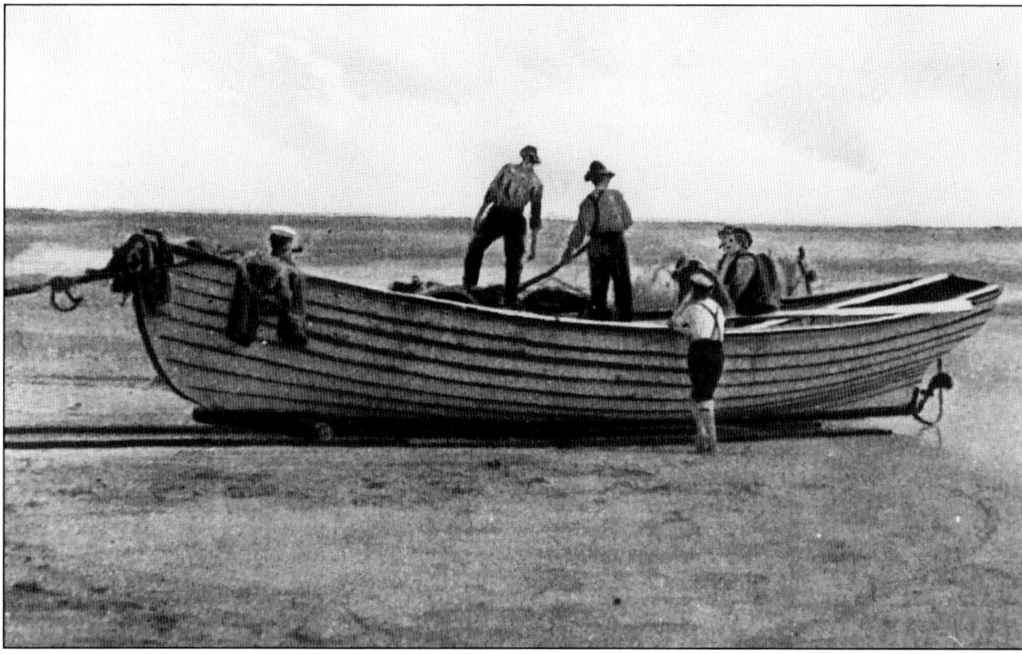

As the pound fishermen unloaded the day's catch, representatives from New York and North Jersey fish retailers (including Fulton's Fish Market) were ready to buy. Among the oddities brought in from the pounds were giant sea turtles. In 1924, a 1,500-pound tuna was brought in at Manasquan.

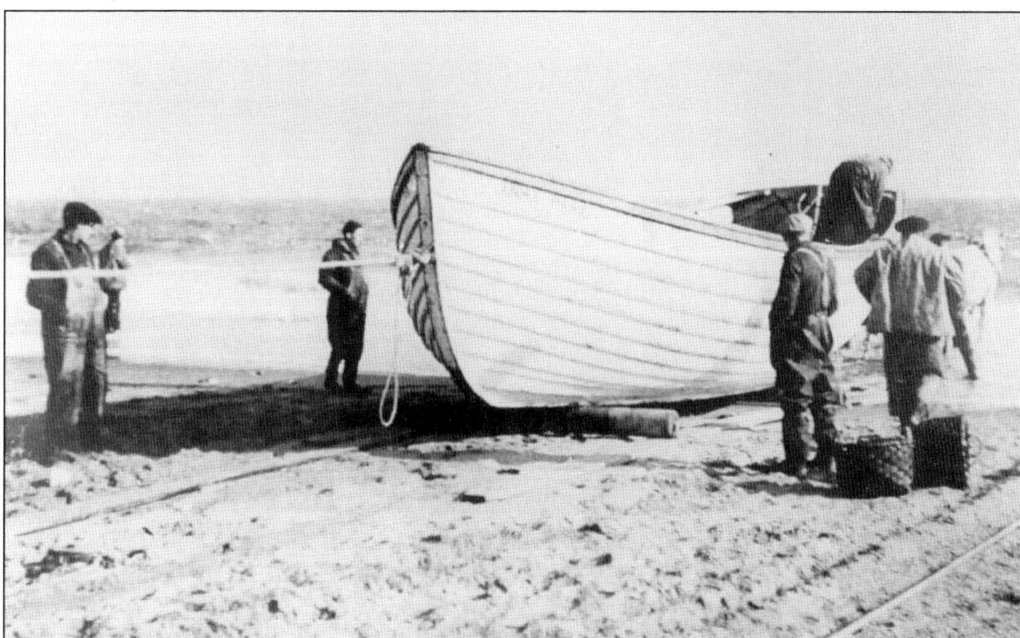

The Jersey Shore fisheries were very successful, as these were once prime fishing grounds because of the many shipwrecks off the coast and the clean, healthy water. The last fishermen—in 1947—to operate in Manasquan were Hilding Swensson (and his son Albert) and Nels J. Nelson.

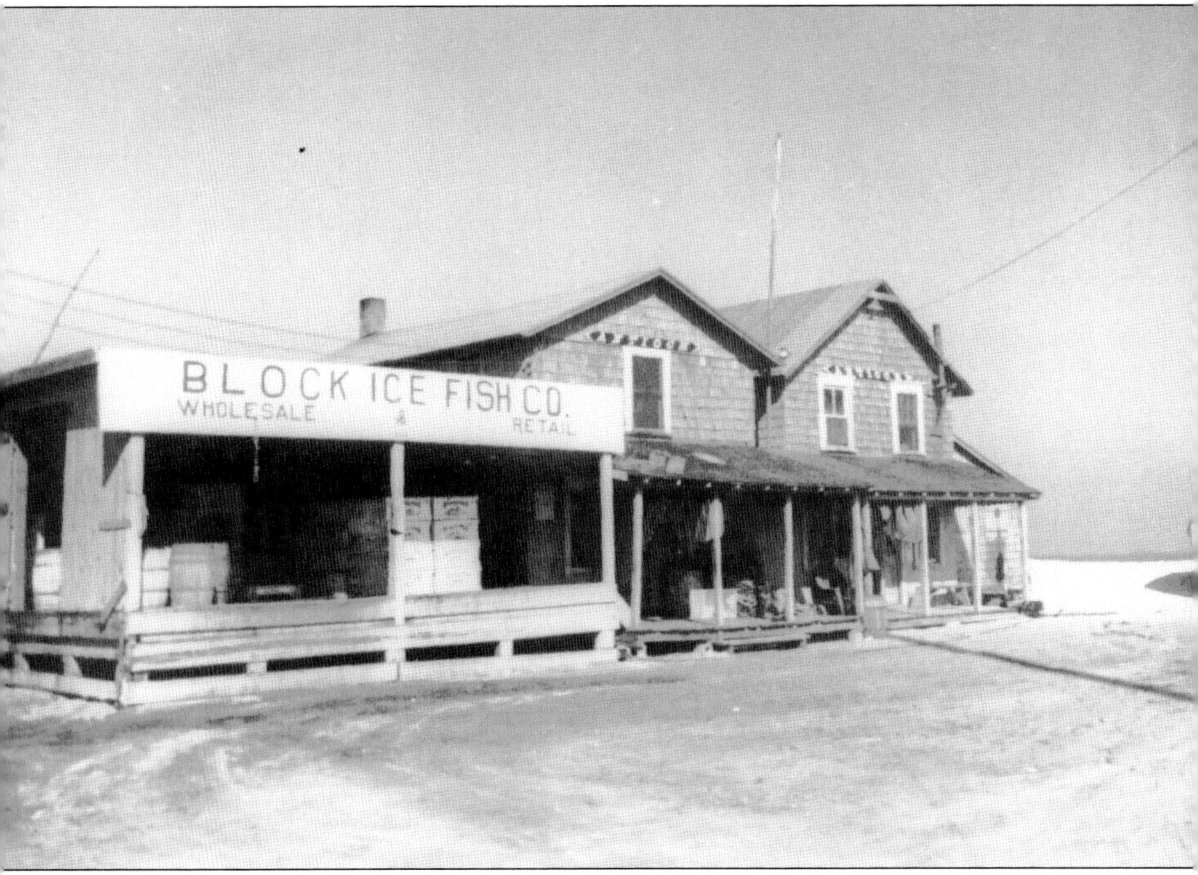

The Block Ice Fish Co.—about 1930—was located on the beach at Ocean Avenue just north of the parking lot for the present Sea Watch. The structures were home to fishermen and served as a wholesale-retail fish business. The signs above the windows are the nameboards from the *Antioch*, a barkentine carrying lumber from Savannah, Georgia, to New York City, which was driven ashore at this site on March 26, 1913. Historians note that the *Antioch* was the last barkentine wrecked off the coast and that all those on board were saved.

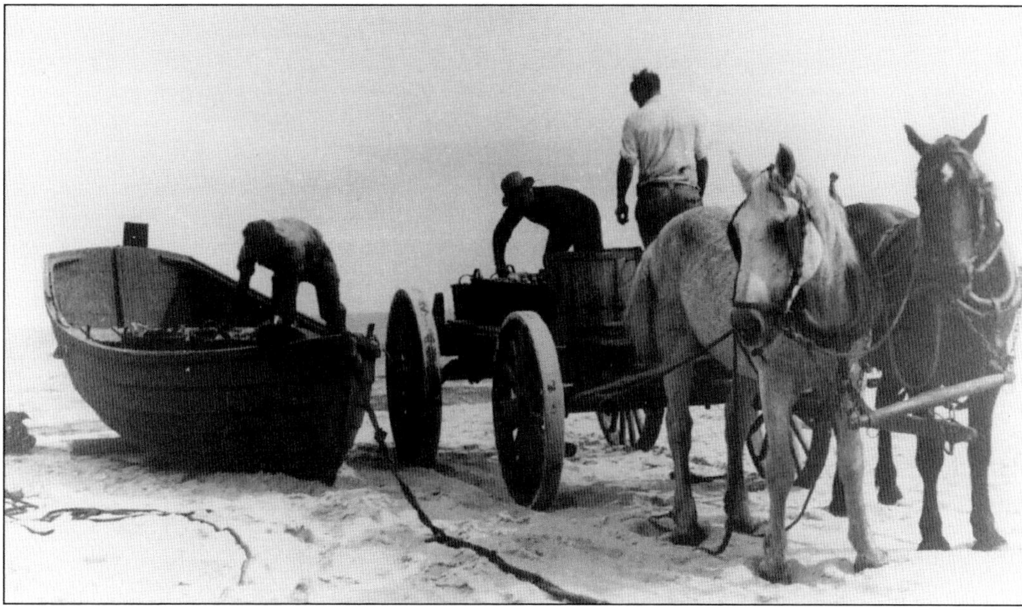

Workhorses, block-and-tackle, and rollers were used to bring the heavy pound boats up past the high watermark when the day's work was completed. In the 1920s and 1930s, Big Sam Holmes of Brielle had the job of hitching up the teams that were used to pull the boats up the beach. The dray carts were also used to transport the fish to the packing plant for icing and boxing for shipment.

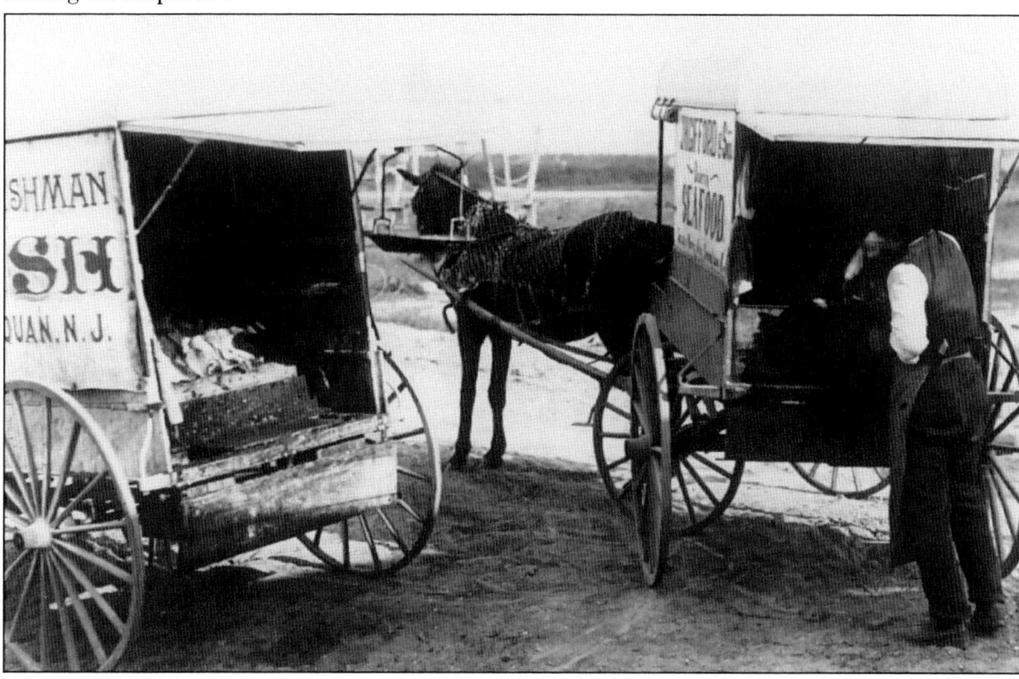

Not only were horses used to carry the baskets up the beach to the packing facility, but at the turn of the century they also were used to transport the product to the train station. This cargo is headed into town to the railroad station where it will be on the evening train to New York City (or Philadelphia).

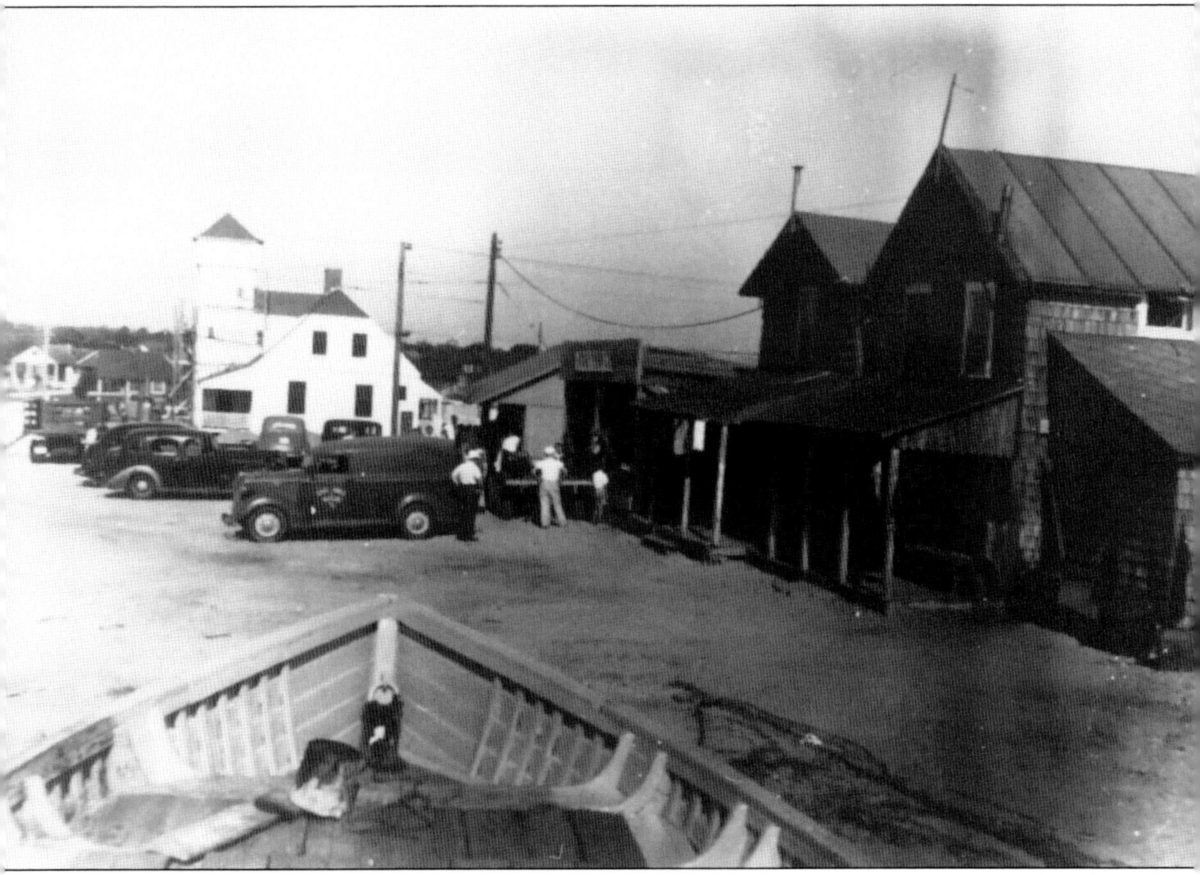

Fishermen at the Star Fish Company prepare to load fresh catch into trucks which replaced the horses. The wholesale-retail fish company was founded as the Manasquan Fish Company and had been owned by Leonard Newman. When he died in January 1940, Hilding Swensson, Mr. Newman's boat captain, and his son, Albert Swensson, operated the business for about seven years. After World War II, higher operating costs of the pounds, new automation, and large trawlers working offshore all combined to close the pound fisheries.

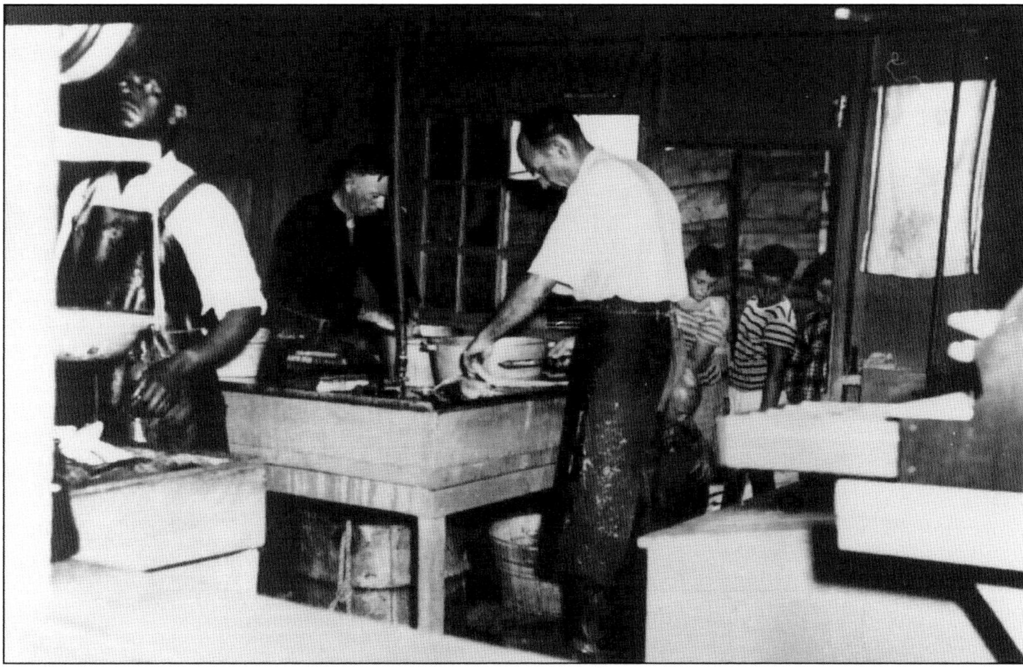

Summer visitors—young children—watch the men working at the Manasquan Fisheries, later known as the Star Fisheries. The processing and packing plant was located on the north end of the beachfront. At the plant, the day's catch was sorted, weighed, and packed on ice for sale and shipment.

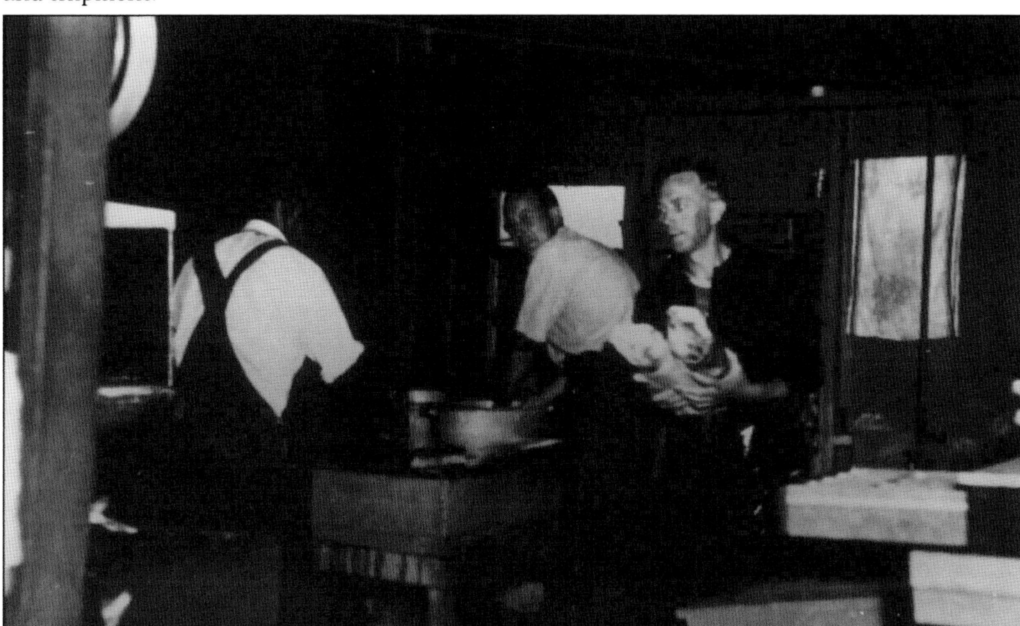

Men clean, weigh, sort, and pack fish in a plant located on the north end of Manasquan Beach near the current site of the Sea Watch. Conditions were crude and the work was hard. Some of the early owners of the fish pounds were John Woolley, Theodore Bennett, Harry Height, and George Height.

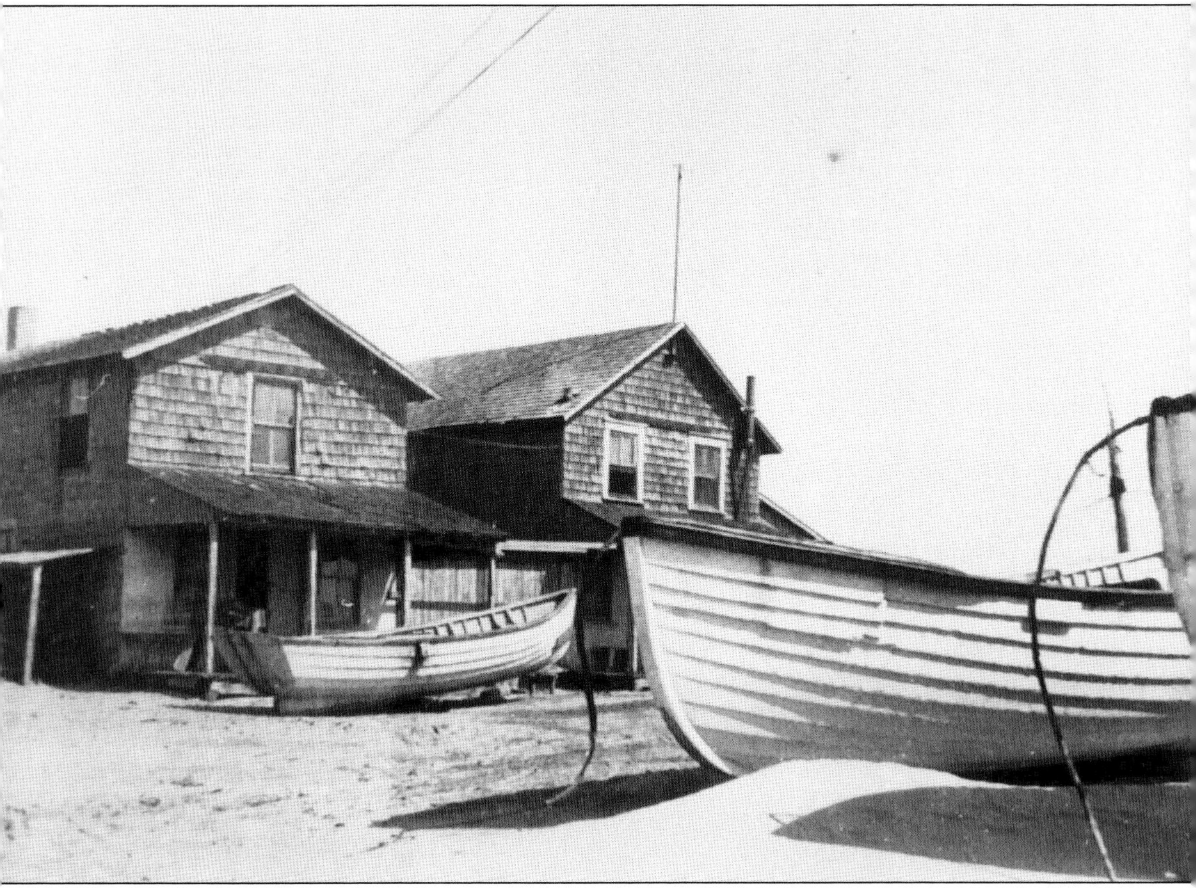

This photograph illustrates the massive size of the pound boats used for an industry that saw its demise at Manasquan Beach some 50 years ago. At one time fishermen were working the pounds from Seaside to Sandy Hook. Today, local fishing fleets out of Brielle, Point Pleasant Beach, and Belmar have made sport fishing a year-round recreational industry for anglers. Notice that some of the clapboard beach bungalows have changed little in the same time.

Seven

Opening the Manasquan Inlet

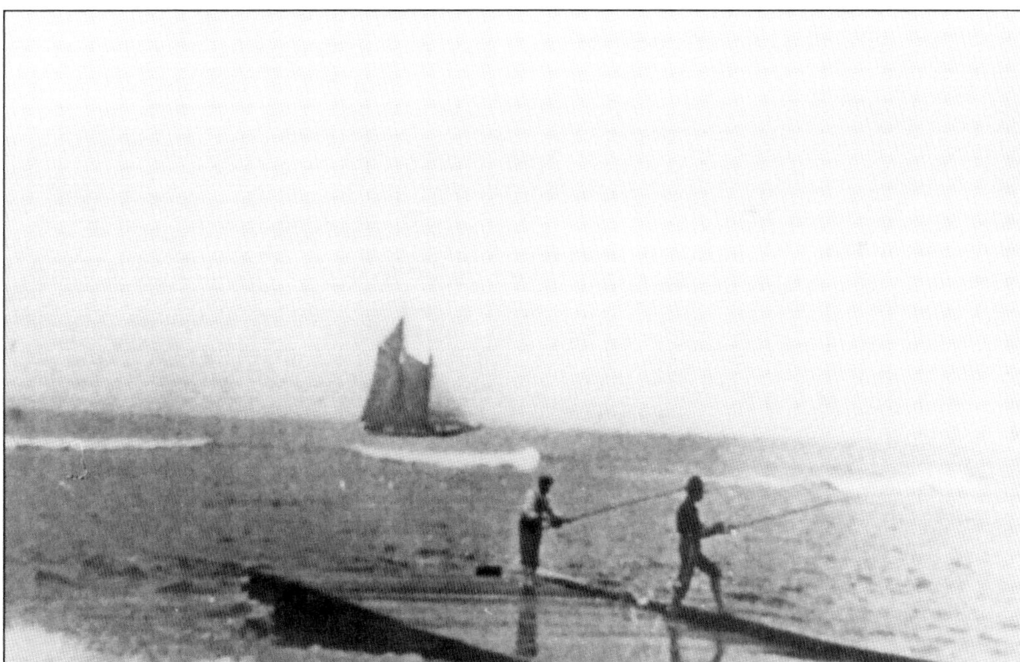

This is a unique view of what existed before the permanent construction of the Manasquan Inlet. These two fishermen are standing on a makeshift pier jutting out into the Atlantic Ocean, where the present-day jetty now stands. Note the impressive sailing ship headed south, very likely out of New York Harbor.

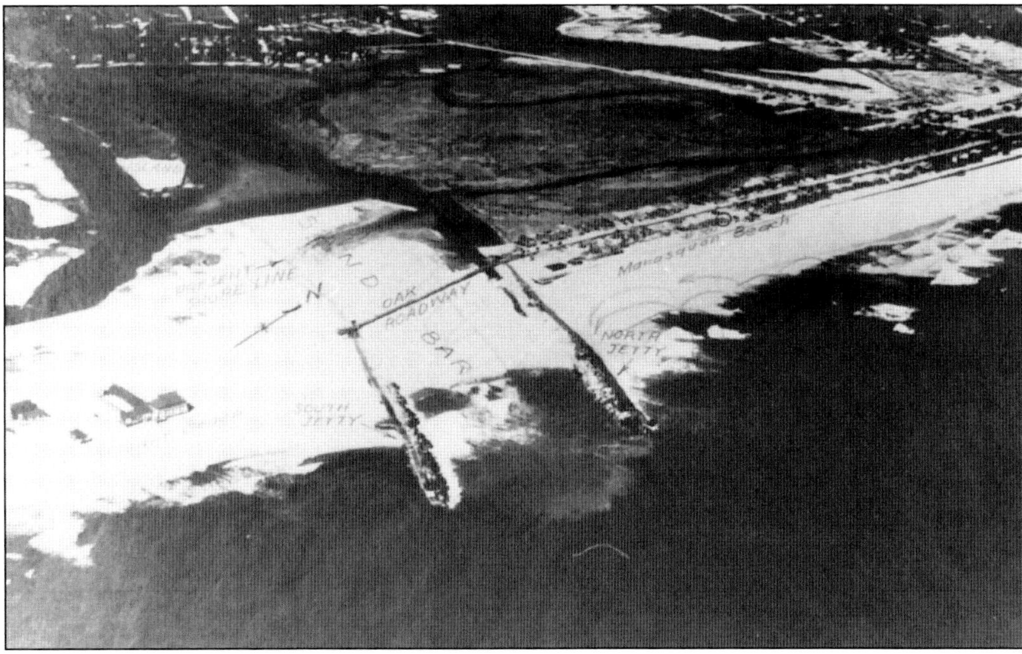

This aerial view—dated August 1929—shows the wooden trestle bridge connecting the north and south jetties over the sandbar between Manasquan and Point Pleasant Beach that would eventually become the inlet. This photograph was used for survey purposes.

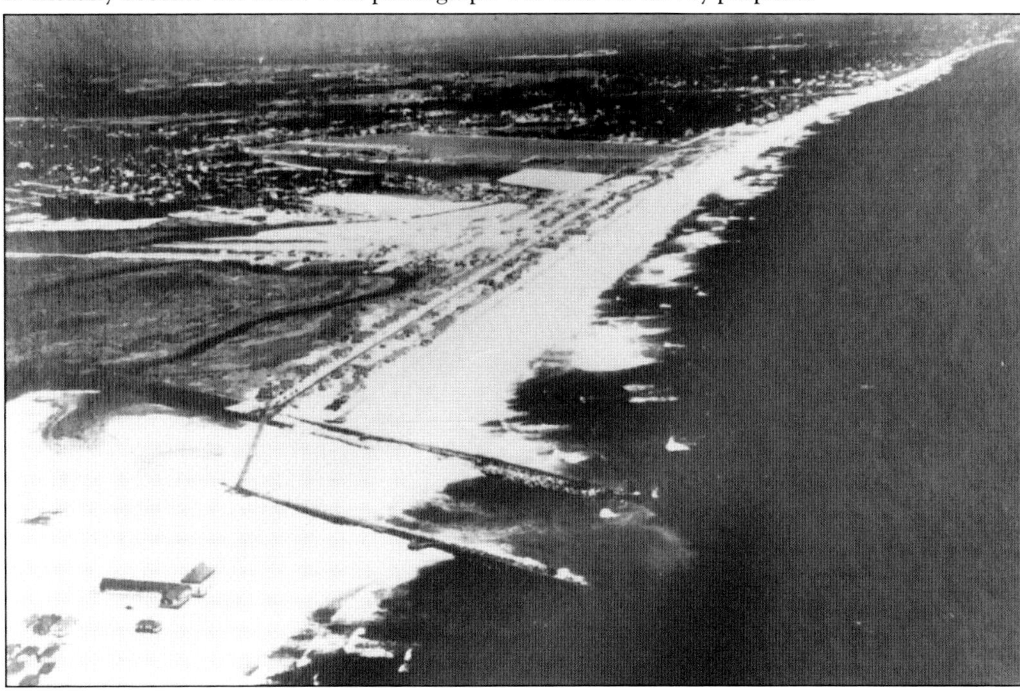

This October 1930 aerial view, taken by the New York District of the Corps of Army Engineers, illustrates the trestle bridge and the jetties. Notice the development of the Manasquan beachfront and Jenkinson's Pavilion on the beachfront in Point Pleasant Beach. There always was an inlet at or near its current location, but it would often shoal up or close over.

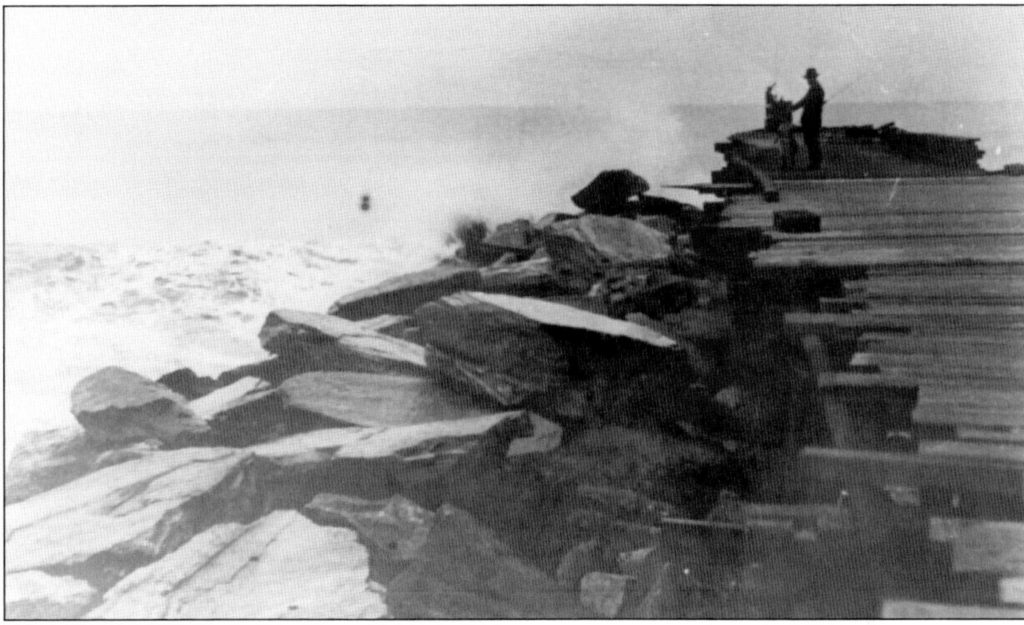

Lewis Warren Randolph, with his son Warren, inspects the contractor's work at the inlet. Mr. Randolph of Newark was the resident engineer sent to Manasquan by the New York District of the Corps of Army Engineers to survey the inlet area, to supervise construction of the jetties, and to reopen the permanent Manasquan Inlet.

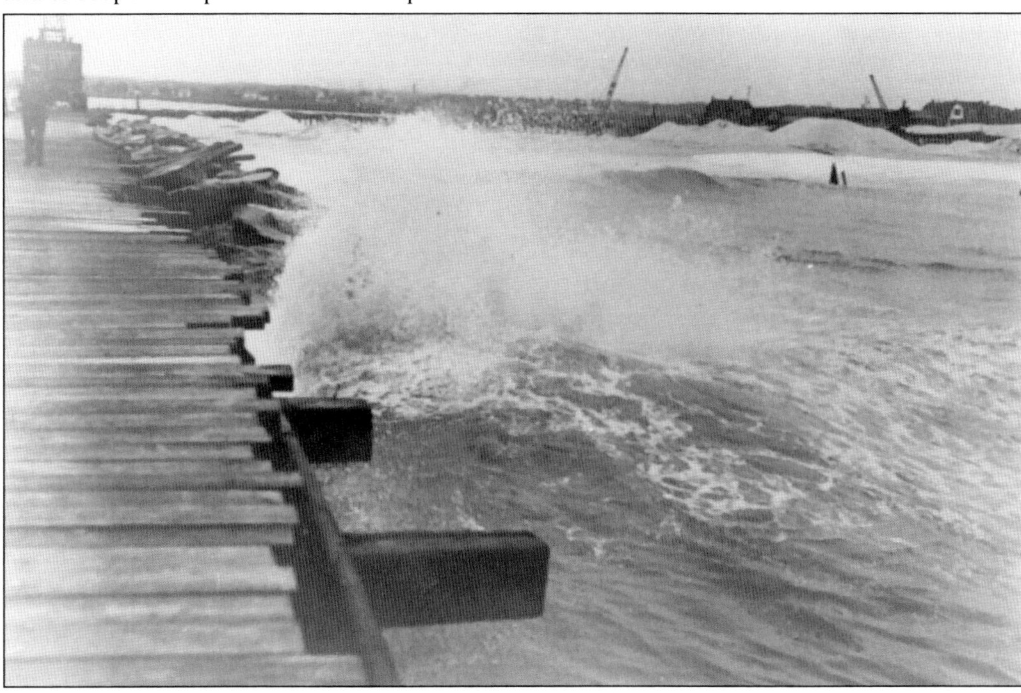

With work underway in this 1931 photograph, the derrick maneuvers rocks into the jetty frame. The crane, like the trucks transporting the rocks, uses the same temporary wooden trestle. Jesse A. Howland & Son Contractor of Sea Bright won the bid to construct the jetties. This part of the overall project was to be completed in 180 days for $179,912.

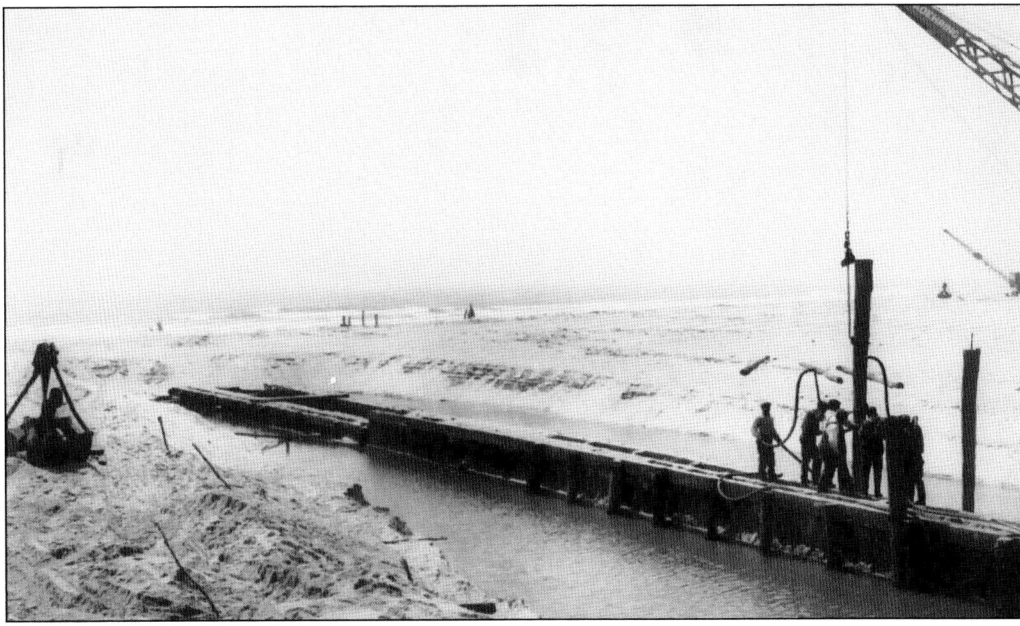

This view shows the wooden bulkheading used to brace the rocks which will form the jetties. During work on the inlet, part of the old bulkhead on the north side of the inlet was incorporated into the inlet's newly constructed bulkhead. The final cost of opening the Manasquan Inlet was $600,000. The federal government provided $300,000, and the other half was provided through state and local funds from towns including Manasquan, Brielle, Point Pleasant Beach, and Point Pleasant Borough.

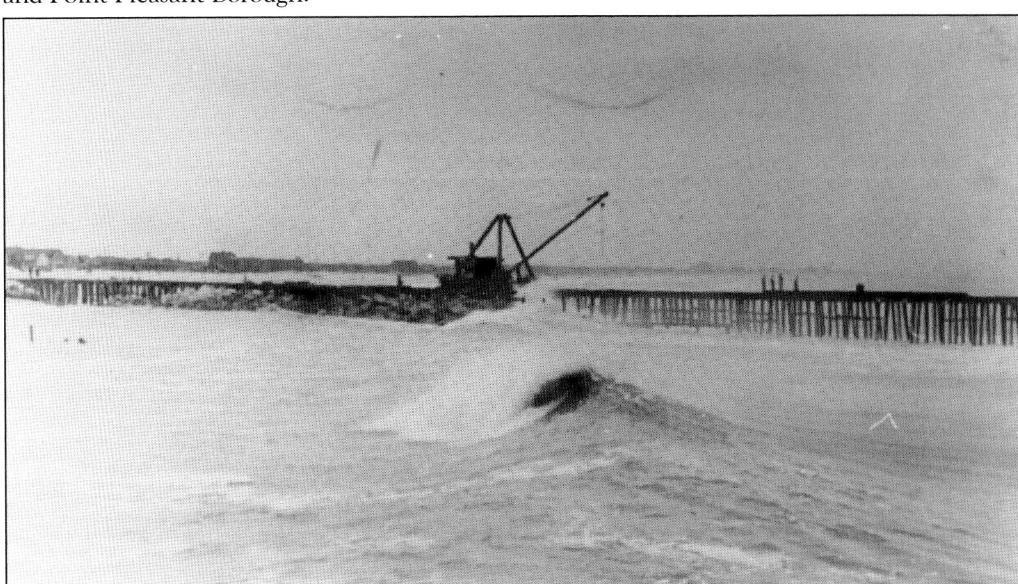

Using rocks obtained during the excavation done for the New York City subway, plans called for two parallel jetties, 400 feet apart, with a channel at least 4 feet deep at low tide. The north jetty was to be 850 feet long with an additional seaward end to be 500 feet, using timber with a steel piling core connected at the inshore end with 200 feet of stone jetty. The south jetty was to have the same configuration.

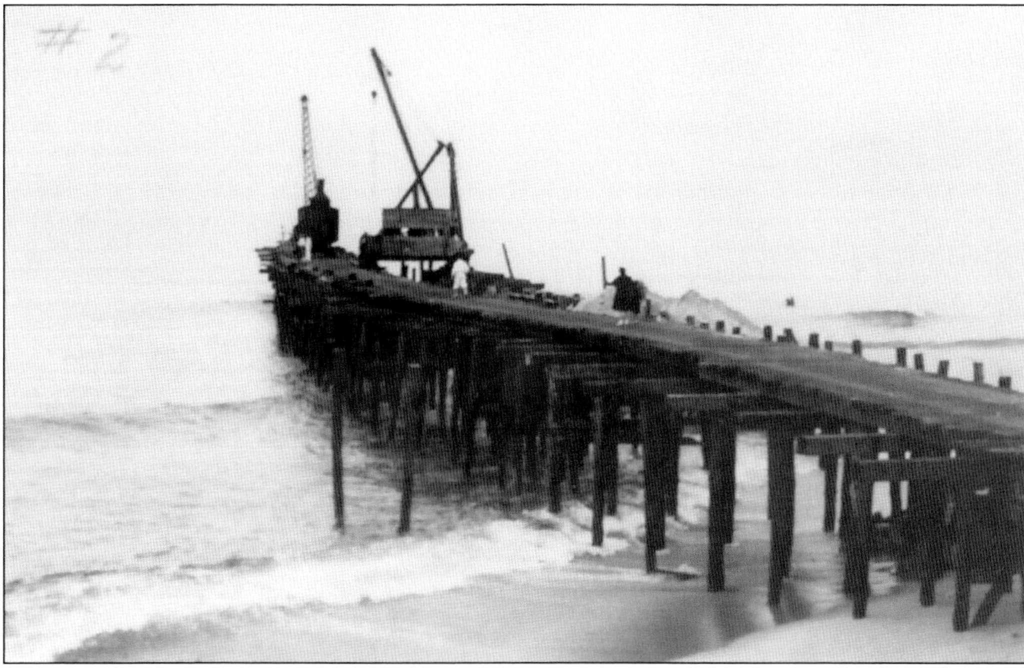

Derricks work on the jetty during calm seas. When the ocean became too rough, work on the project was temporarily halted, and equipment was stored in the garage of Mr. Randolph's home on Wyckoff Avenue in Manasquan, where he and his family had relocated for the duration of the project.

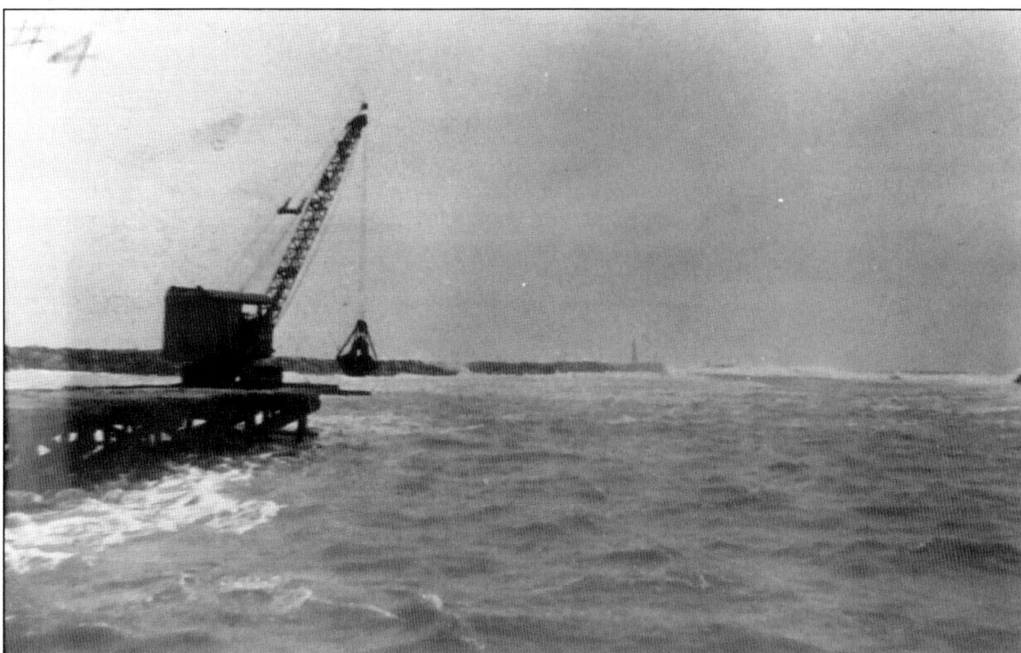

This stiff-leg derrick placed the rocks that had been transported by truck two at a time from the Main Street Railroad Station, east on Main Street and south on First Avenue to the south end of Manasquan Beach. At that site, the trucks continued out over the trestle.

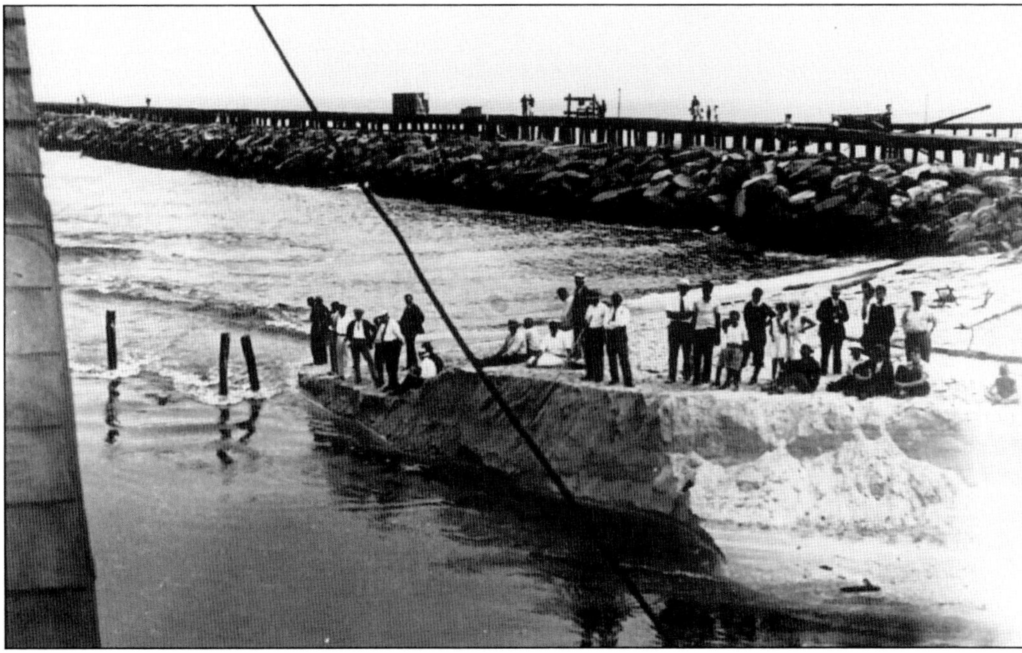

There was high local interest in creating a permanent inlet between Manasquan and Point Pleasant Beach. In 1922, an organization comprised of 63 men called the Manasquan Inlet Improvement Association completed a questionnaire provided by the Army Corps of Engineers. By 1924, the association had received their reply: the War Department believed if the improvement was to be completed, it should be accomplished at local expense.

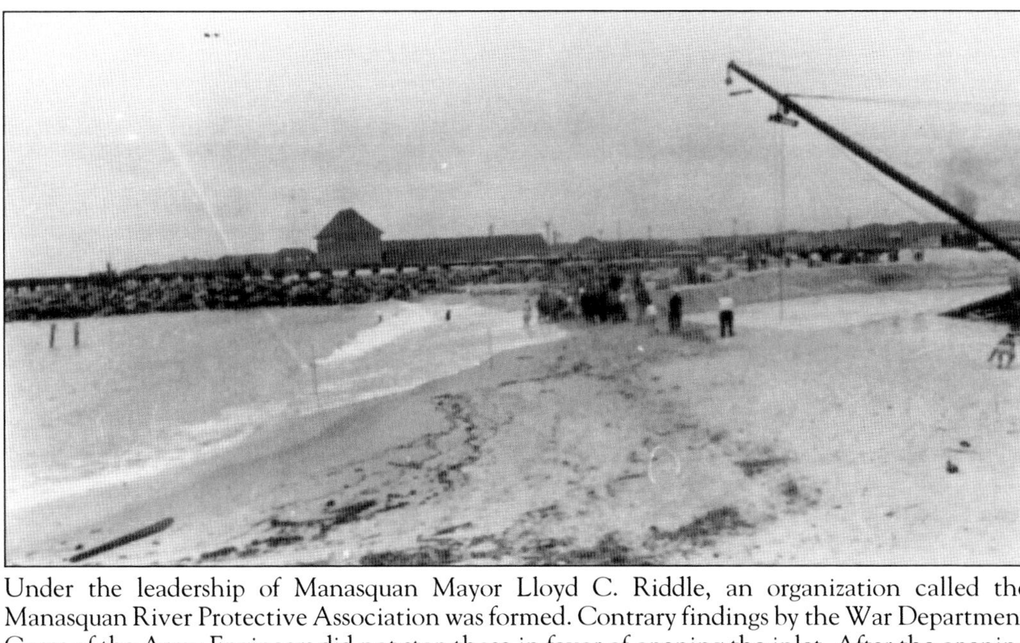

Under the leadership of Manasquan Mayor Lloyd C. Riddle, an organization called the Manasquan River Protective Association was formed. Contrary findings by the War Department Corps of the Army Engineers did not stop those in favor of opening the inlet. After the opening of the Manasquan-Bay Head Canal (now Point Pleasant Canal) in 1925, the association pressed government officials even harder to construct a permanent opening for the Manasquan Inlet.

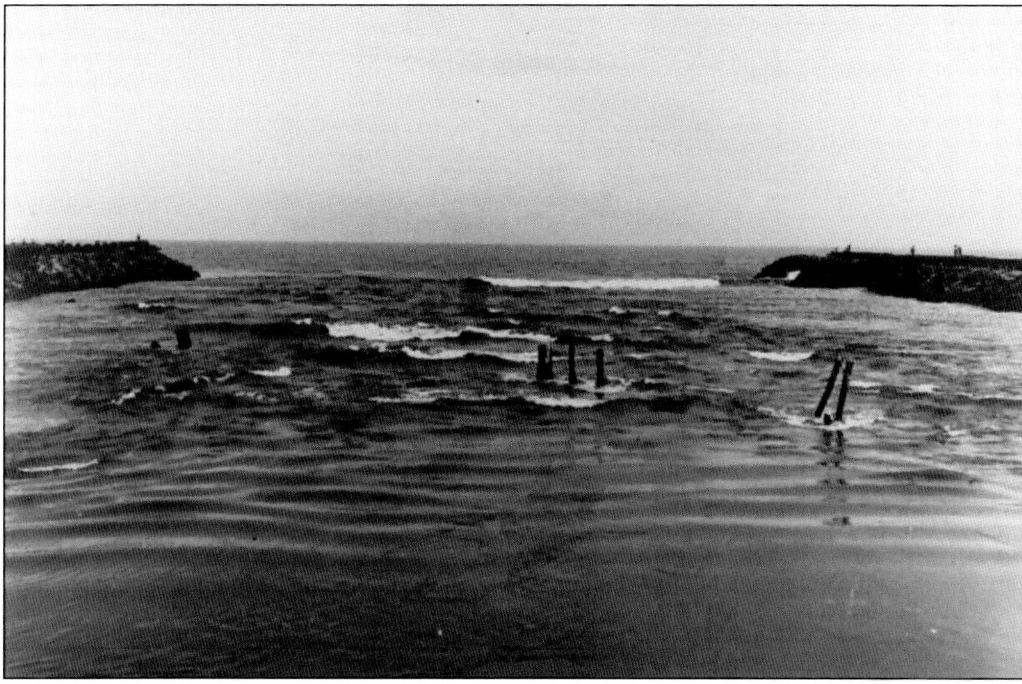

In 1924, the War Department stated that "the principal ground upon which the adverse conclusion is based is that the prospective commercial use of the improvement does not warrant the large cost of providing a permanent channel through the inlet."

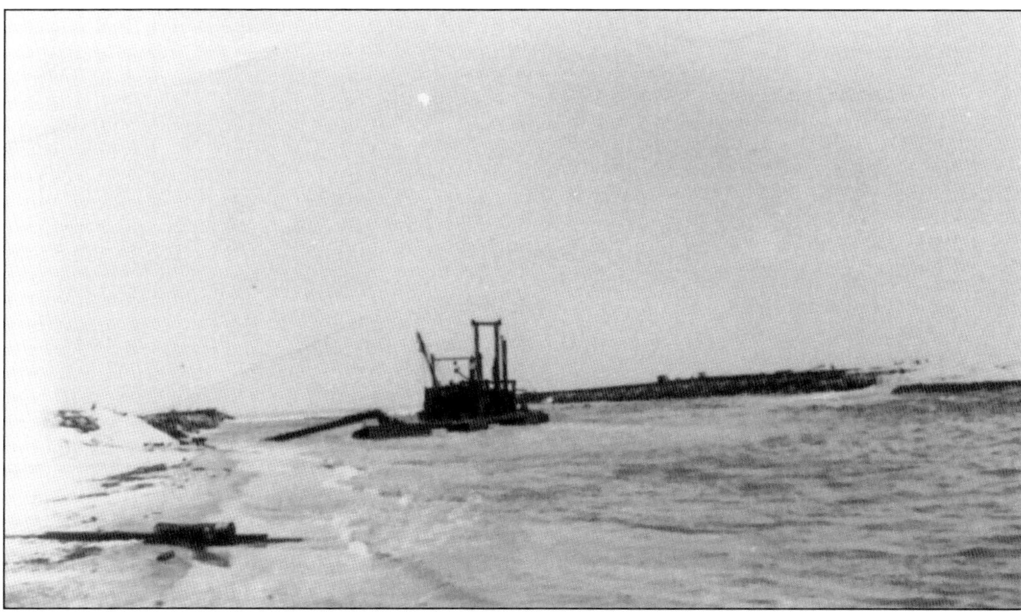

In November 1927, 37 residents from Manasquan, Brielle, Point Pleasant Borough, and Point Pleasant Beach traveled to Washington, D.C. to press the federal government for the opening of the Manasquan Inlet. They refused to give up because they saw the important value for easier accessibility for the transport of goods, a safe harbor for ships, and the opening of the area for pleasure and fishing boats.

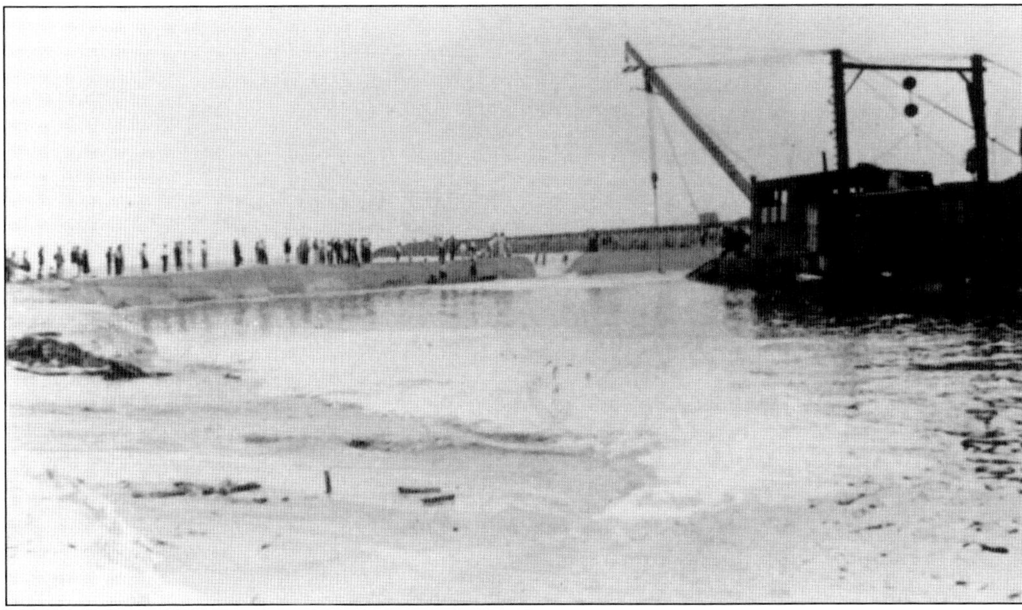

Area residents watch the dredge make a final cut across the sand barrier at the newly constructed inlet on July 3, 1931. The inlet had been opened on February 10 of that year with a 20-, then 40-foot opening, but a sandbar soon closed the opening. Work continued on a more successful opening, which duly occurred on the July 3 date.

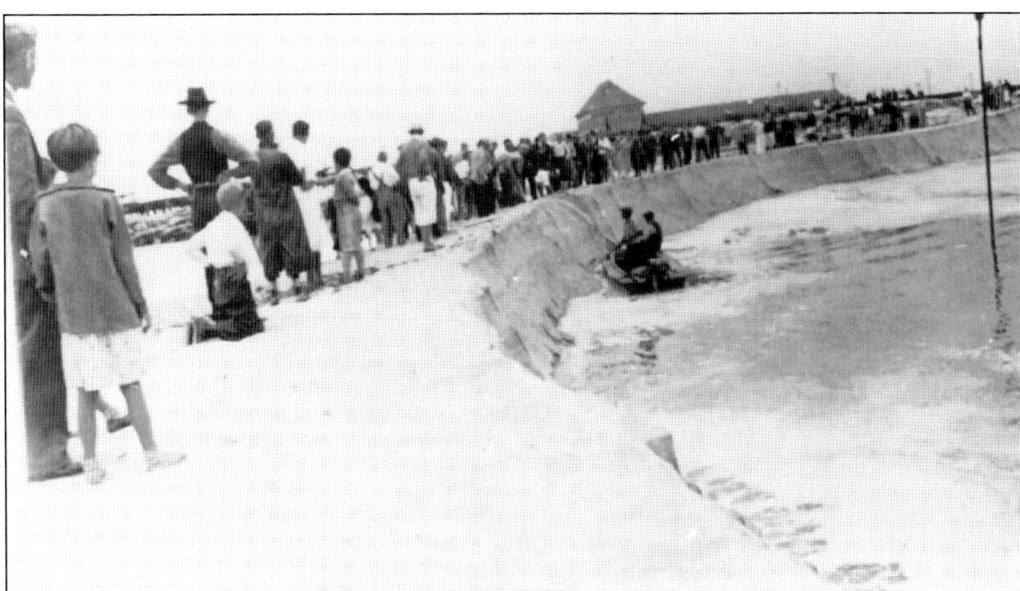

On July 3, 1931, Lewis Warren Randolph (in rowboat) makes the first trip through the new inlet. Within a week of the opening, the Hill Dredging Co. completed a channel to a minimum depth of 8 feet at low water, making the inlet permanent.

Manasquan Mayor Lloyd C. Riddle (right), who served as president of the Manasquan River Protective Association, joins George C. Kloss (center) and Councilman Edward R. Emmons at the Manasquan Inlet gazebo in August 1932 during the gala opening of the waterway.

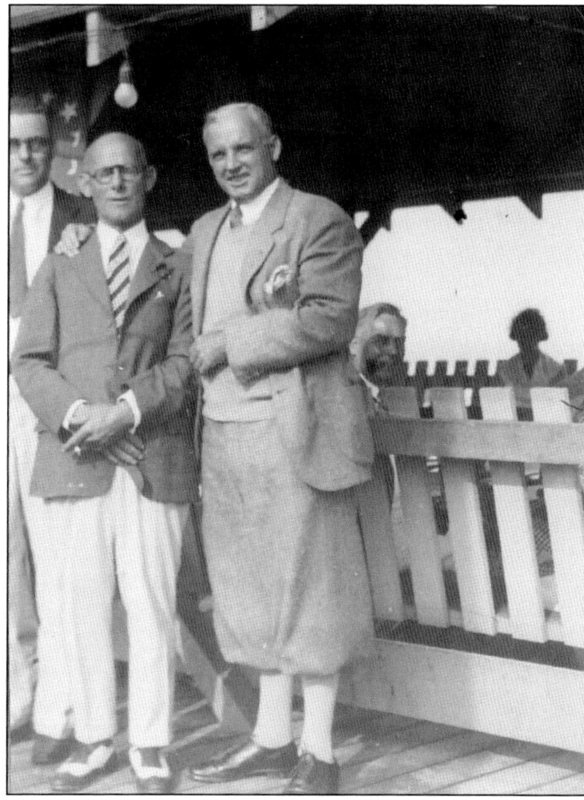

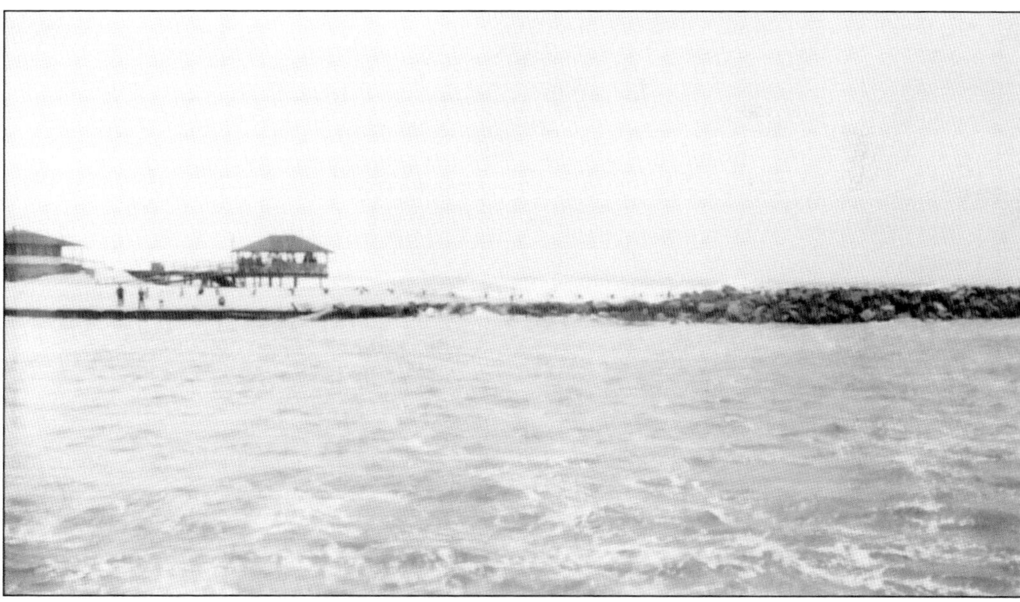

On the evening of February 10, 1931, during a snowfall, the inlet was opened for the first time, with more than 100 persons watching the Atlantic Ocean meet the Manasquan River (including Manasquan Mayor Lloyd C. Riddle, president, and other members of the Manasquan River Protective Association). This pavilion was constructed prior to the opening of the inlet.

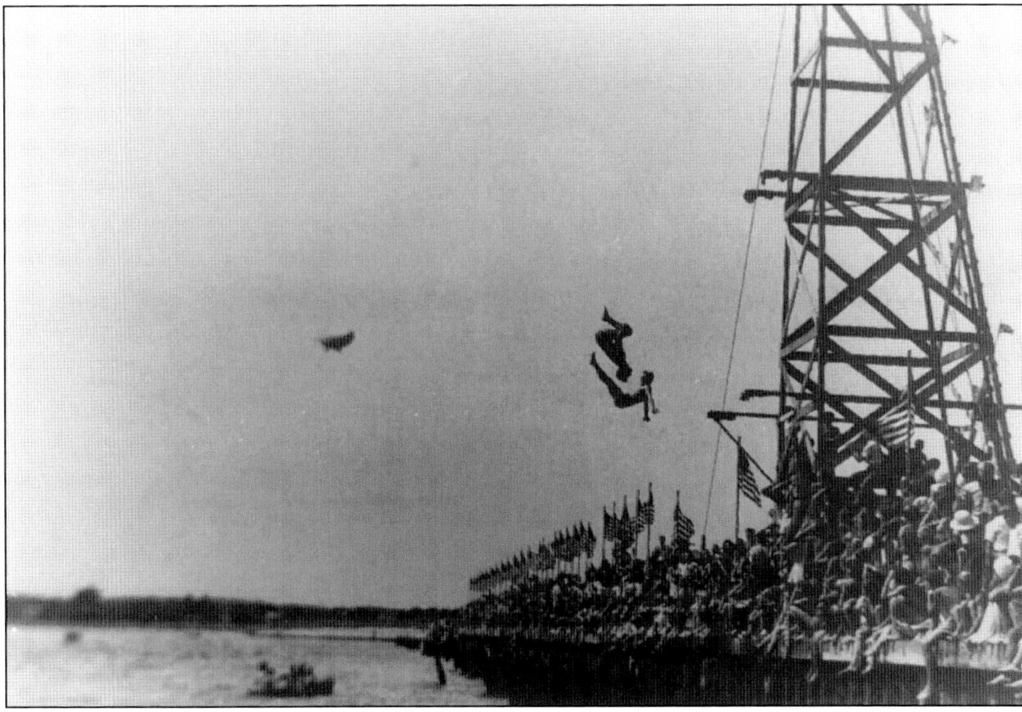

Thousands attended festivities in 1938 following the completion of the esplanade at the Manasquan Inlet. In this photograph, a 150-foot tower was erected, and exhibitionists performed diving acts into the inlet, including one man who dived into the water with a flaming pack on his back.

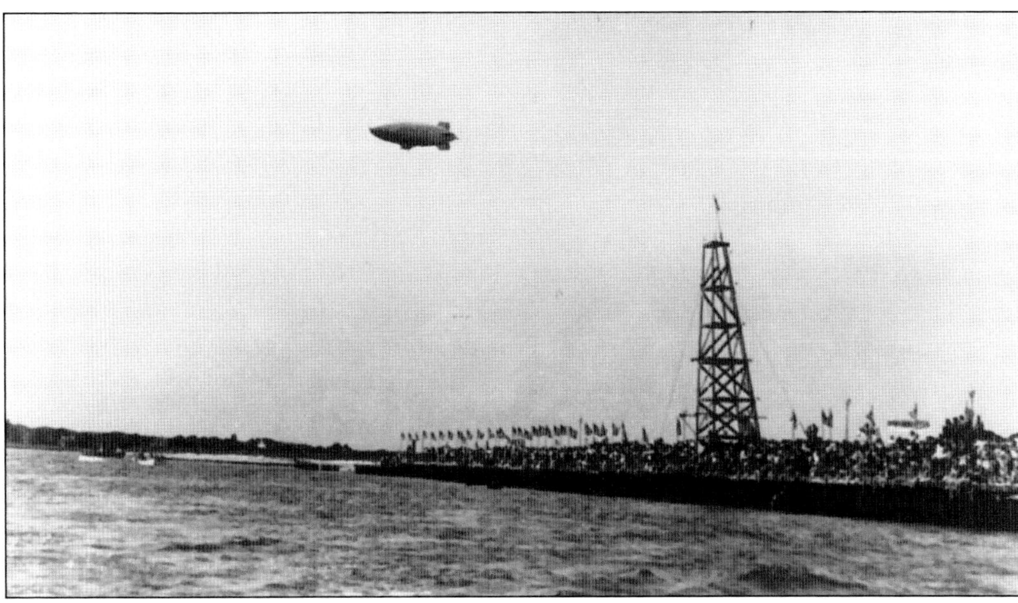

A triumphant gala continued for residents and visitors attending the celebration to mark the completion of the inlet esplanade. During the festivities, a blimp from Lakehurst (New Jersey) Air Station can be seen passing overhead, as American flags line the esplanade on what is now Riverside Drive.

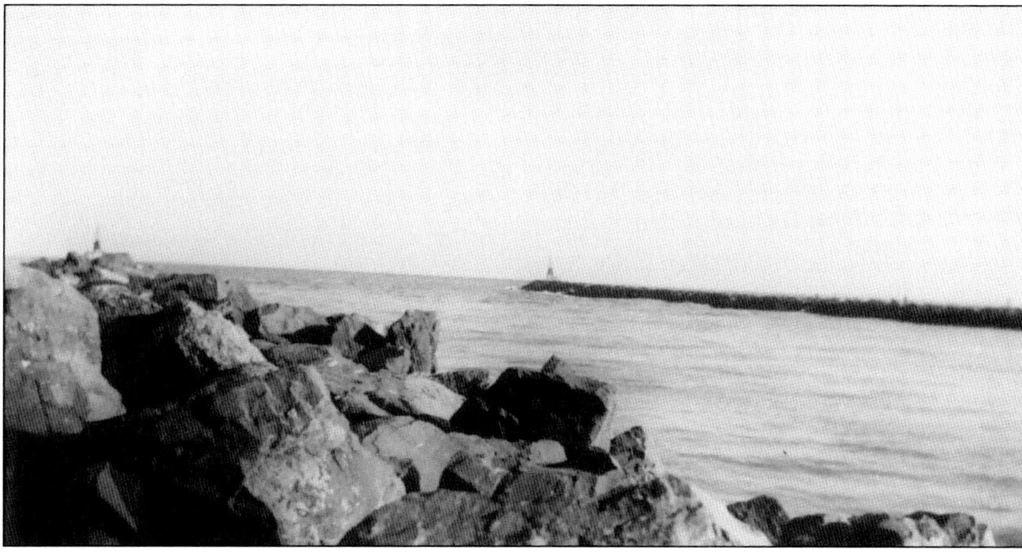

Dredging sand out of the Manasquan Inlet continued through 1932, when the project was finally completed. Some shoaling has continued since that time, but constant monitoring and dredging has kept the inlet open for traffic. This scene of the inlet—looking east—was taken in the 1940s about 15 years after the permanent opening of the waterway.

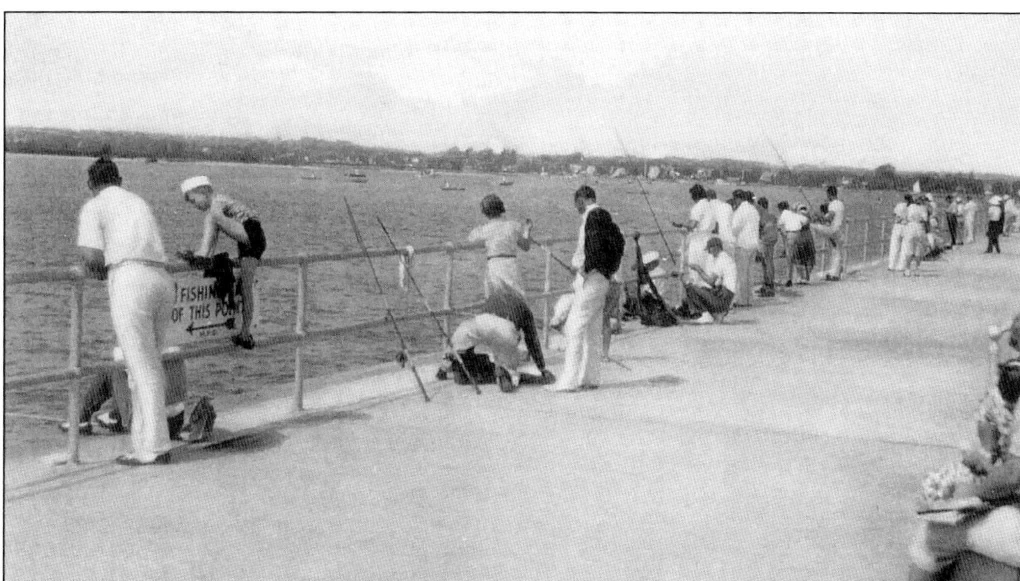

A summer day at the Manasquan Inlet—as seen in this 1940s postcard—illustrates many of the same activities local residents and visitors enjoy today. According to William Nelson's *History of the New Jersey Coast*, published in 1902, the Manasquan Inlet had closed because of a Spanish brig which years prior had been wrecked in the Manasquan River, and loaded with iron, had become embedded in the sand.

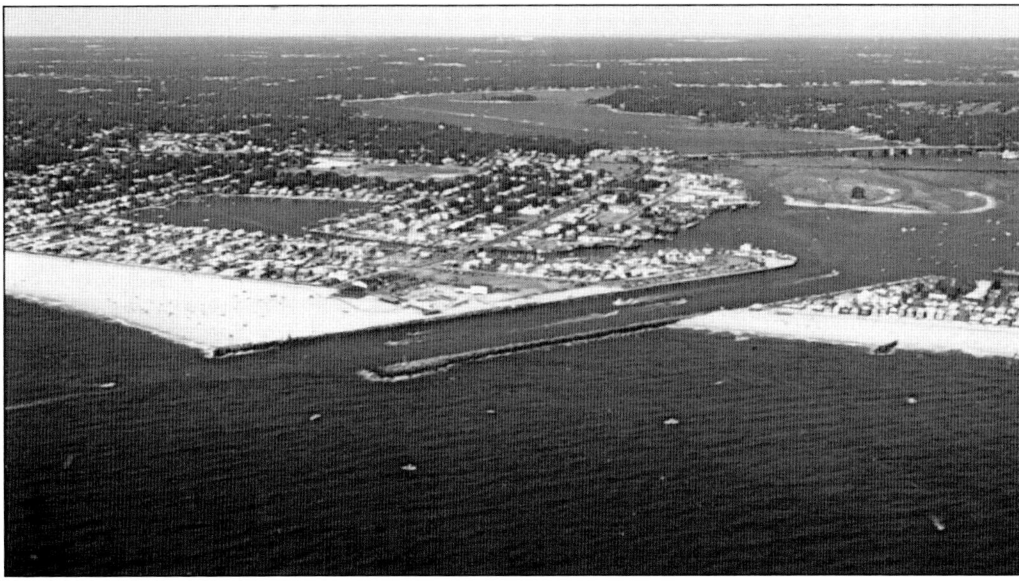

This breath-taking aerial view of the Manasquan Inlet taken in 1976 shows its incredible size—for a man-made waterway some 70 years ago. With great vision, the leaders of this community, as well as those in surrounding boroughs, realized the value of the inlet even before the federal government cleared the project.

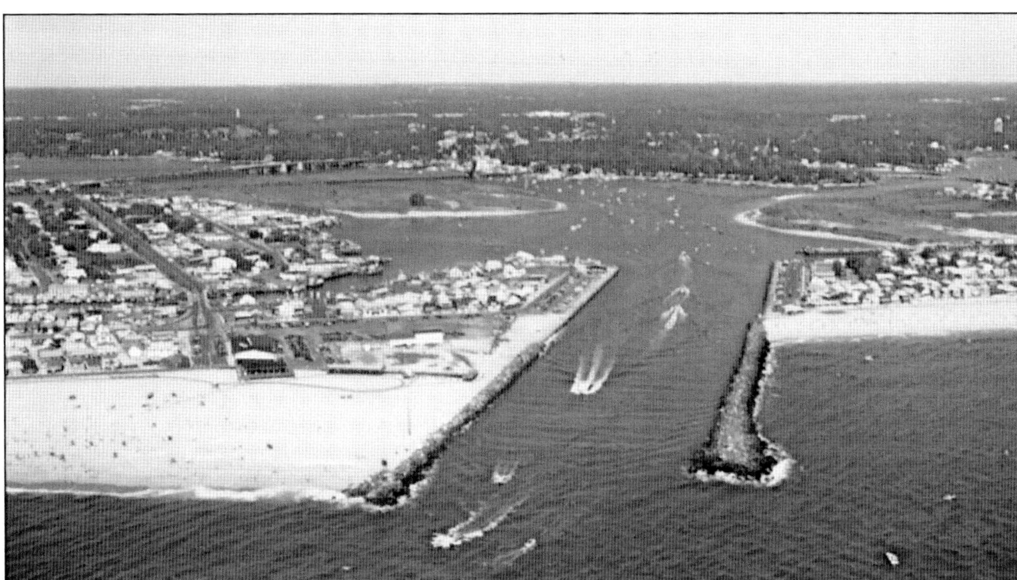

The Manasquan Inlet is the beginning of the Intracoastal Waterway—connecting bodies of water that lead boaters on an inland waterway, often paralleling the Atlantic, to Florida. In this aerial view, as well as the above photograph, the condominiums on the Point Pleasant Beach side of the inlet had not yet been constructed.

Eight

The Beach and Boardwalk

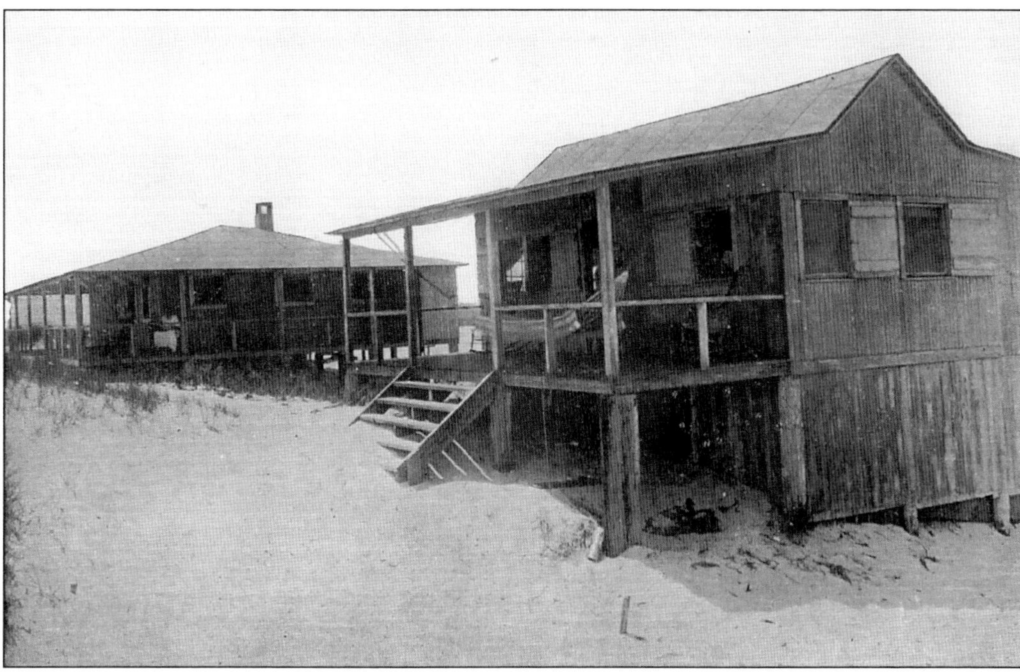

The earliest visitors came to the beach in the early 1800s for the healthy sea air, fishing, and relaxing. Mostly men, they pitched tents and lived rough. As the charm of this life became more popular and access to it was made available to all as train transport grew, families began to appear along the shore. The tents and shacks were built of makeshift materials, including driftwood and boat wreckage. These structures—located at the south end of the beachfront—were among the first two constructed on the beachfront.

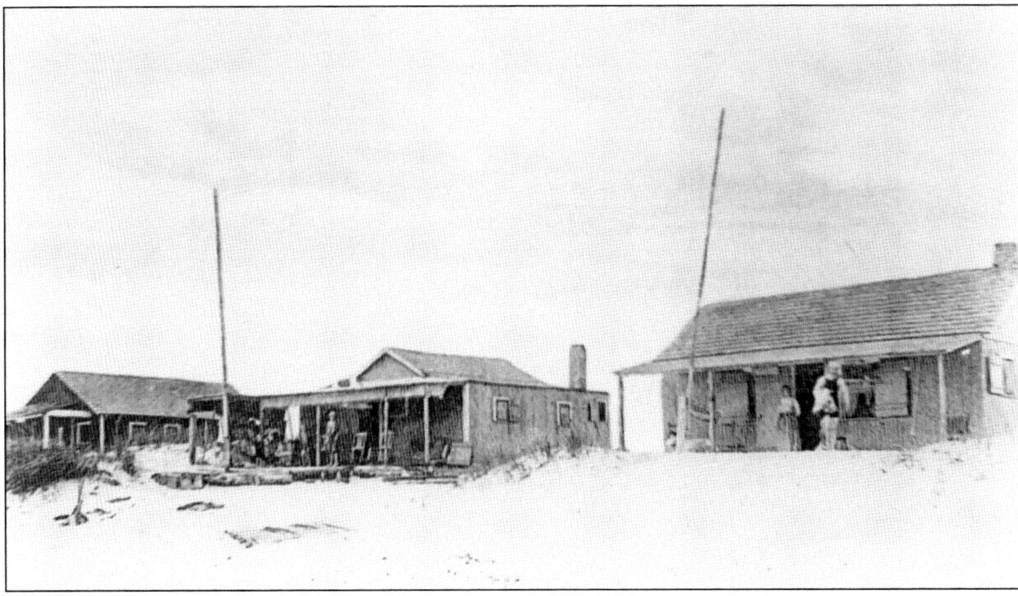

Many built houses on land owned by Henry H. Yard of Sea Girt (formerly Wall), president of the American Timber Co., who owned an area from the northern tip of Belmar to the southern end of Manasquan. Mr. Yard had acquired the property from the Board of Proprietors of Eastern, New Jersey, in 1893. At one point in the early twentieth century, some of this land had been owned by the Sea Coast Realty Co.

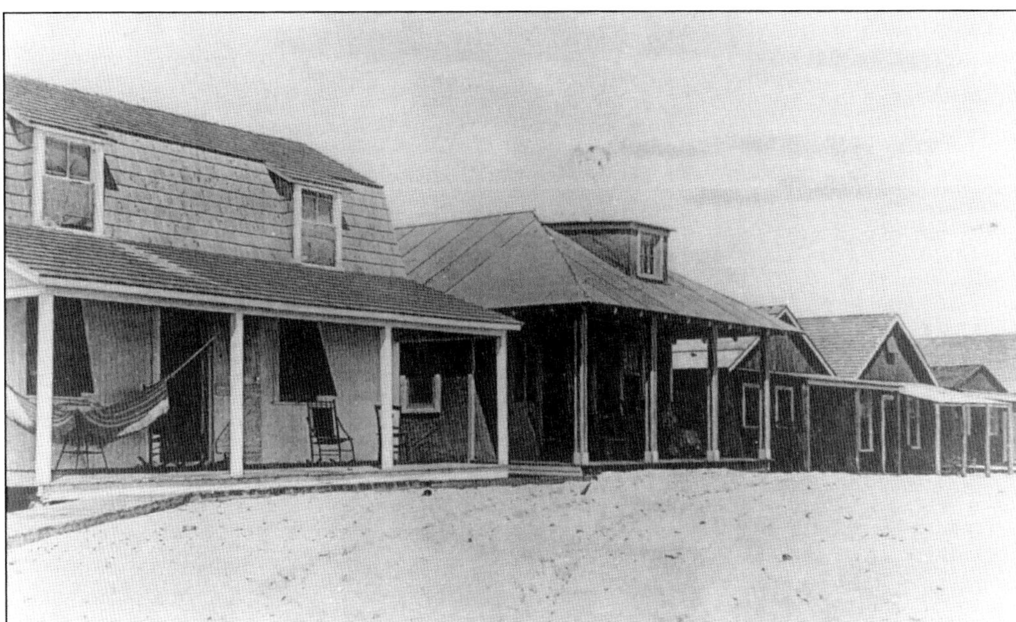

Nearly all of the bungalows had wooden porches that were furnished with hammocks and rocking chairs, where people could sit to watch the tides change and the waves swell. The homes did not have plumbing, heat, or electricity—those amenities came later. Notice that there were plenty of windows to let in the fresh sea breezes.

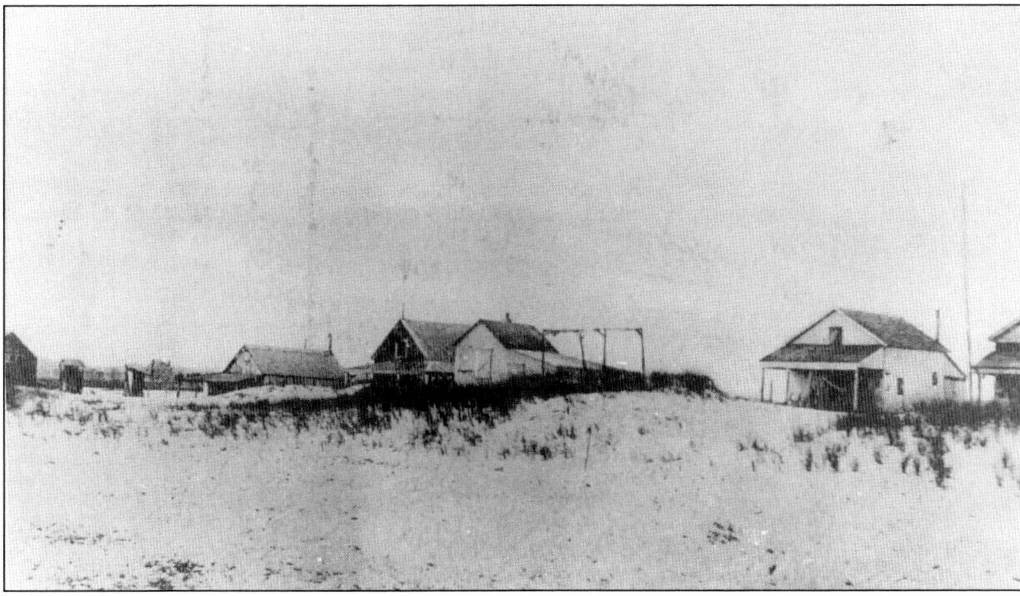

With no electricity or plumbing, many homes were built with fireplaces for warmth on stormy days or cool nights, and outhouses—visible in the photograph—were a necessity. Fresh water came from various wells, and the water turned brackish in heavy weather. Also, roads had not yet been established, and visitors to the beachfront—many arriving by train—loaded their belongings on horse-drawn carts and, walking, followed the wagons east.

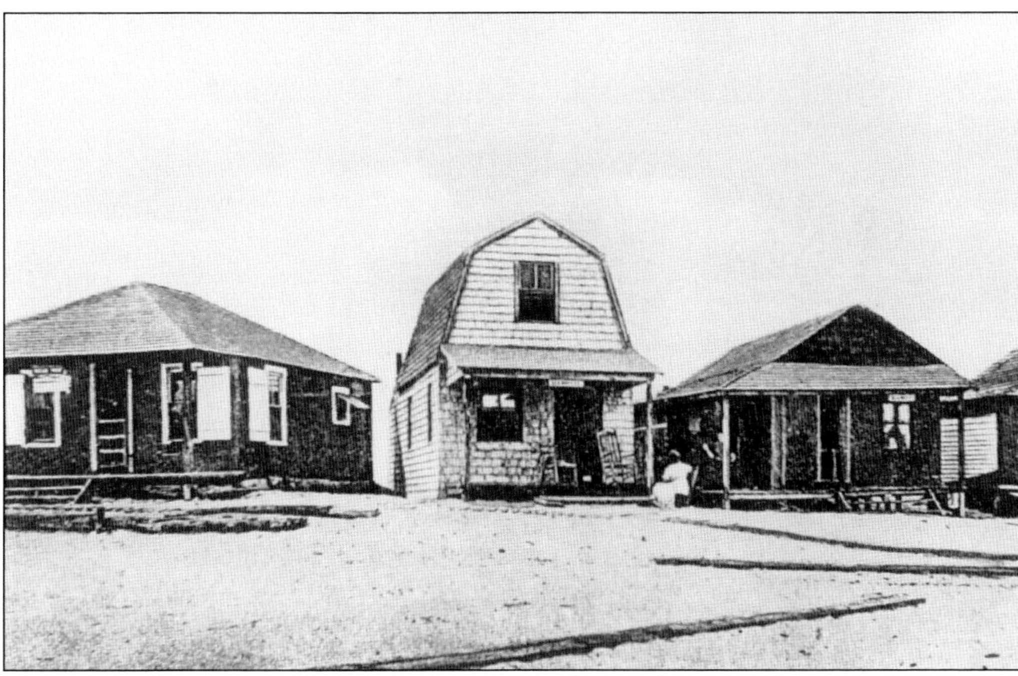

These shacks—just west of the beachfront on Brielle Road—look today much the same way they did when they were constructed 60 years ago. The bungalows had no street addresses. Rather, they had names on signs at the entrances—Sea Air, Grand View, Shoestring Lodge, or numbers—such as Shack No. 5.

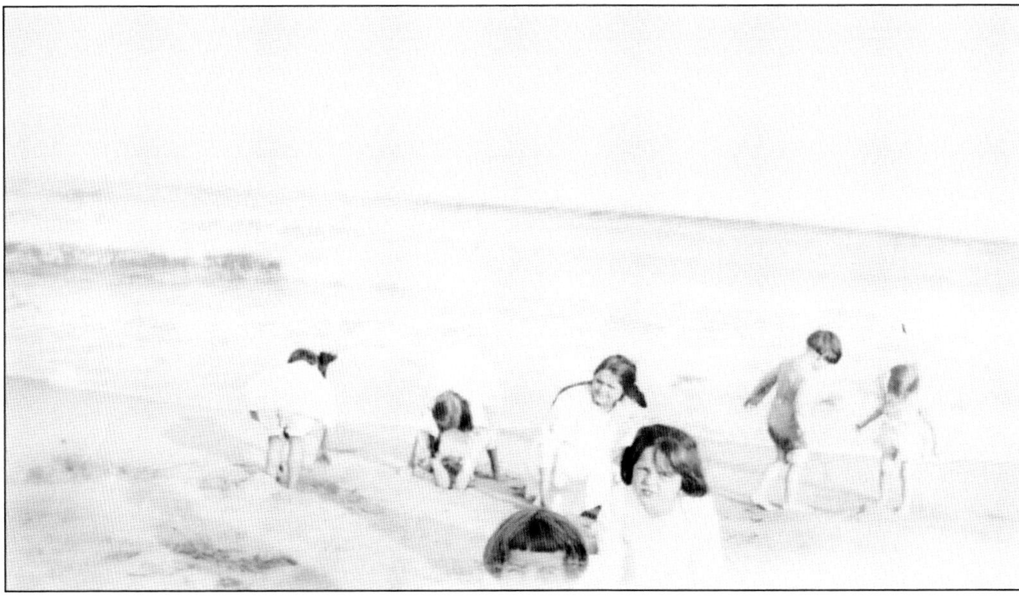

On a wonderful day in the mid-1920s, cousins (from left to right) Nancy Riddle, Joyce Linch, Grace Riddle, Esther Riddle, Robert Riddle, William Linch, and Vera Linch dig in the sand at Manasquan. In a rare beach gathering, Mayor Riddle's children and his sister's children enjoy the sand and surf. Mrs. Mills, the former Esther Riddle, is a resident of Toronto, Canada, who is still a summer resident of the borough.

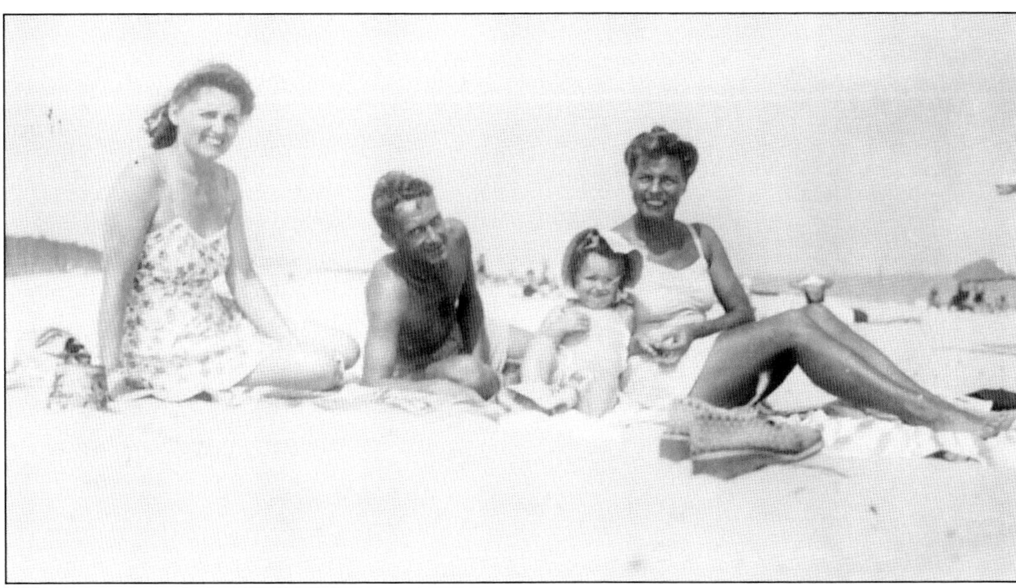

Grace Riddle Green (at left) and John and Nancy Riddle Lewis relax on Pompano Avenue beach in Manasquan with Kathy, the Lewis's daughter, in 1948. Grace and Nancy were daughters of Mayor Lloyd C. Riddle and were lifelong residents of the borough.

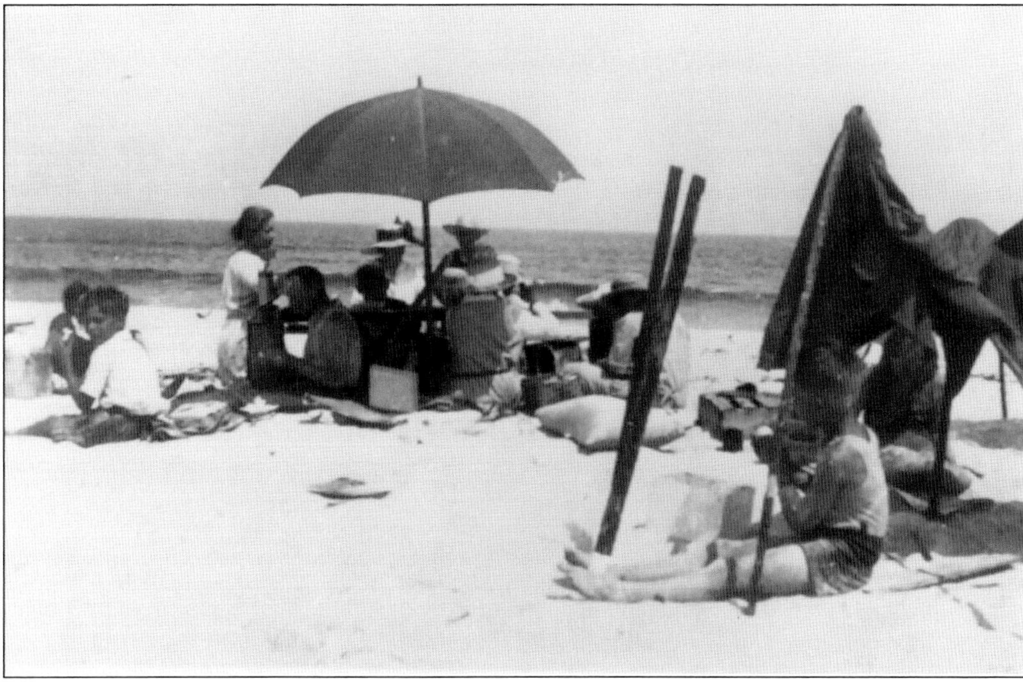

A family enjoys a day at Manasquan Beach in the 1930s—with a picnic, swimming, and relaxing under the umbrella not much unlike today—except for the fashions which were drab, covered more, and took much longer to dry. Today's beach scenes show brighter colors, more toys, and much larger crowds.

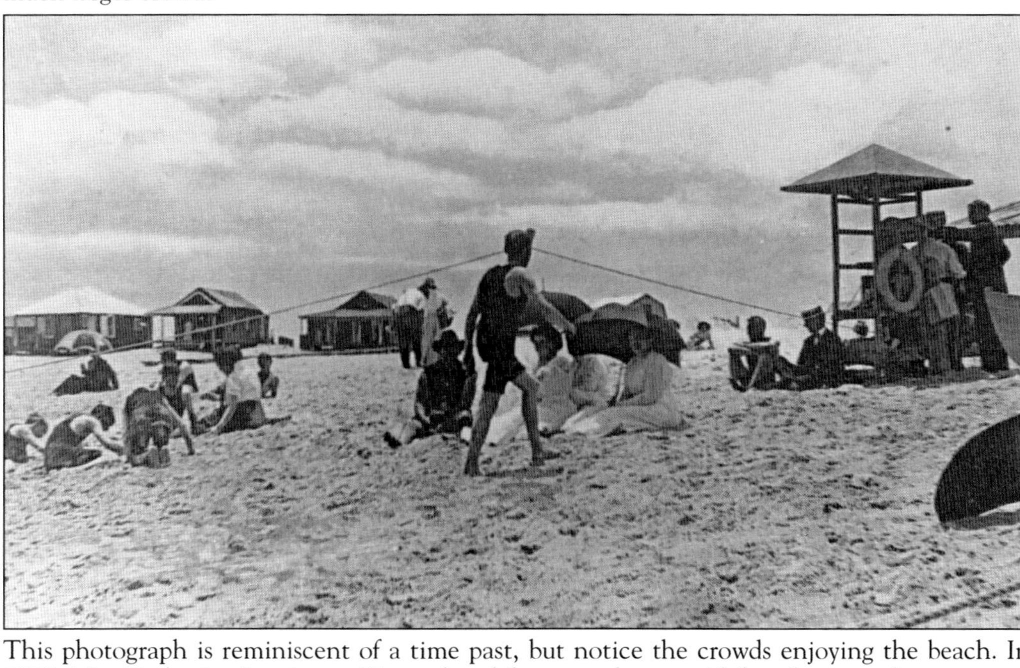

This photograph is reminiscent of a time past, but notice the crowds enjoying the beach. In 1976, Mrs. Katherine Leming, a 40-year beachfront employee, said that she started at a wage of 35.5¢ an hour. Season badges were available for $1; beach access was 50¢ on weekends, and 25¢ on weekdays. Also, in 1976, season badges for bathers had increased to $9.

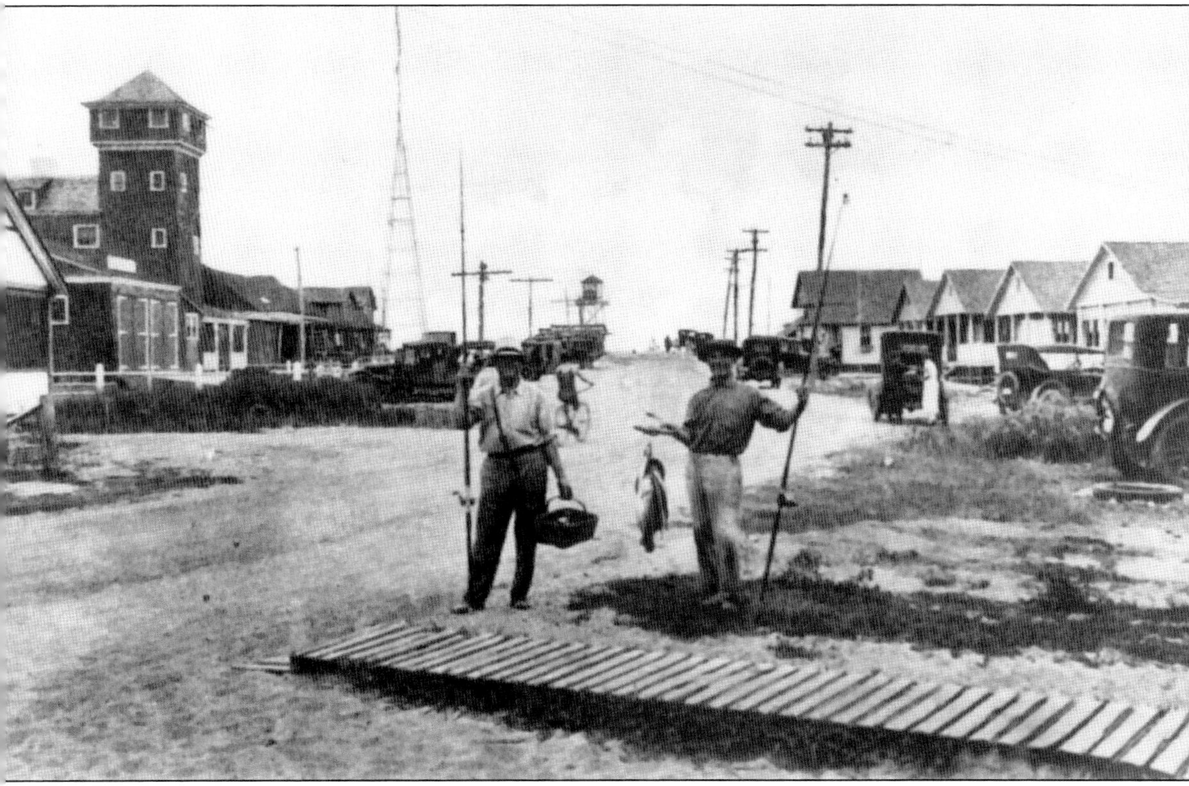

Happy fishermen with rods and the day's catch proudly display them for friends. From this c. 1915 photograph looking east to the beachfront, the houses on Ocean Avenue have changed very little during the last five decades, but the sand path is now a paved road with sidewalks and curbs. In the left of this image, the U.S. Coast Guard Station is visible. Earlier this decade, the station was decommissioned.

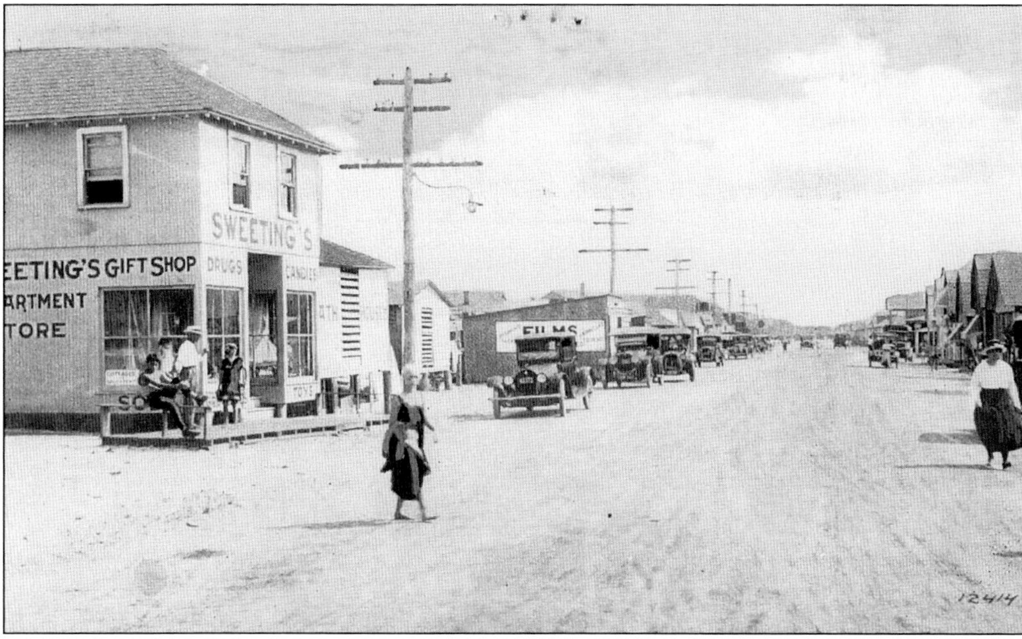

Sweetings Gift Shop and Department Store on First Avenue in the beach area of the community was owned and operated by Dr. Edward J. Sweeting. At the time this postcard photograph was taken in 1915, the road was still a dirt path.

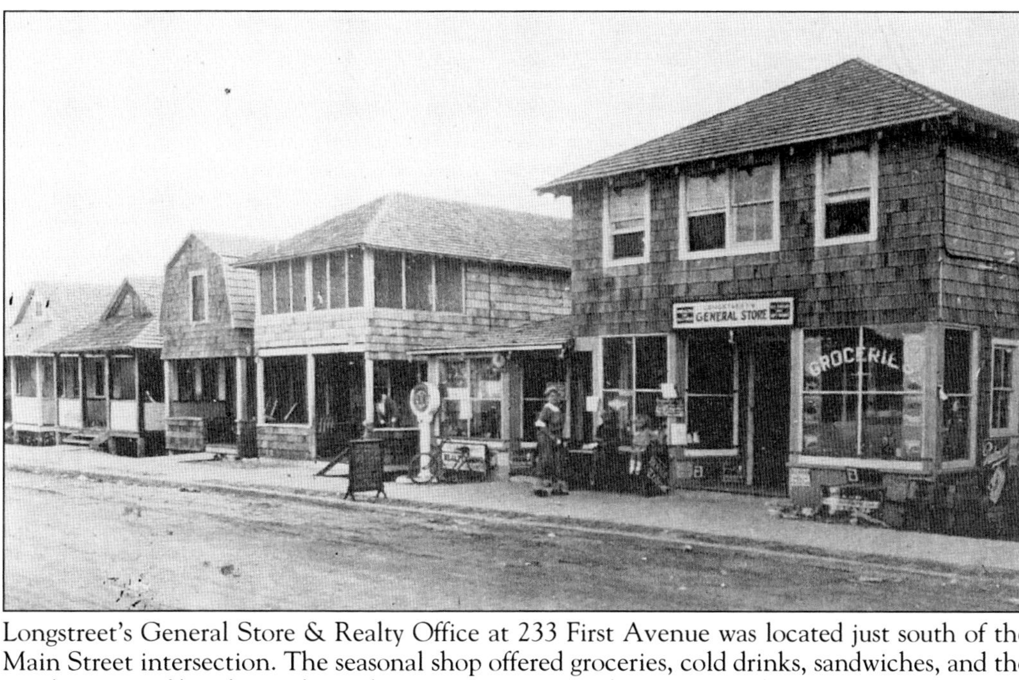

Longstreet's General Store & Realty Office at 233 First Avenue was located just south of the Main Street intersection. The seasonal shop offered groceries, cold drinks, sandwiches, and the usual variety of beach supplies. The image captures a glimpse of the beach community in the late 1920s.

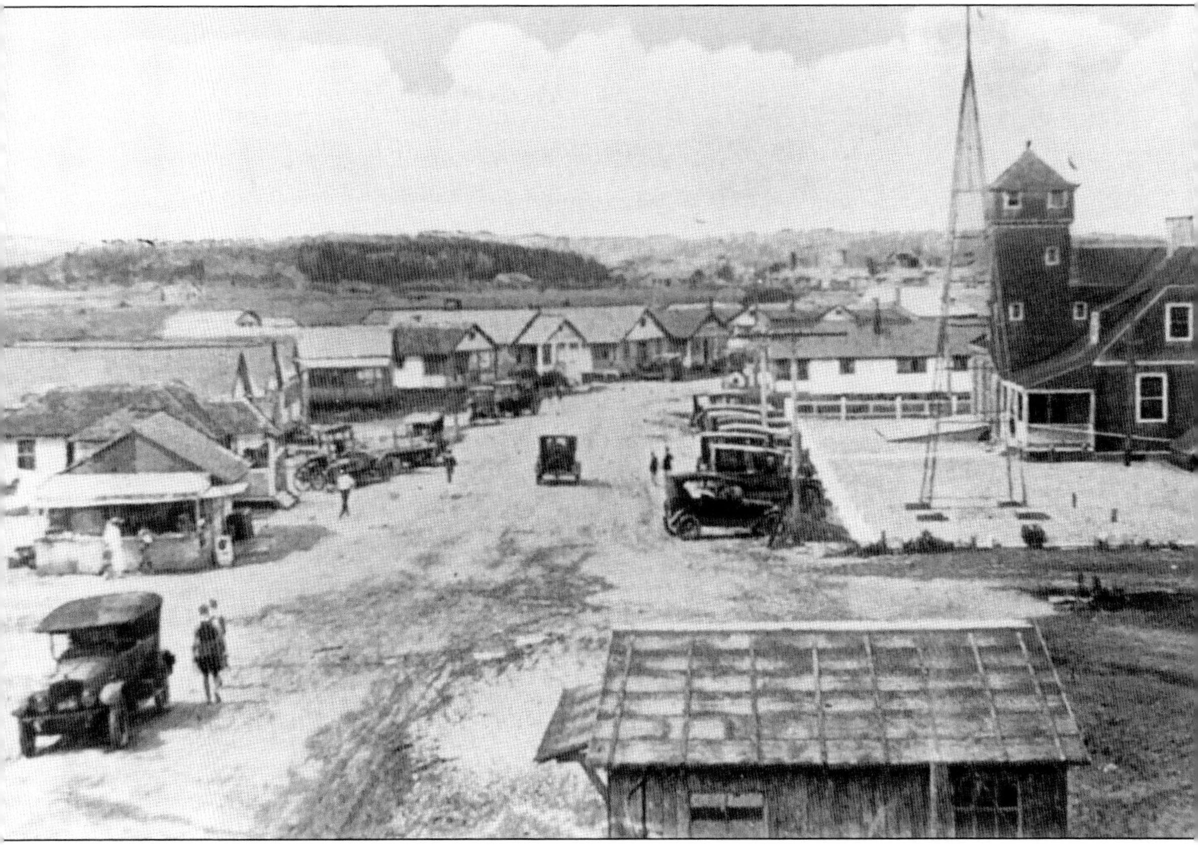

The Ocean Avenue entrance to the beachfront was a busy area. On the north side of the street is the Squan Beach Life-Saving Station, and on the southwest side of Ocean and First Avenues is the Corner Store, a convenience shop serving this well-established, but seasonal neighborhood. The roof of the fisheries packing plant is visible in the foreground.

Georgia Geiser relaxes with a friend on the Manasquan beachfront in the 1920s. Her father moved his family—including five other children, Ralph, Alwyn, Theodore, Harriet, and Paul—from Newark, where he operated a plumbing business, to Manasquan during the summer months. As a Manasquan resident, he earned his living as a fisherman, and the family enjoyed the benefits of a more peaceful, healthy environment.

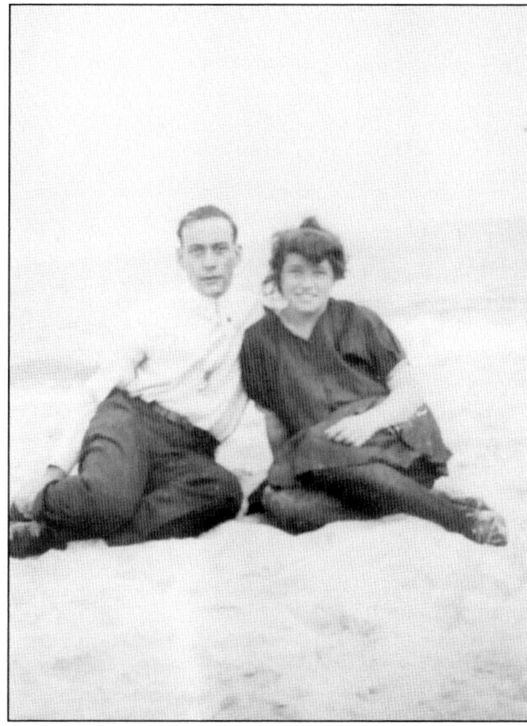

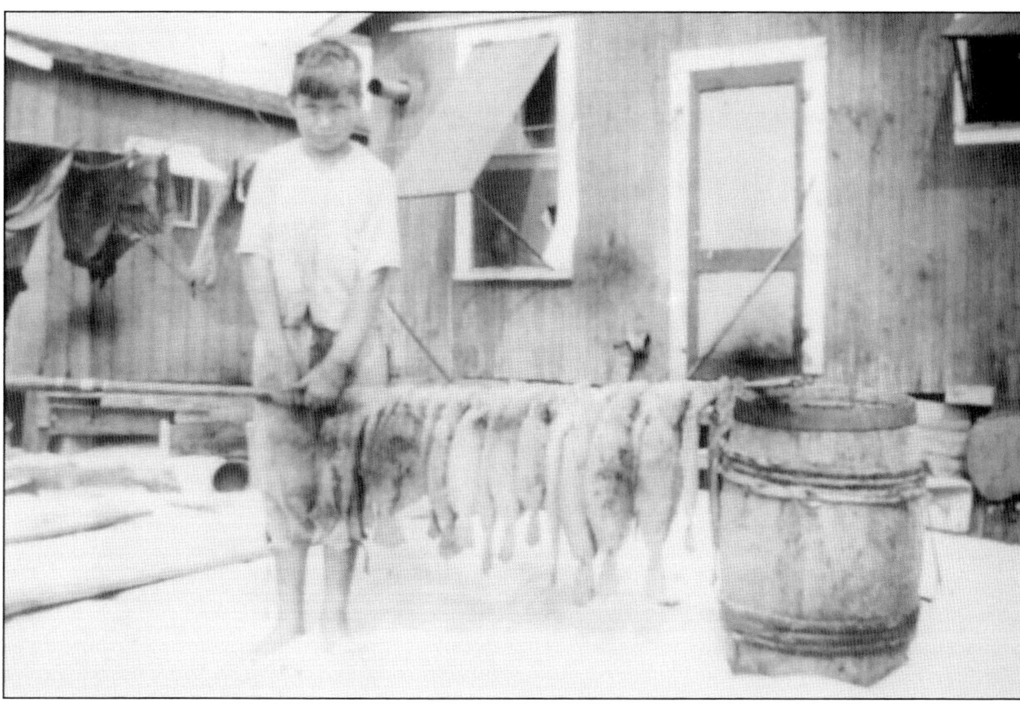

Paul Geiser, about ten years old, displays his catch of the day at his family's summer bungalow on the beachfront. The house was built by his father, George T. Geiser, and two of Paul's brothers, Ralph and Alwyn, in the early 1920s. Paul married Ruth Vail, a local artist best known for capturing coastal scenes, particularly those of Manasquan.

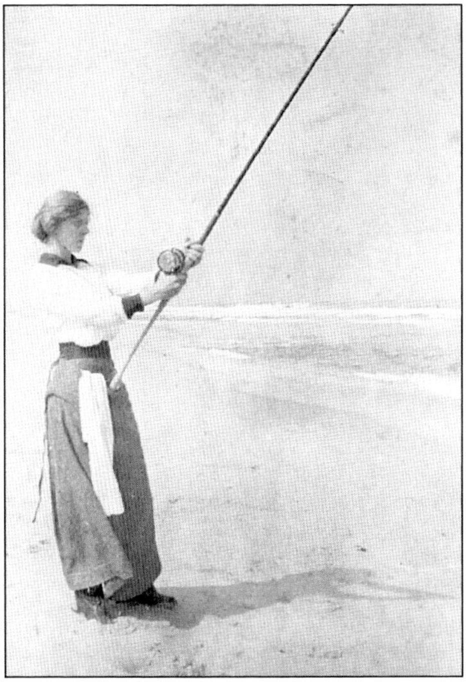

Stella Phillips enjoys a day of recreation at Manasquan Beach. Shown here in this 1914 photograph, Stella wore traditional women's clothing of the time—even for a day of fishing at the beach. Her great-grandson, Steven E. Phillips, remembers stories he heard from his grandmother, that Stella's catch of the day rivaled area fishermen.

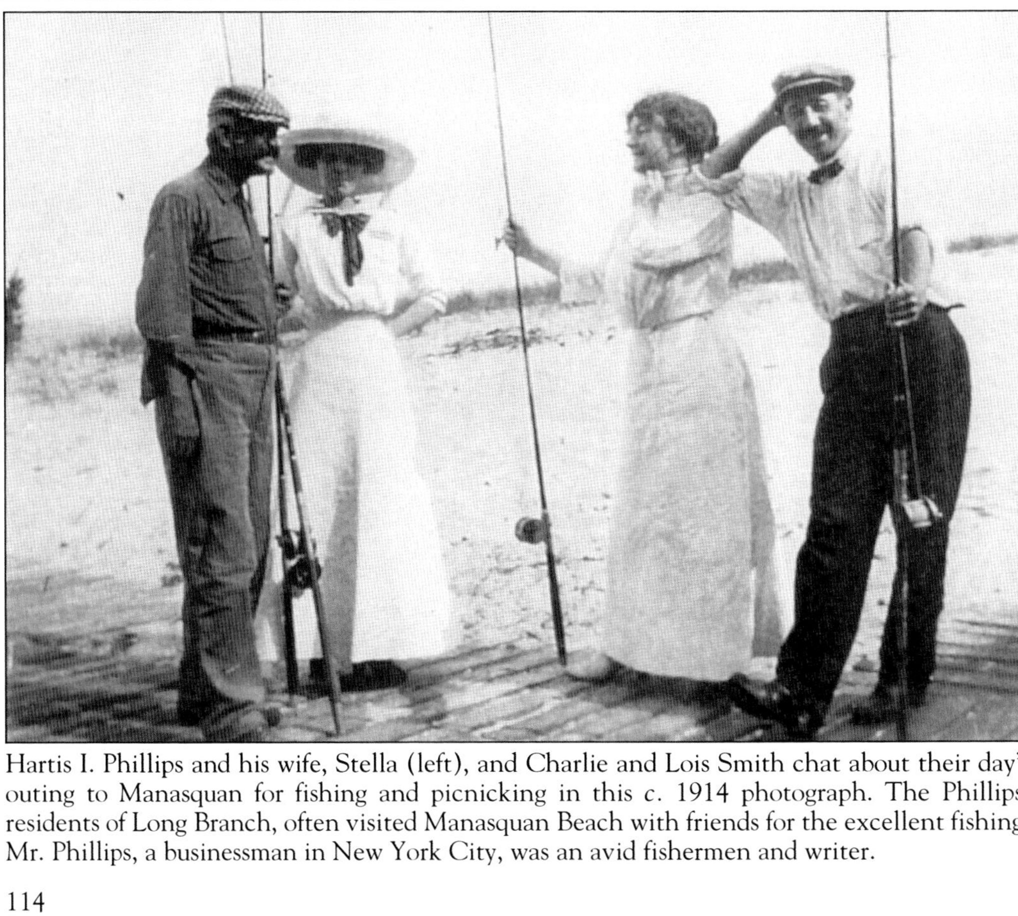

Hartis I. Phillips and his wife, Stella (left), and Charlie and Lois Smith chat about their day's outing to Manasquan for fishing and picnicking in this *c.* 1914 photograph. The Phillips, residents of Long Branch, often visited Manasquan Beach with friends for the excellent fishing. Mr. Phillips, a businessman in New York City, was an avid fishermen and writer.

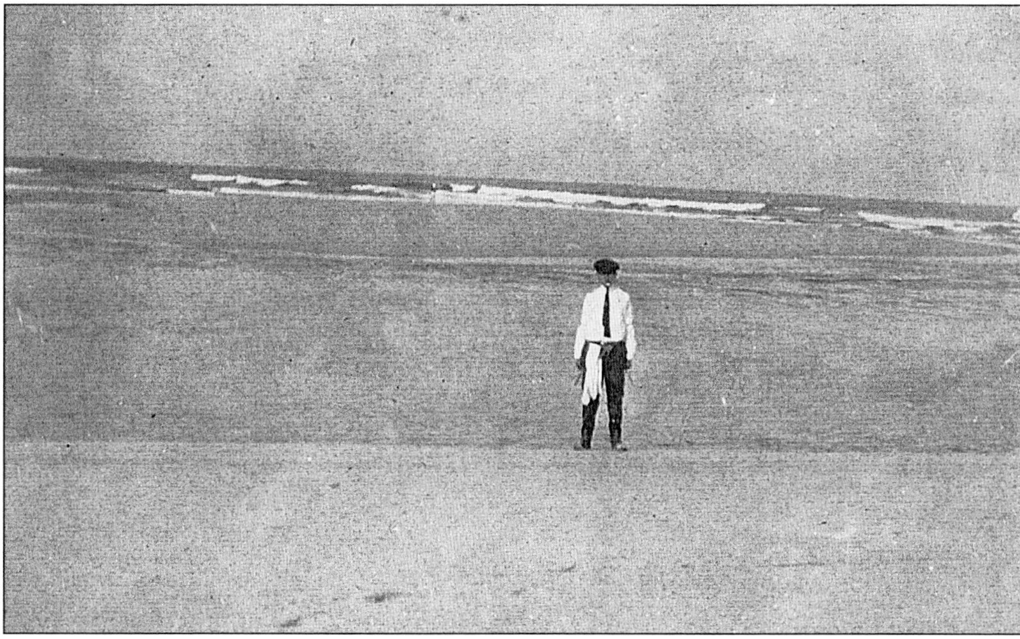

Adrian H. Phillips, whose family visited Manasquan Beach in the early 1900s, stands near the site of the present Manasquan Inlet. This photograph, taken in 1913, illustrates the emptiness of the beachfront before construction of the permanent inlet. He enjoyed Manasquan so much that he was a summer resident of the borough from 1955 until 1971, maintaining a home on Riverside Drive.

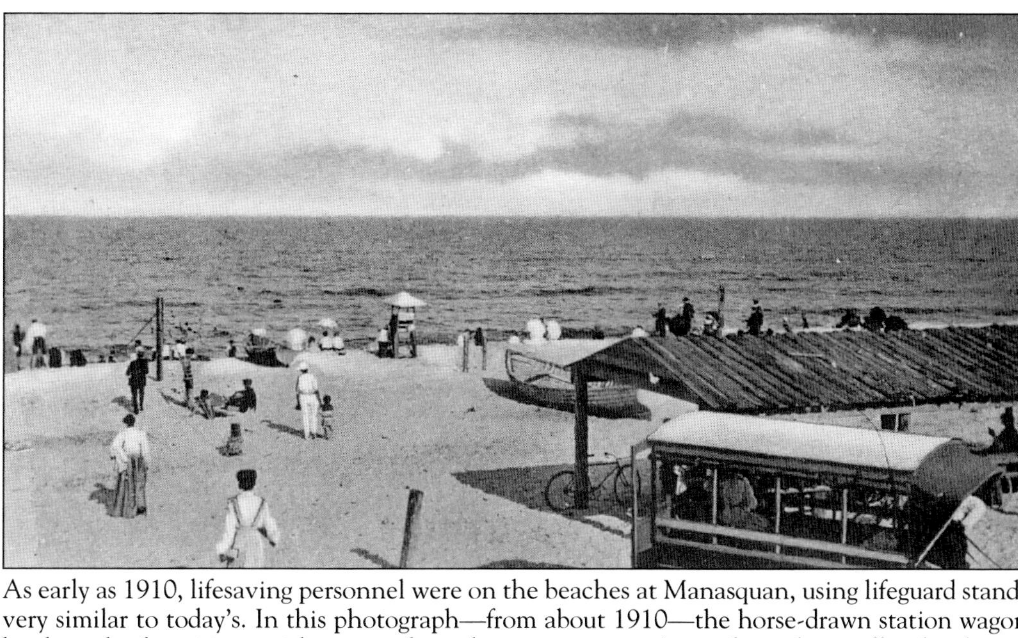

As early as 1910, lifesaving personnel were on the beaches at Manasquan, using lifeguard stands very similar to today's. In this photograph—from about 1910—the horse-drawn station wagon has brought day visitors with picnics from the train station. A wooden cabana offered welcome shade for women in days when complexions were protected from the sun.

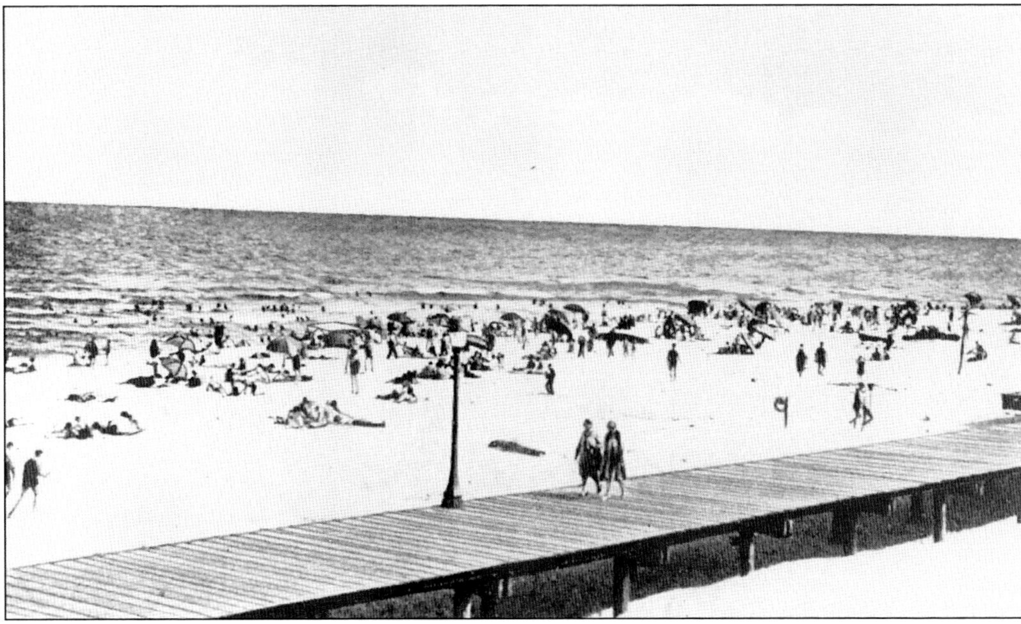

The dedication and celebration of the new boardwalk at Manasquan Beach were held on August 18, 1928. Mayor Lloyd C. Riddle drove the gold spike into the boardwalk signifying its final completion. Dr. Edward J. Sweeting served as chairman and secretary of the event. More than 10,000 attended the festivities that included a speech by New Jersey Governor A. Harry Moore, a fancy dress parade featuring costumes, a band concert, and $1,000 fireworks display.

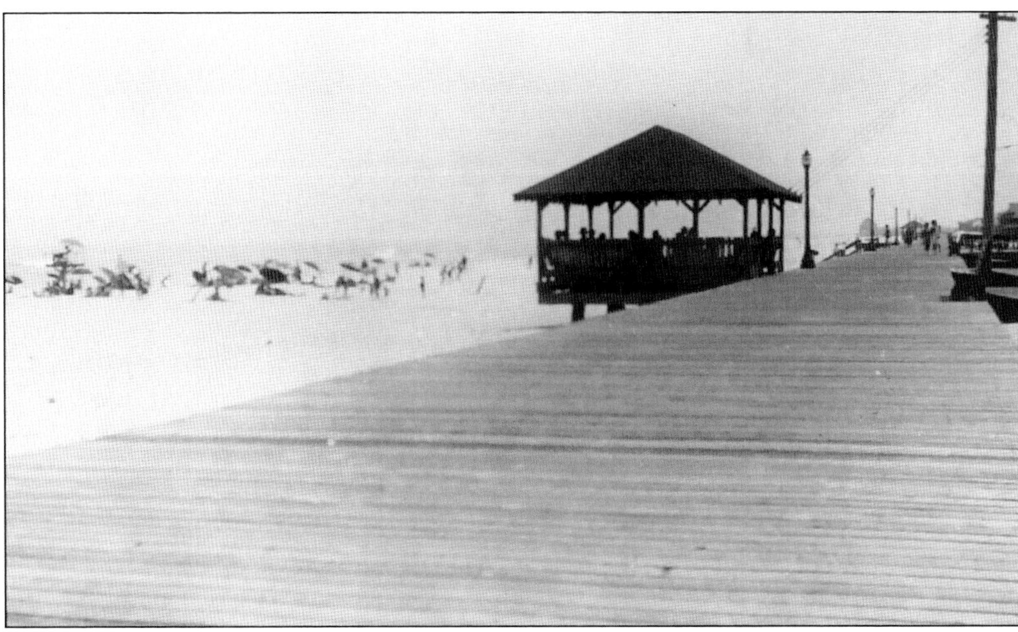

In the 1920s when Manasquan officials talked about building a boardwalk on the beachfront, it is generally believed that the shacks would be torn down and would be replaced with more "respectable homes." A visitor to the beachfront today will see that the exterior of many of these "shacks" remain nearly as they were constructed more than 60 years ago.

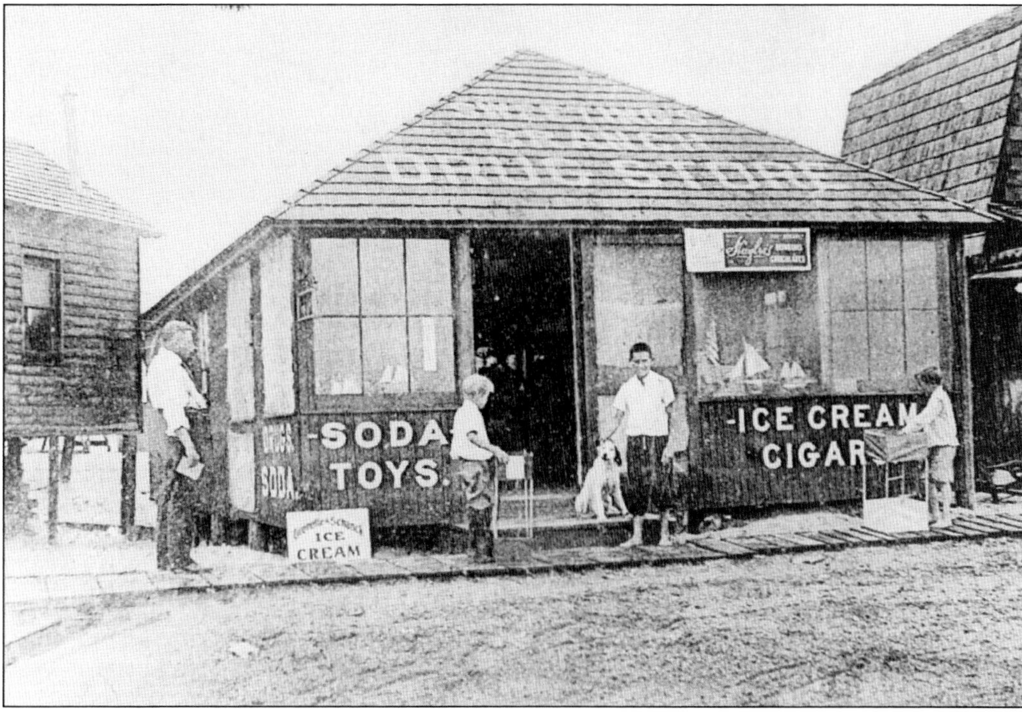

Dr. Edward J. Sweeting opened a second branch location of his popular Manasquan Pharmacy—located in downtown Manasquan in the Borden Building—on the Manasquan Beach at Main Street during the 1930s. The bungalow pharmacy offered beach sundries, sand toys, ice cream, and cold drinks.

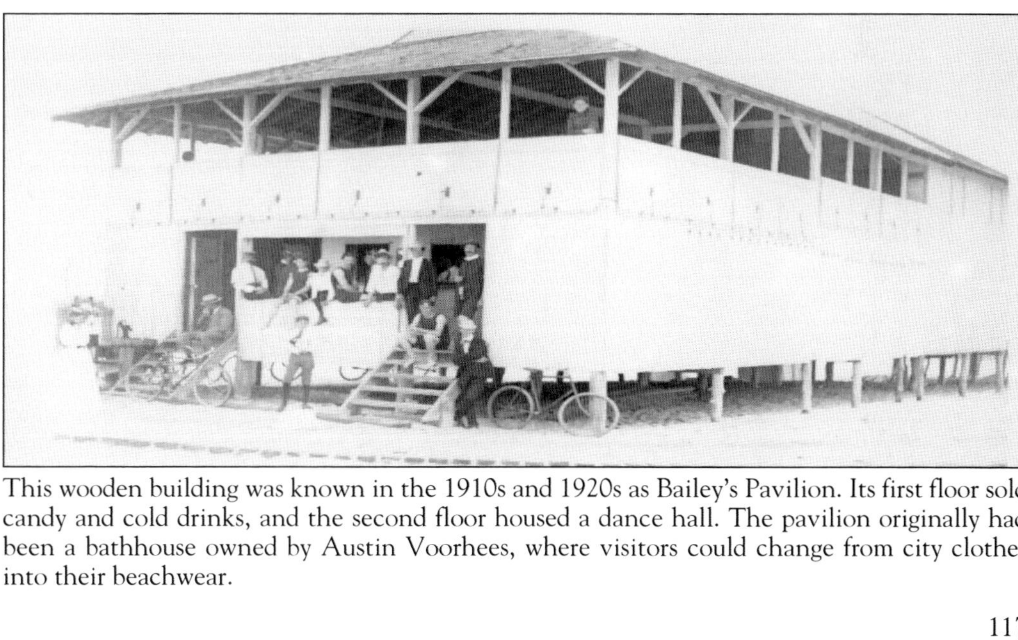

This wooden building was known in the 1910s and 1920s as Bailey's Pavilion. Its first floor sold candy and cold drinks, and the second floor housed a dance hall. The pavilion originally had been a bathhouse owned by Austin Voorhees, where visitors could change from city clothes into their beachwear.

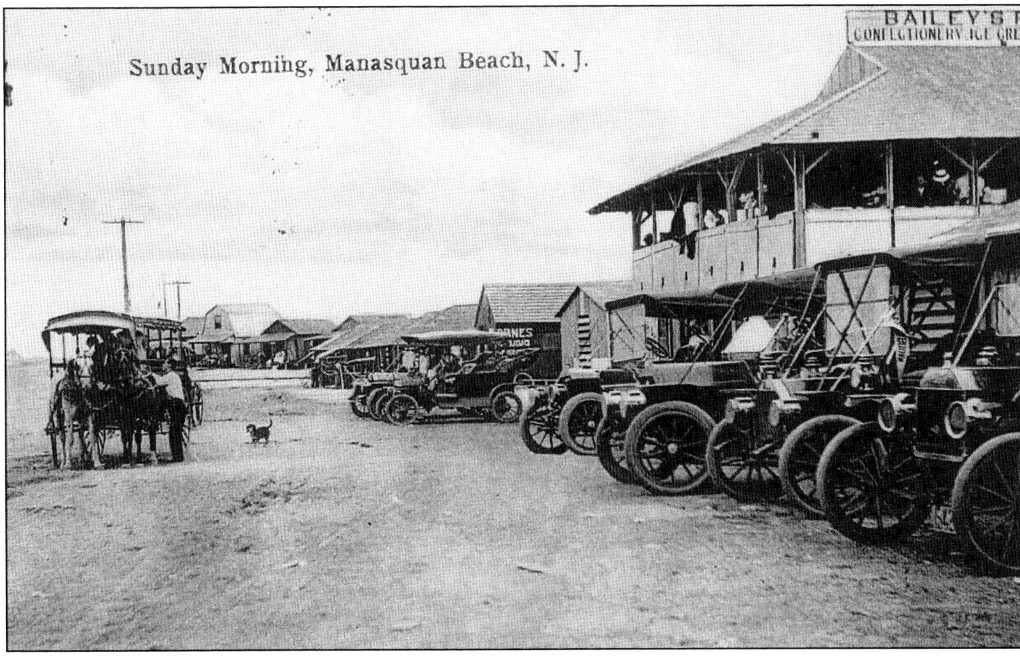

In this postcard of Bailey's Pavilion on a Sunday morning, all has not changed in the decades since this image was taken. Although horse-drawn wagons and turn-of-the-century motorcars no longer transport visitors to the beach, crowds arrive in large numbers by other means of transportation to enjoy the sun, sand, and surf.

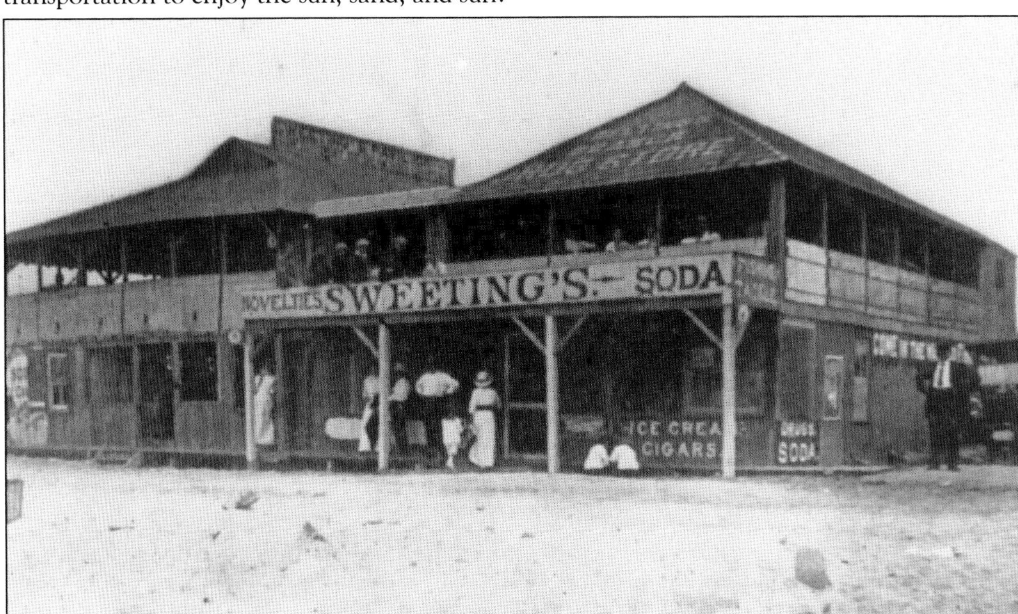

The Sweeting Pavilion, originally Bailey's, was bought by Dr. Edward J. Sweeting. The second floor featured a dance hall where residents and visitors danced to live music on summer nights. Fresh ocean breezes and iced drinks cooled the overheated dancers. It was one of the oldest structures of its kind along the New Jersey coast, perhaps because it was built on pilings for stability and safety from high tides and storms.

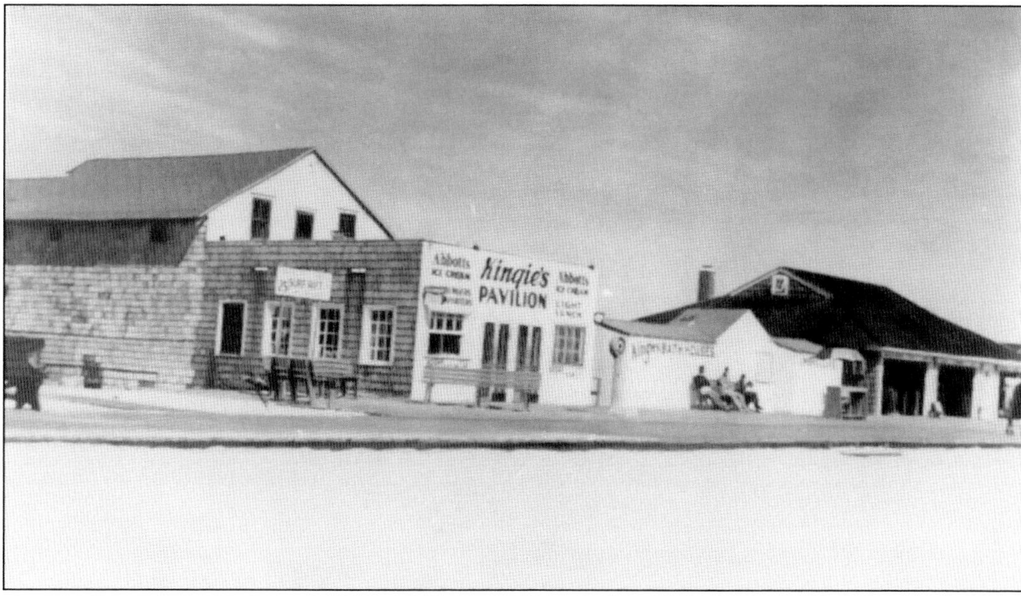

Many a fine time was spent playing ping pong and pinball at Kingie's Pavilion on the beachfront south of Main Beach, according to local residents. The residents, teenagers at the time this photograph was taken in the 1930s, also said that soft drinks and ice cream at Kingie's were always refreshing. Kingie's was owned and operated by W. Kingman Potter. Prior to Mr. Potter's ownership, the arcade and luncheonette had been called Metcalf's Pavilion.

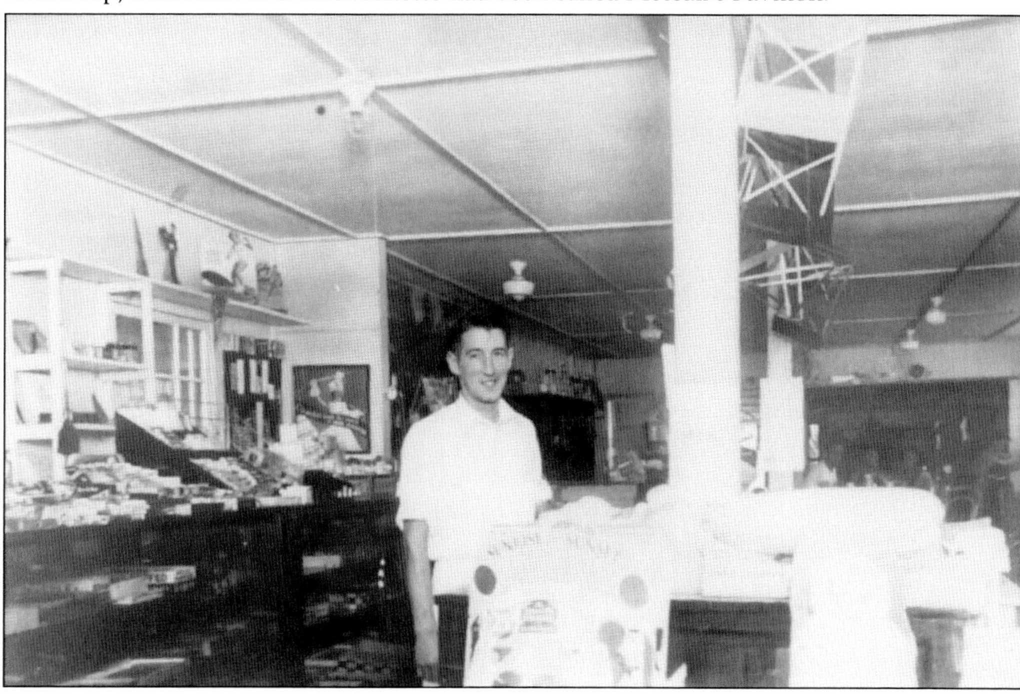

W. Kingman Potter, owner of Kingie's, smiles for this late-1930s photograph inside his beachfront store. One of Kingie's most popular attractions was the pinball machines, always very attractive to Manasquan's teenagers; he also offered luncheonette food and stocked candy, drinks, and beach toys. Note the paper box kites hanging from the ceiling.

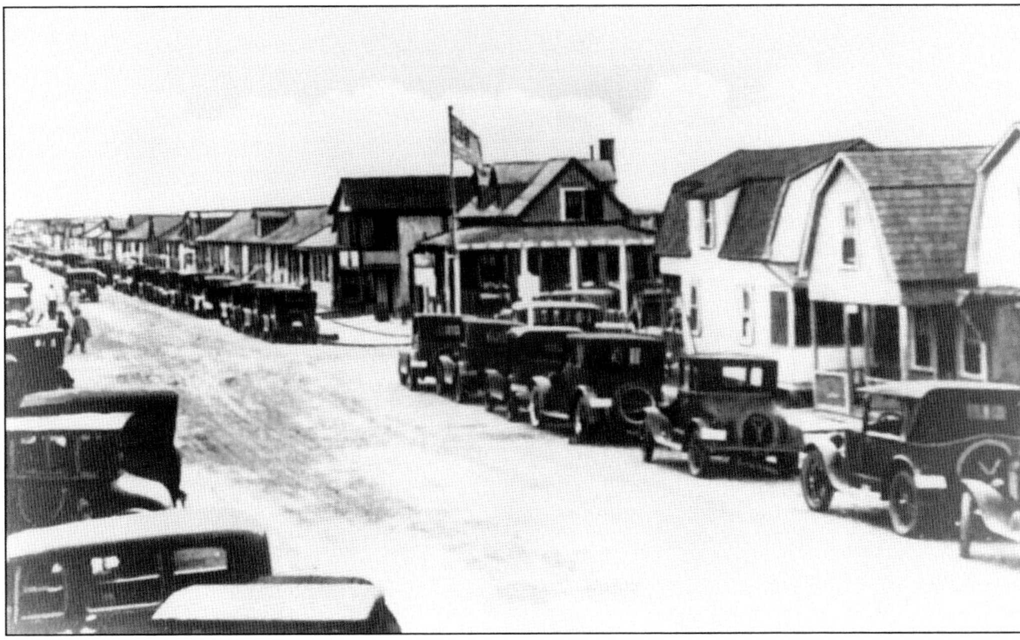

This view of yet-to-be paved First Avenue, looking south toward the Manasquan Inlet, shows an automobile parking situation similar to the present day. Note Brielle Road on the right, by the flagpole. Like most Americans of the period, anyone in the area who owned a car took the family out for a Sunday drive, often ending up by the Atlantic Ocean.

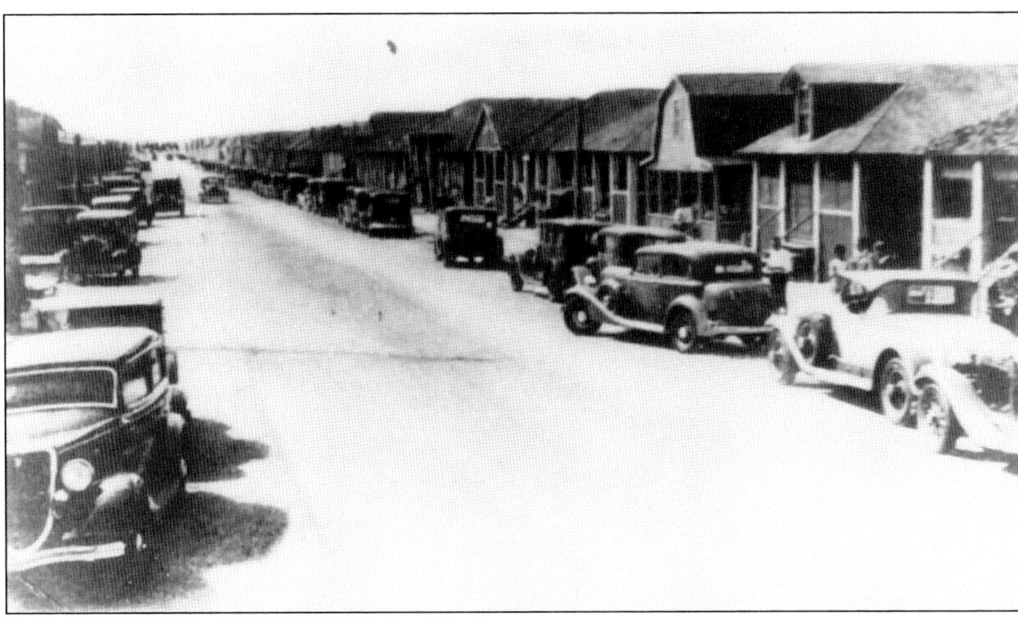

Many of the early summer cottages on First Avenue (the row of houses after the oceanfront bungalows that stretches the length of the beachfront community) were developed by Obadiah Herbert, a resident of Marlboro, in the late 1890s. This picture, *c.* 1920, also shows many similarities to the present day.

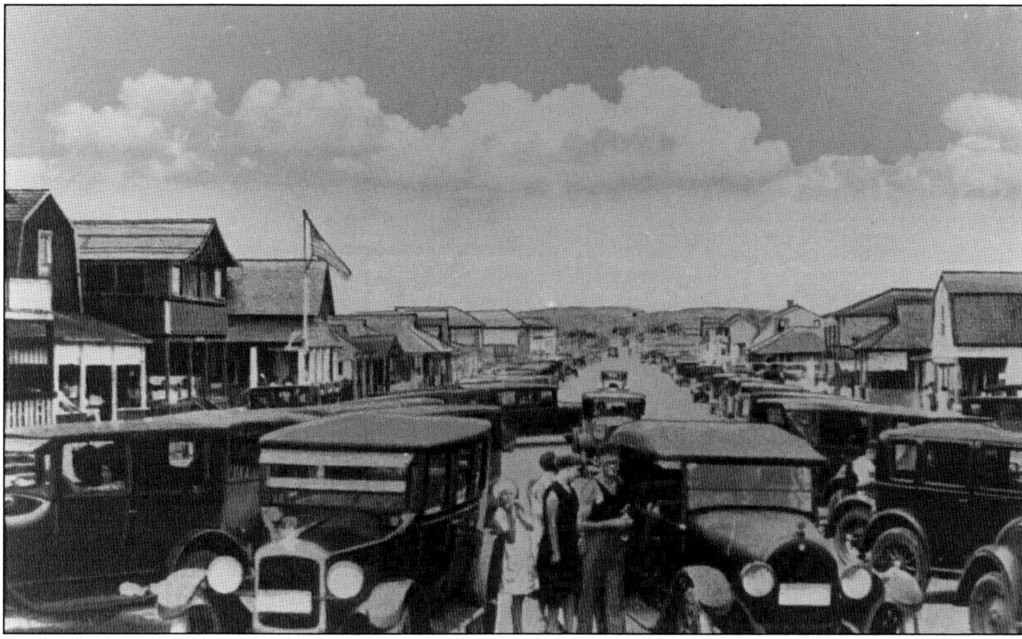

A summer Sunday in the 1920s shows the growing popularity of Manasquan Beach. This view looks west along Brielle Road. These houses, once summer homes owned by families from North Jersey and New York, may look much the same today, but are enjoyed by groups of young people who take them for the season.

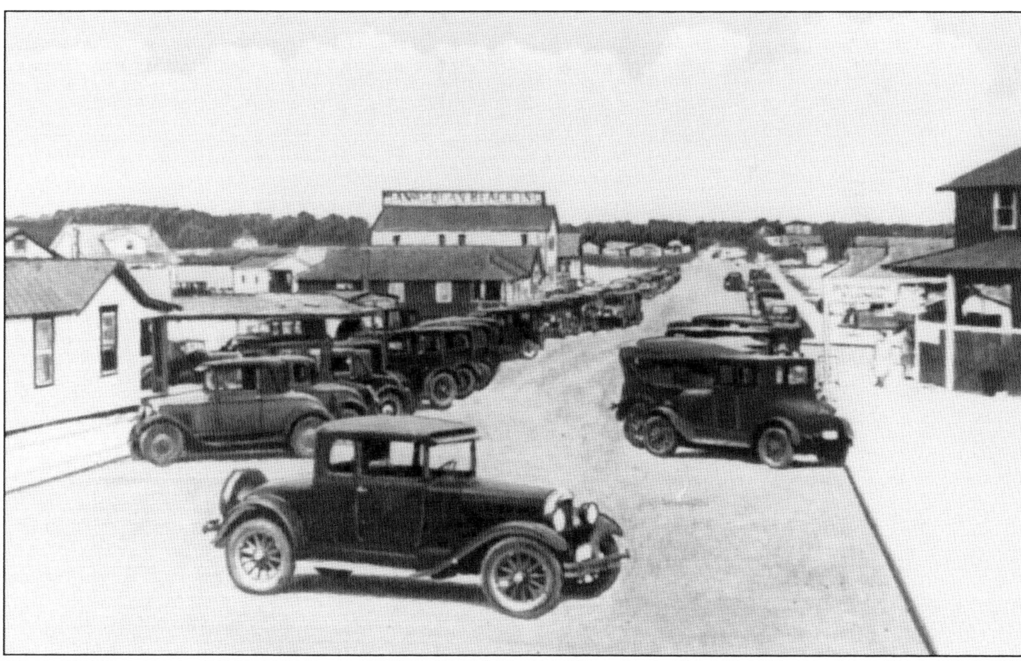

This 1939 scene of Main Street in the beach area illustrates the growth in population. In the left corner, the real estate firm owned by Dr. Edward J. Sweeting is visible. Manasquan Beach, Inc., owned and operated by Harry Ries, is yet another real estate business ready to assist visitors to the area with the purchase of a home or rental accommodation for the summer season.

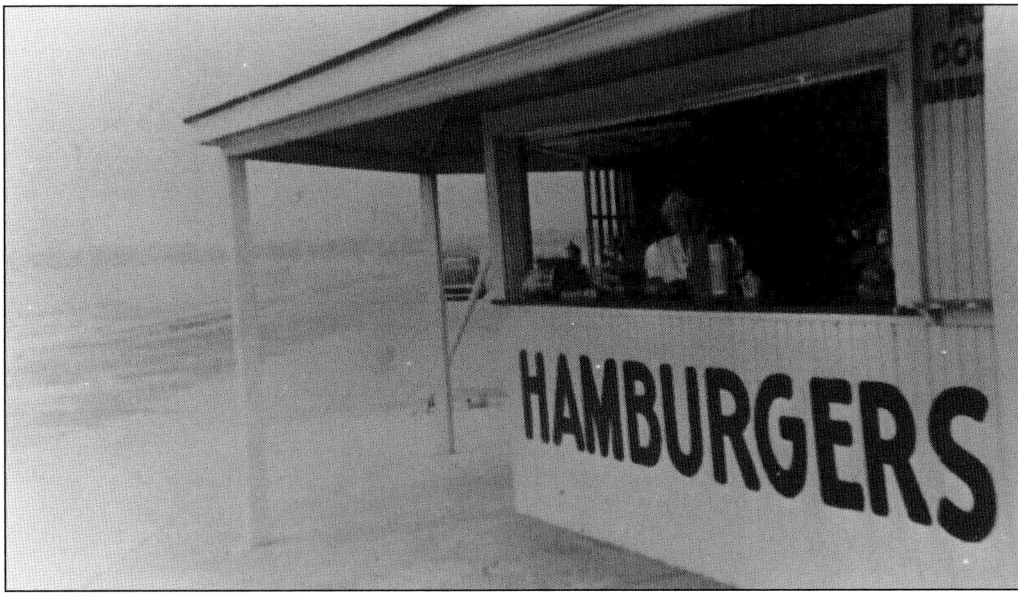

Hamburgers, ice cream, and cold drinks have been the fare at Randy's at the inlet, Manasquan Inlet and First Avenue, since 1934. Built in just ten days, the establishment was owned by Lewis W. Randolph, who opened the eatery after completing his work as the resident engineer with the Army Corps of Engineers, supervising the construction of the jetties and the opening of the Manasquan Inlet.

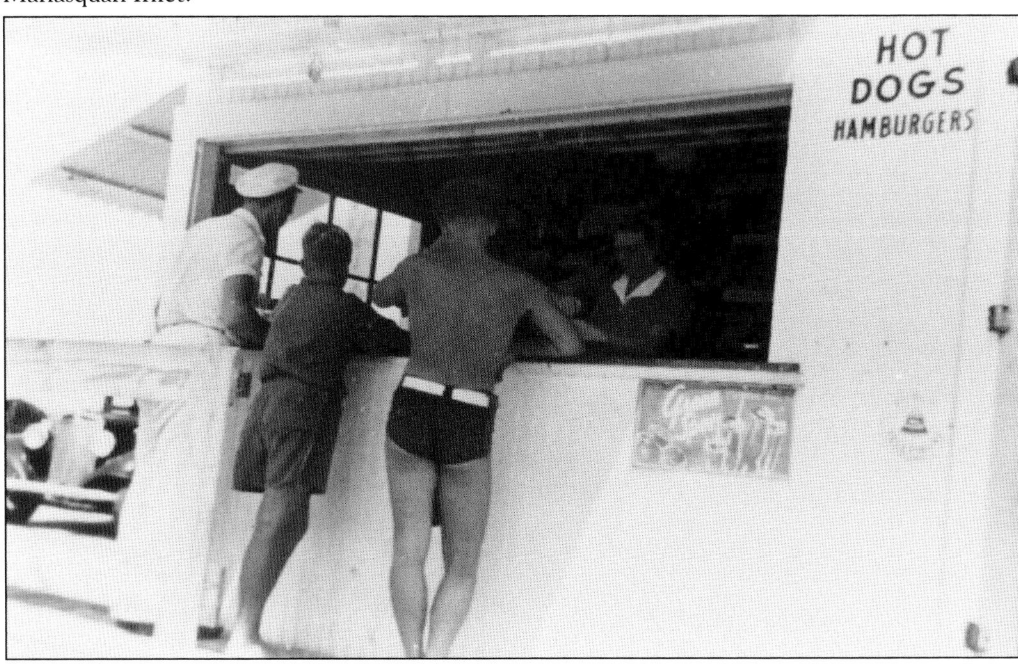

Patrons order their burgers and sodas from the counter at Randy's during the summer of 1936. They were no doubt being waited on by Mrs. Mary Stevens, Lewis Randolph's mother-in-law, who relocated from North Jersey during the summer months to help run the stand with Mr. Randolph and his wife, Helen (her daughter). The whole family, including children, lived on the second floor of Randy's during the summer season.

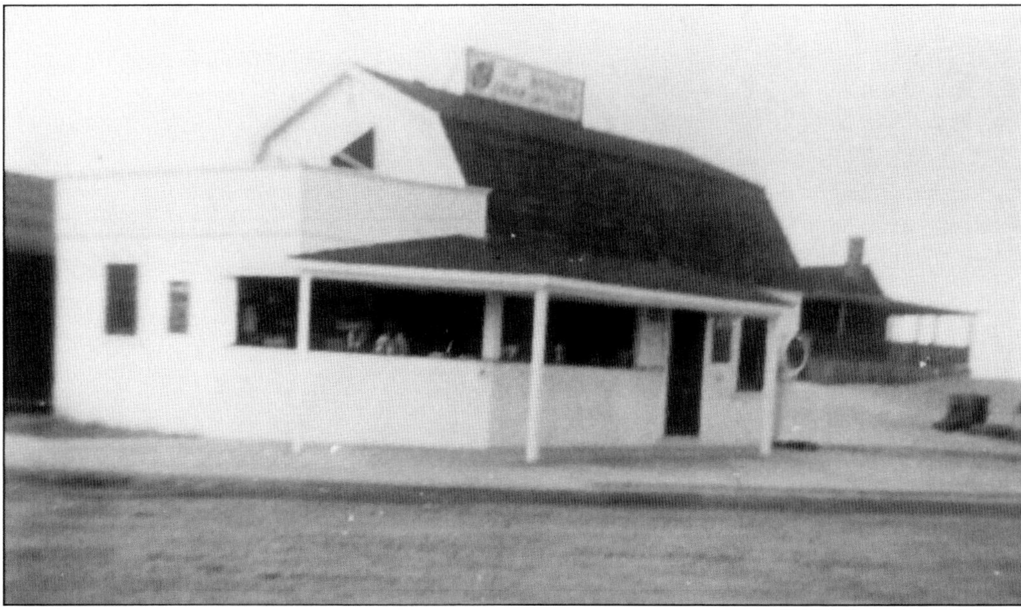

Randy's at the inlet also featured a dining room with three tables, seats, and a telephone booth. The Randolphs ran the stand until 1947, when they sold the business to Fred Carlson, a Manasquan resident. Many present and former Manasquan residents and visitors recall the blissful aroma from the combination of grilling hamburgers and onions and sea air.

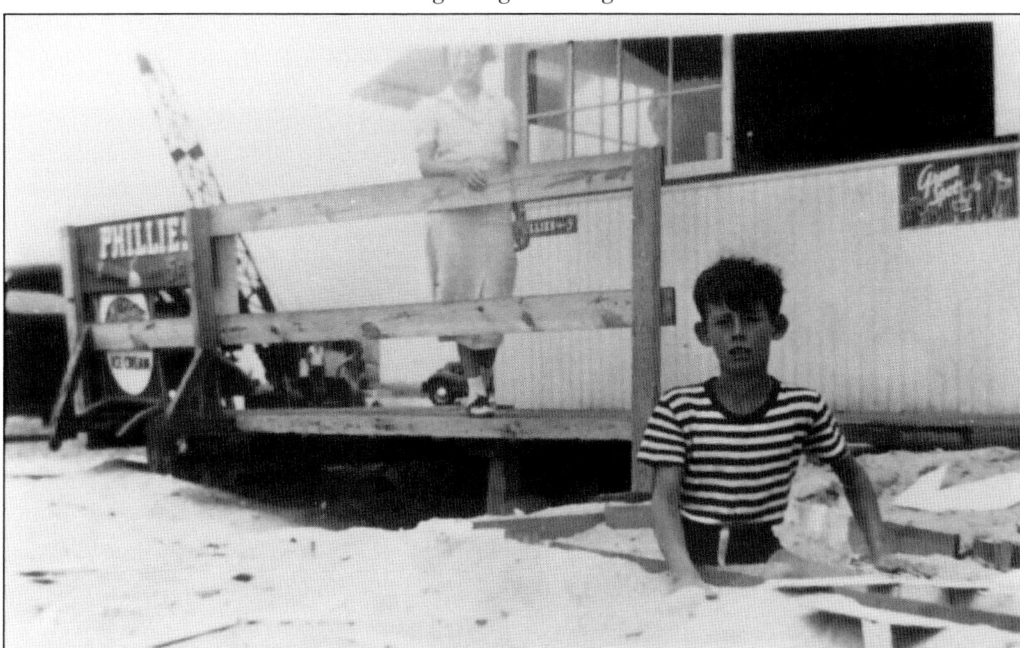

Lewis Randolph's son Warren, who lives in Manasquan today, plays in the sand outside Randy's in this picture from the late 1930s. He remembers the opening of the Manasquan Inlet supervised by his father and the use of the dining room of Randy's as a temporary morgue during the *Morro Castle* disaster in 1934.

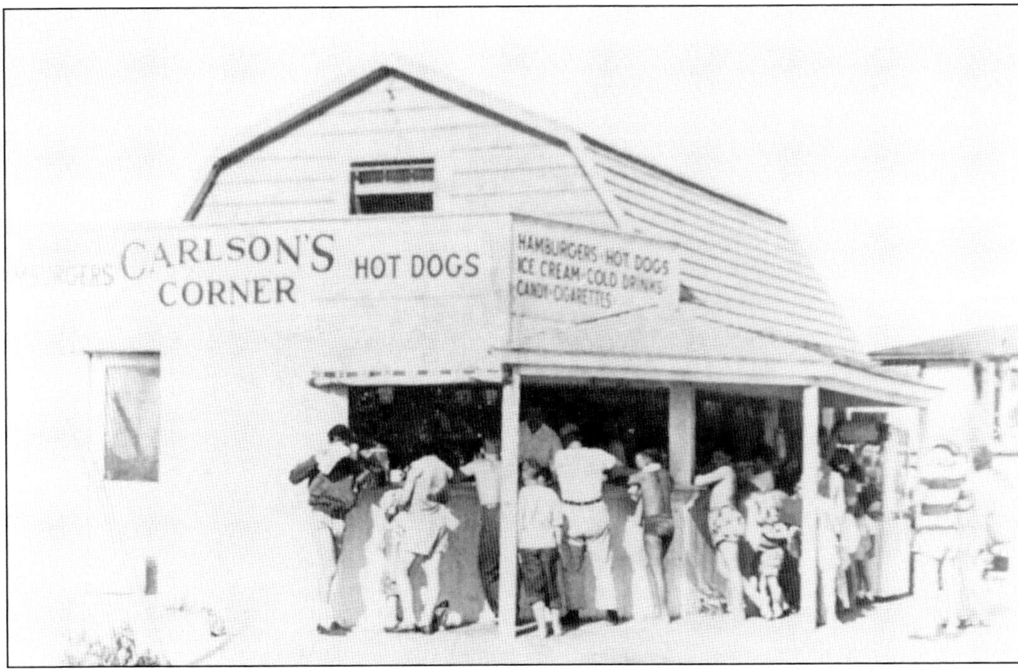

Carlson's Corner has always been a popular snackbar for beachgoers, surfers, and anglers. Some of the best surfing and fishing take place just east of the snackbar on the Manasquan Inlet beach, a specifically designated beach for both of the ocean sports. Fishing and surfing contests also are held at this location, as well as a community Easter Sunrise Service in the pavilion.

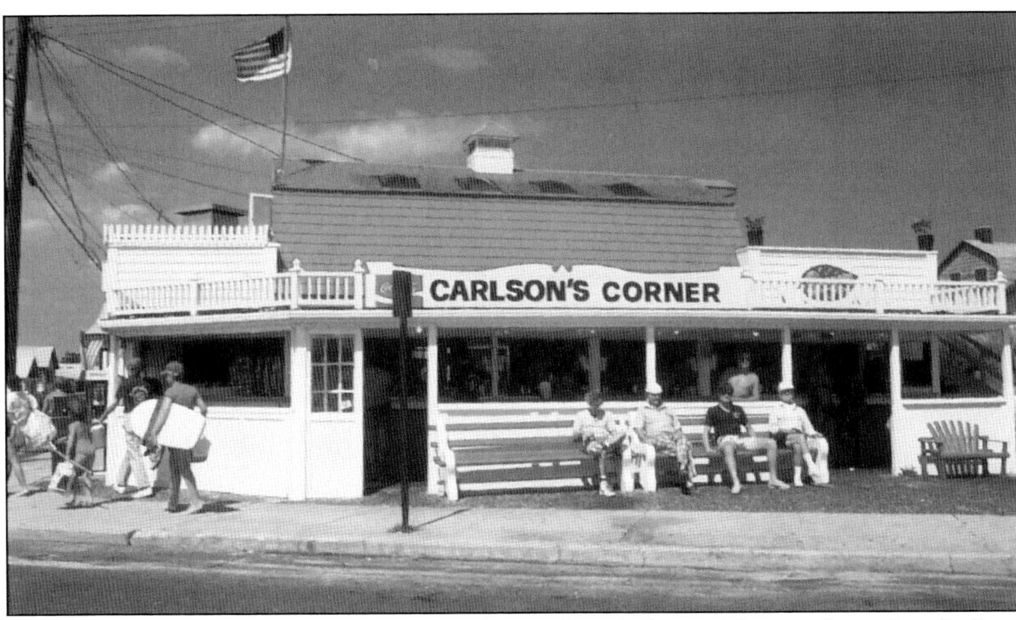

Beachgoers and fishermen visit Carlson's Corner in this 1985 view. The stand—with its brilliant red roof—looks much as it did 50 years ago. The reverse of this postcard calls Carlson's a "surfer's and fisherman's hangout," which it remains today, owned by Larry Ross of Manasquan, who continues to serve burgers, fries, hotdogs, and soda—and "Mom's brewing more coffee, inside."

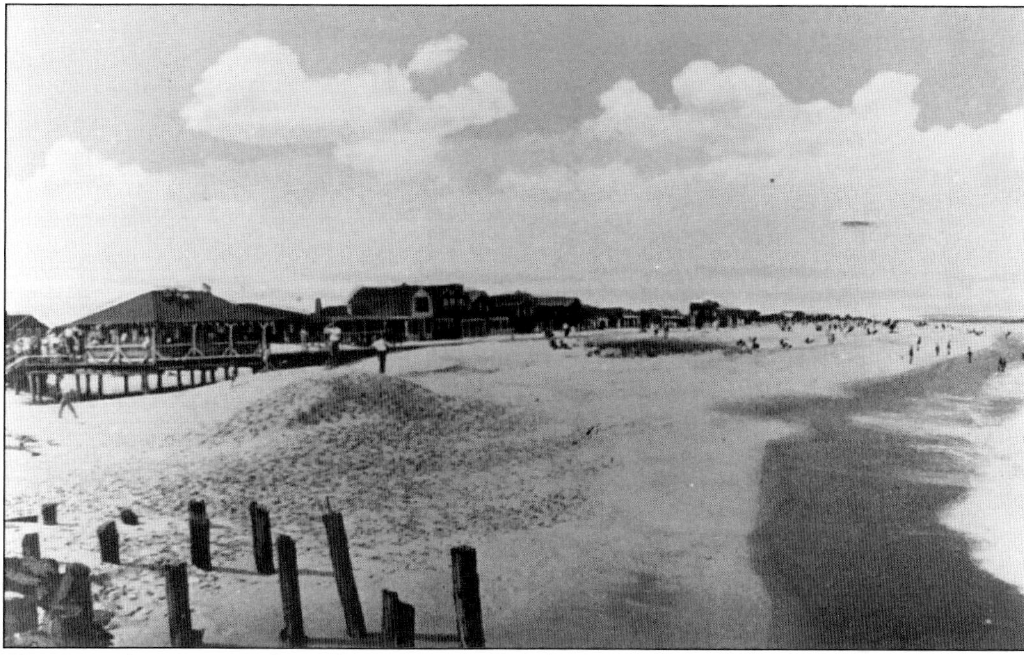

Wooden pilings remain from the temporary jetty built by the Army Corps of Engineers during the construction of the permanent jetty and Manasquan Inlet in the 1930s. This picture was taken just after the completion of that project and shows a nice wide beach thanks to all the sand pumped out of the shoaled-over inlet. The pavilion remains today, as do many of the original houses along this stretch of beachfront.

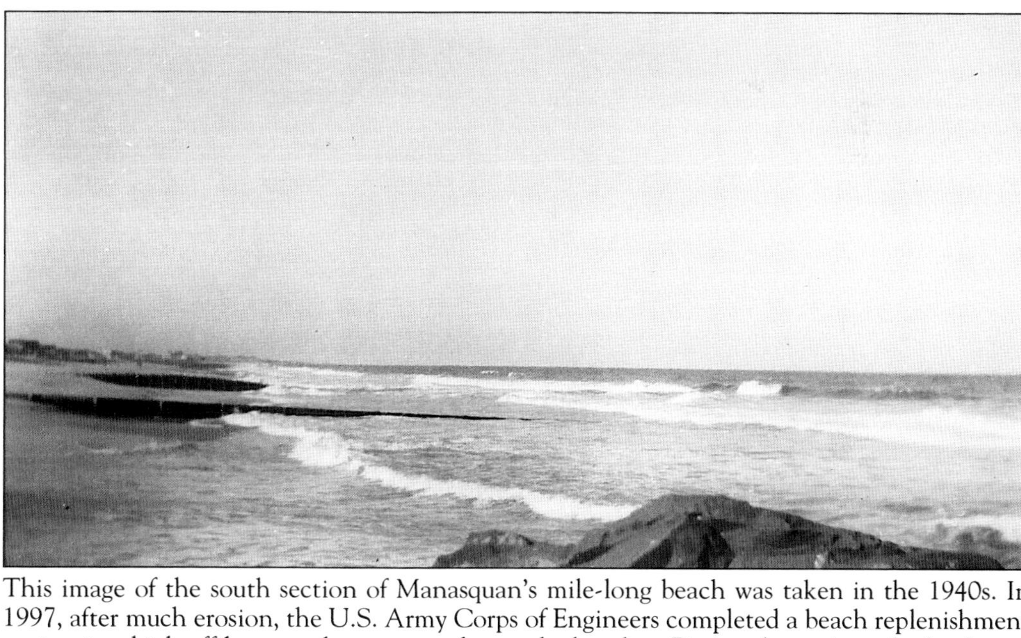

This image of the south section of Manasquan's mile-long beach was taken in the 1940s. In 1997, after much erosion, the U.S. Army Corps of Engineers completed a beach replenishment project in which offshore sand was pumped onto the beaches. During the project, the landscape of the beach was dramatically altered.

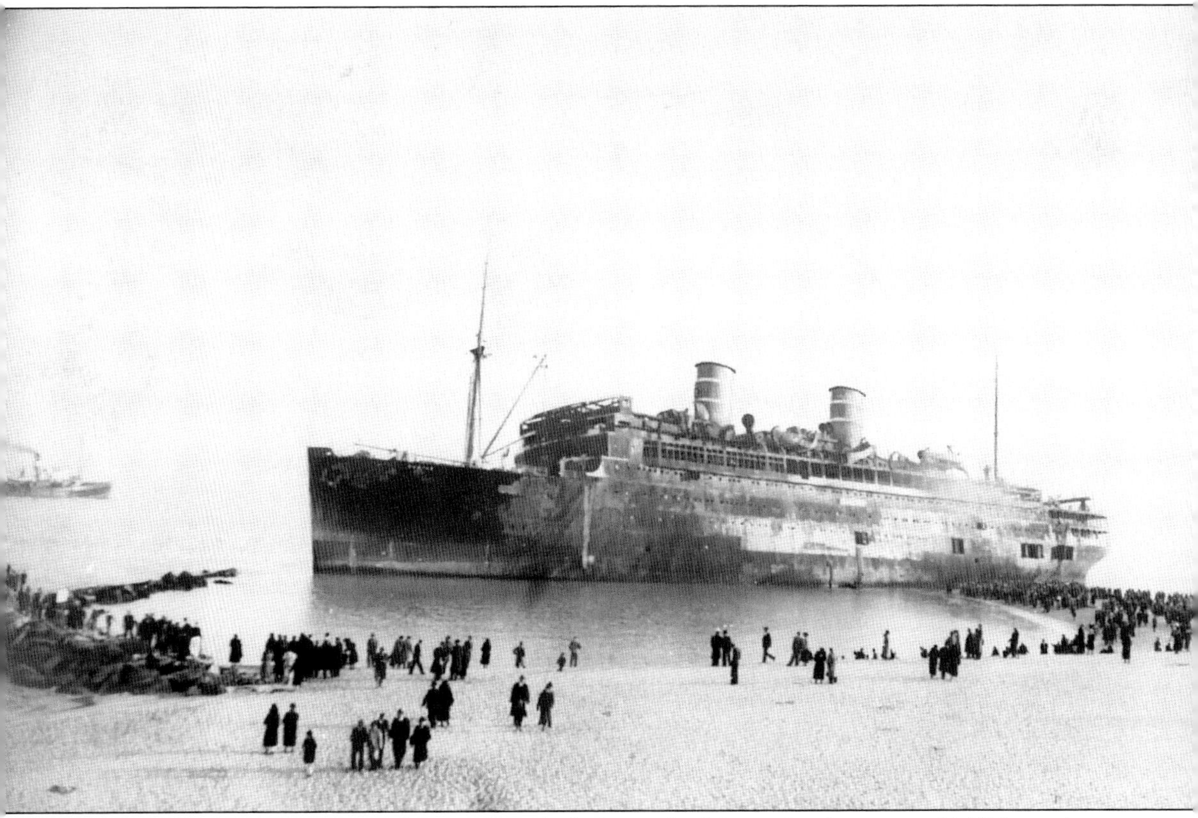

En route from Havana, Cuba, to New York City, the *Morro Castle* was an 11,500-ton luxury liner that caught fire and burned off the coast of Asbury Park (by Convention Hall) on September 8, 1934. Captain John Bogan, with his charter fishing boat the *Paramount* out of Brielle Basin, was one of the first to brave the high seas and strong winds to save passengers. The dining room at Randy's, on First Avenue and the inlet, served as a makeshift morgue. Manasquan resident Lewis W. Randolph, who had served as chief project engineer for the opening of the inlet, was responsible for the eventual removal of the *Morro Castle* to New York, where what was left of it was scrapped.

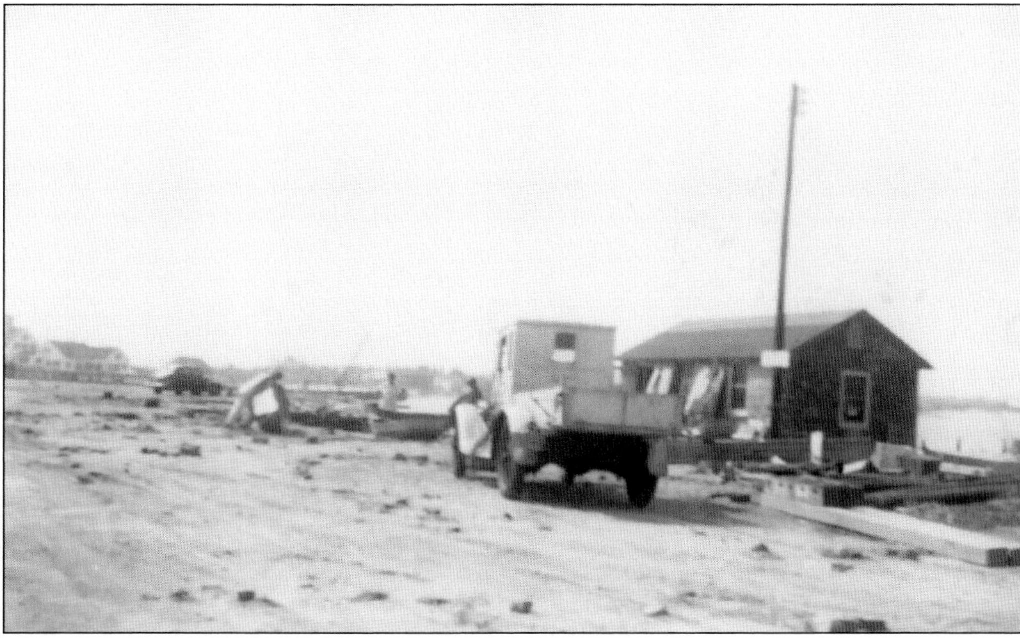

Ed Manley's Bait & Tackle Shop on Third Avenue at the Manasquan Inlet supplied fishermen with the usual fishing staples. Also, Mr. Manley rented rowboats. He operated the bait shop from the late 1940s until the mid-1950s. The Point Pleasant Beach Coast Guard Station can be seen to the south across the inlet.

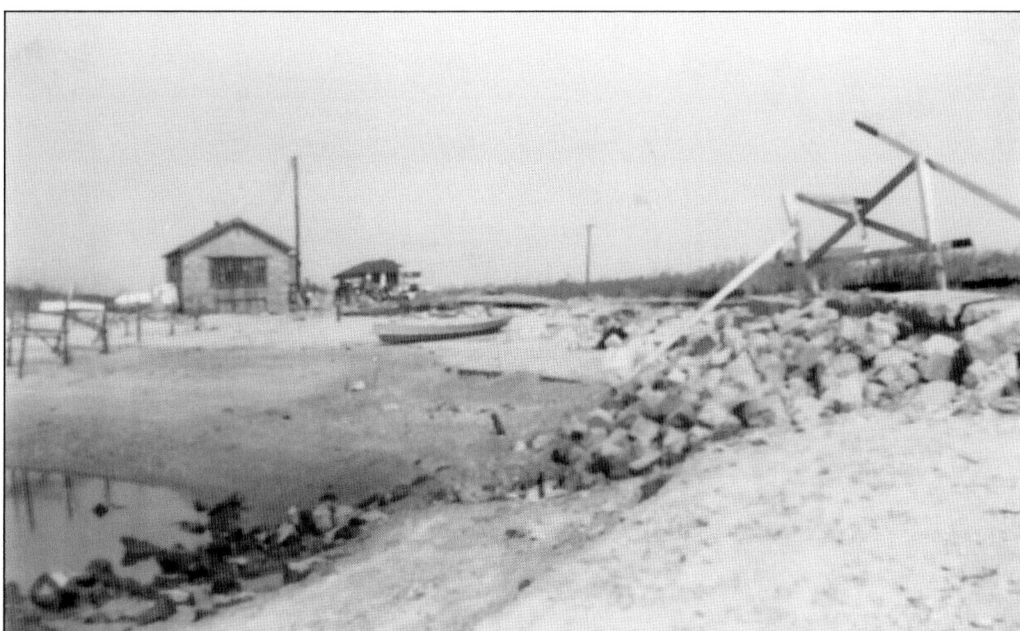

The view north from Ed Manley's Bait & Tackle—on property now known as Fisherman's Cove—illustrates the barren, unpopulated area of the community. Full development of the area east of Third Avenue to the beachfront did not take place until the early 1980s. As for Manley's bait shop, it was torn down and replaced by a larger establishment.

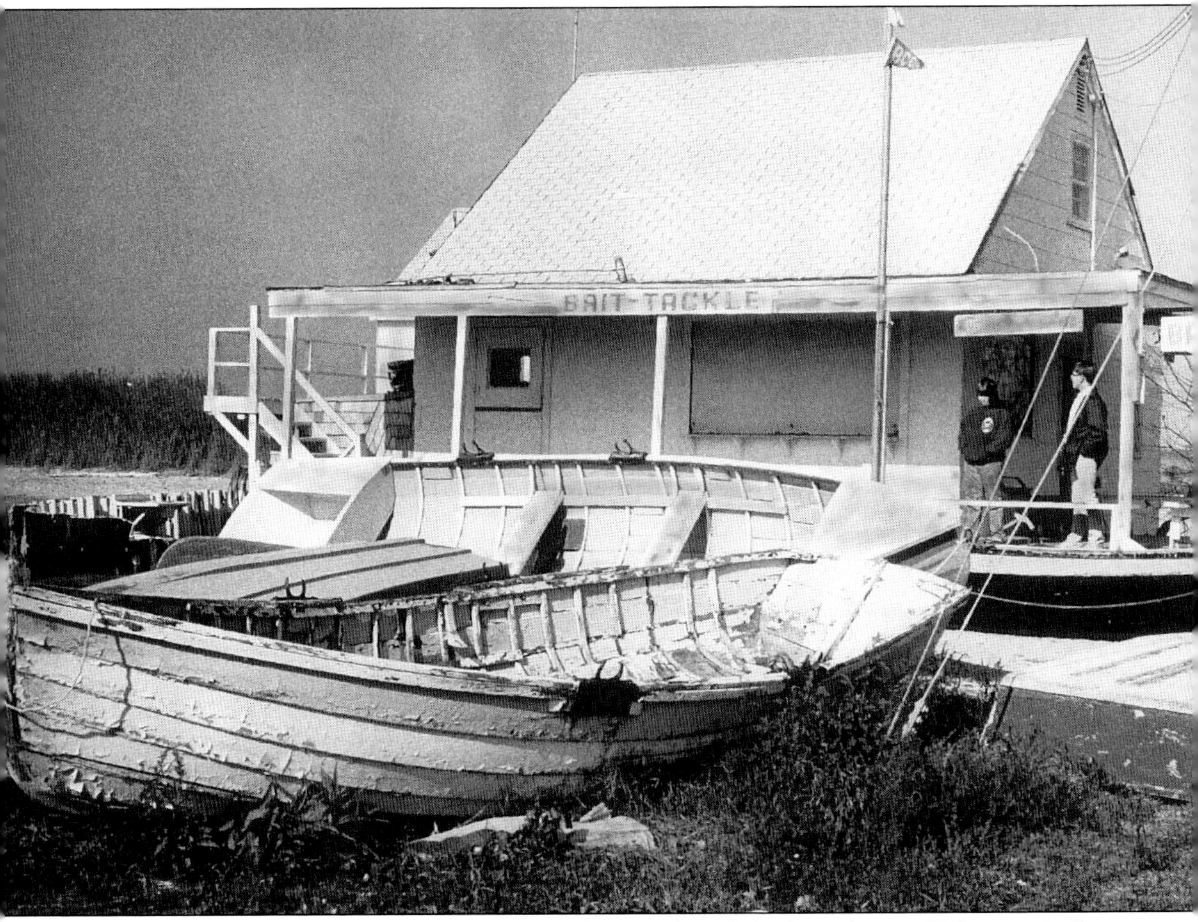

In 1958, Ruth and Clement Danish of Linden purchased the bait shop at Fisherman's Cove. Within three years, the Danishes moved their family of six children to Manasquan. They ran the shop until September 1996. This view, taken in 1984, shows the bait shop with wooden dories beached just steps from the shop's porches. From the porch, magnificent sunsets could be viewed to the west over the Manasquan River. In seashore tradition, summers were ended with a clambake at the Fisherman's Cove bait house. The building and the 63-acre Fisherman's Cove tract on the Manasquan River were acquired by Monmouth County to be used as a nature and passive recreation area.